Basque Ger

Margaret Bullen graduated in Modern Languages (French and Spanish) from the University of Bristol (UK), in 1987; and pursued postgraduate studies at the Institute of Latin American Studies, University of Liverpool, from where she received her Ph.D. in 1991.

She is a professor at the University Studies Abroad Consortium (USAC) by agreement with the University of the Basque Country (Donostia-San-Sebastián), where she has been teaching since 1993, offering courses on Basque and Iberian Culture and Basque and Spanish Gender Studies. She also taught on the Masters program organized by the former Seminar for Women's Studies.

She works too in the Farapi Consultancy of Applied Anthropology, based in Donostia-San-Sebastián, specializing in issues of gender, migration and diversity.

Her research interests bridge the areas of the Basque Country and Peru, and focus on the themes of gender, identity, migration and socio-cultural change. Tristes Espectáculos (Sad Sights), her latest research on the confrontation between equal rights and the defence of tradition, is soon to be published by the University of the Basque Country Press.

Margaret Bullen

Basque Gender Studies

Basque Textbooks Series

Center for Basque Studies
University of Nevada, Reno

For Teresa del Valle,

without whom Basque Gender Studies
would not be what they are today

This book was published with generous financial support from the Basque Government.

Cover prints by Lola Sarratea.
Floral illustration of eguzkilore by Xamar.

Library of Congress Cataloging-in-Publication Data

Bullen, Margaret, 1964–
Basque gender studies / Margaret Bullen.
p. cm. -- (Basque textbooks series)
Includes bibliographical references and index.
ISBN 1-877802-31-X (paperback)
ISBN 1-877802-32-8 (hardcover)
ISBN 1-877802-33-6 (compact disk)
1. Women, Basque. 2. Women—France—Pays Basque. 3. Women—Spain—País Vasco. I. Title. II. Series.
HQ1162.B84 2003
305.48'89'992--dc22

2003024152

Published by the Center for Basque Studies
University of Nevada, Reno /322
Reno, Nevada 89557-0012.

Printed in the United States of America.

Contents

Acknowledgments

Heartfelt thanks go out to all those who have contributed to the writing of this book. To all the Basque women and men who over the years have shared their knowledge and experience with me.

To Joseba Zulaika for his initiative in producing this series and his faith in me to produce this book.

To Cameron Watson and Linda White for their suggestions and ideas in the early stages.

To Teresa del Valle for opening the door of Basque Gender Studies to me at the Seminar of Women's Studies and for generously placing at my disposal her library and her store of wisdom.

To Txemi Apaolaza, Carmen Díez, and Mari Luz Esteban, who have been a constant source of inspiration and encouragement.

To all those who have kindly given me photographs, articles, and other material. To Gunnlaugur SE Briem and Fabian Hidalgo for their patient help with the graphics and book design, and to Mark Woodworth for his affable editing.

To Iñaki, Mikel, Beñat, and Aritz, and to Asun and Aristi, in a special way.

Part One. Introduction to gender theory

1 · Women's studies to gender studies

As we approach the study of gender in the Basque context we need first to open the door onto Gender Studies in general and from there take our pointers to guide us in our exploration of Basque Gender Studies. To this end, we will begin with an overview of the development of gender theory from its first formulation as an effort both to focus on women in different areas of study and to redress earlier male bias through the evolution of a concept of gender and its consolidation into a strong body of theory.

What is particularly interesting in the history of gender theory is that it has a pragmatic parallel in the history of feminism. Teresa del Valle, a prominent Basque anthropologist whose work we will be quoting throughout this book, places emphasis on the relationship between gender theory and feminism, finding that as a social movement feminism provides a base that lends credibility to the developing body of theory. She also points out that feminism is essentially a movement for social change, originating in the suffragettes' fight for equal rights and their continuing struggle for social justice for women (del Valle, 2000:10). Gender theory should then build upon the way "inequality is created, transmitted and validated" (del Valle, 1993:6) and the manner in which change is demanded or brought about by different social groups pushing for greater equality.

The identification of women's subordination in different walks of life has been at the core of Gender Studies from its birth. At the end of the sixties and beginning of the seventies a growing awareness of women's universal oppression was emerging and the question rang out loud and clear: Why? The quest to uncover the reasons for inequality between men and women has led to a greater knowledge of both women's and men's situation in society and to an increasingly sophisticated body of theory. The knowledge of how gender inequality maintains and reproduces itself eventually leads to knowledge of how change has been brought about, or could be. This returns us to the purpose of feminism, which as Janet Saltzman Chafetz, a leading sociologist in feminist theory, so rightly says is "committed to changing systems of gender that are inequitable to women" (1990:7).

The scientific field has drawn from and contributed to feminist practice and vice versa. The dialogue has not always been straightforward but it is through the interaction, discussion, and sometimes disagreement between the two that new ideas have emerged and crucial concepts have been molded. Gender theory is one of the most dynamic areas of Cultural Studies today and right on the cutting edge of the fight for greater equality in contemporary society as a whole—and no less in the Basque society we are concerned with here.

The suggested readings for this book are in English and the theory we study takes into account the major texts on gender, many of which were originally written in English. However, I believe a book on Basque Gender Studies cannot ignore the vital work that has been done by scholars both from the Basque Country and from different areas of the Spanish State. Consequently, here in this chapter and throughout the book, I will be referring to works—with or without English translations—which must be considered in the study of gender in the Basque context. In each chapter, as well as the required or recommended readings, I will include a bibliography of some of the key texts in Spanish or Basque that bear upon the subject in hand. At the end of each section,

Battleground
The history of gender theory is paralleled in the history of feminism, essentially a movement for social change, originating in the suffragettes' fight for equal rights and their continuing struggle for social justice for women. As a social movement, feminism is the battleground where theory and practice meet.
Illustration by Seymour Chwast.

---

you will find definitions of several key words used in the text.

In the rest of this chapter we will look at the evolution of Gender Studies, a term that encapsulates its own history and that we will trace from its beginnings as "Women's Studies" in which the focus was on women, with the express intention of bringing female social actors out into the light and redressing the imbalance accruing in the literature through years of emphasis on men. We will go on to see how the concept of gender is adopted in order to include both women and men and shift the focus to the relations between them.

Women: From Passive to Active

The concern with the subordinate status of women in society and feminism's fight to redress this social imbalance from the sixties led to a general questioning of the way in which women were represented in the social sciences. The overall conclusion was two-fold:

1. There was a marked predominance of information on male activities.
2. Where women were represented, they were seen from a male perspective.

It is not that women were always absent from the social sciences but rather that they were viewed in a way that reflected androcentric assumptions that were a direct product of male bias in Western society. That is to say, they were treated as passive objects of study and not as active social agents in their own right.

The anthropologist Henrietta Moore, in the first chapter of her now-classic book Feminism and Anthropology (1988), explores the way in which women had been neglected in anthropology, a field on which, together with sociology, we will draw amply in this book. Moore finds that women had been overlooked not in the sense that they had been left out (since women had always been included in the ethnographic accounts traditionally concerned with kinship and marriage), but rather in the way they were represented. On the one hand, anthropology's interest in kinship meant that the women mostly appeared in a reproductive role as mothers and in a subordinate role as wives. On the other hand, the accounts of women were often derived from conversations with male informants and reflected either the male view of their womenfolk or the interpretation of the anthropologist that was refracted by their maleness or femaleness: "The male ethnographers spoke of the women as profane, economically unimportant and excluded from rituals. The female researchers, on the other hand, described the women's central role in subsistence, the importance of women's rituals and the respectful way in which they were treated by men." (1988:1)

Women were there: the problem, then, was not their presence but their representation. The way they were portrayed can be summed up by the much-quoted phrase of the famous anthropologist Bronislaw Malinowski who defined anthropology itself as the "study of man embracing woman." The emphasis is clear and the vision it conveys says much about the gender order reflected.

The feminist critique of the social science's representation of women was the fruit of a new consciousness forming among women reflecting upon or militating for equal rights, questioning old assumptions, and developing innovative ways of perceiving human relations. The Spanish sociologist María Jesús Izquierdo (1998) explains how the interest in women as an object of study begins when a number of females recognize that the sex they share is socially significant. This awareness of being women collectively enables the shift from conceiving of woman as a passive object to which things happen to an active subject who does things herself.

The creation of the category "woman" is the very first step in gender theory: it permits the construction of a

Not just about women
The realization that gender is about both women and men and the relations between them led to a shift in focus and a wider angle on the systems that support social inequality.
Photo: Alain Pagoaga

---

political subject (i.e., possessing a power potential, capable of exerting authority and influence, with a right to express themselves and have a say) as well as an object of analysis (i.e., "woman" as a topic of study). In this first stage, "woman" emerges as a homogeneous category, expressed in the use of the singular rather than the later preferred plural "women."

The emphasis was on equality between women based on the shared biological condition of being females and the social implications attached to their sex. Other forms of difference (such as class, ethnicity, or sexual preference) were initially obscured by this blanket term, but would later challenge the universality and uniformity of the category.

"Add Women and Stir"

If representation was the problem, then one of the first things that had to be done was to correct the male bias perceived to be distorting the picture portrayed of women. This was done initially by women researchers concentrating on what the women studied were doing and describing this in detail rather than relying on male accounts of what women did. Attention was then paid to women's actions and words, and a new body of material was built up in which women were brought to the fore and seen to be social and political actors who were significant in their own right, rather than secondary objects of a study whose main focus was elsewhere.

It was also necessary to widen the angle on what women were observed to be doing. As we have said, they were not actually invisible in earlier studies, though they were represented almost exclusively as mothers and in terms of their reproductive role within the kinship system. It was time to take in other spheres of action: their contribution to production or their participation in the exercise of power and decision-making.

Although, as Moore indicates (2–3), making women more visible was a first important step in rectifying male bias, it was only half the story. The challenge remained to rework the underlying bias at the theoretical level. It was not simply a case of what Marilyn Boxer called the "add-women-and-stir method" (1982:258): both in the women's movement and in women's studies it was found that just adding or increasing women's presence was not sufficient to vanquish deep-rooted sexist prejudice in analysis.

"It Takes One to Know One"

The recognition of there being a problem with male bias in the analytical models used in the social sciences led to a theory of "muting" developed by the anthropologist Edwin Ardener (1975:21–23). He argued that there exist dominant groups in society—whether defined by sex, age, class, or ethnicity—that "generate and control the dominant modes of expression" and that silence or "mute" subordinated social groups, including women. It is not just that women lack a voice but that their voice is seemingly unintelligible because they have to use the dominant models and worldviews to make themselves heard. As a result their messages and meanings are distorted or muted.

Following this postulation, it is not sufficient for an ethnographer to talk to women to find out everything about what they do since their worldview and their model of reality cannot express themselves adequately using the terms of the dominant male model. "It is not that women are silent; it is just that they cannot be heard" (Moore 1988:4).

For these groups to become articulate, models of analysis need to be developed that recognize the different male and female visions of the world and their society. This, however, gave rise to another question: if women's models of the world are different from those of men, does that make women better equipped than men to study women? And conversely, does that mean that women are incapable of effectively studying men? As Judith Shapiro pointed out (1981:125), if it takes one to know one, doesn't that ultimately render ineffective the whole enterprise of studying human societies?

Every Woman

The privileged status of women for the study of women—the "it takes one to know one" position—depends upon the construction of a universal category of woman. It was this universal and categorical vision of woman with its emphasis on equality between women that had dominated the first phase of "women's studies" in the seventies.

The collection of articles edited by Olivia Harris and Kate Young (1974) in Anthropology and Feminism are an example of this phase.

However, it was not long before it became evident that the terms "woman" or "man" are social constructions that are "always culturally and historically specific" (Moore 1998:7). They mean different things in different cultural contexts, and it is not the biological similarity but the social difference between women that is meaningful in the social sciences.

The category "woman" thus had to be deconstructed, giving rise to an awareness that there is not one woman but many, that the various and disparate experiences of women must be contemplated in their social and historical context. This eye-opening realization leads to rethinking the "sameness" of women, the experience based on common biological and reproductive similarities and a shared subordination to men. It requires taking into account differences of class, race, and ethnicity that are critical to power relations in society and cannot be "erased simply by commonalities of sex" (Moore, ibid. 9).

The analytical concept of gender was a response to these realizations and provided a breakthrough for feminist studies in the eighties. It countered the previous essentialist assumption of universality and biological reductionism and inaugurated a new emphasis on difference not only between men and women but also among women themselves.

Feminism and Difference

The eighties marked a shift in emphasis away from the concept of "sameness" and toward a sharper awareness of difference between women. This, trend however, met with some degree of resistance from the feminist movement, since the challenging of the universal category of woman shakes the foundations of feminism, based as they are on a shared subordination.

Let us pause for a moment to consider what we mean by "feminism." In everyday discourse, feminism is often used as a bad word, associated with radical politics and an antimale stance. When talking about women's rights, people are frequently quick to add a disclaimer: "Not that I'm a feminist . . . ." Yet feminism by definition refers to the assertion of equal rights for women. The Concise Oxford Dictionary gives us the following definition: "the advocacy of women's rights on the grounds of the equality of the sexes." Expanding on this, Moore suggests it refers to "the awareness of women's oppression and exploitation at work, in the home and in society as well as to the conscious political action taken by women to change this situation" (ibid. 10).

However, as she goes on to point out, this definition returns us to the problem of difference, for it implies:

1. That women as a social group are dominated by men as a social group
2. That an identifiable shared corpus of women's interests exists
3. That a shared political identity exists, over and above differences

Equal rights for women
Feminism strives to raise awareness of women's oppression and exploitation at work, in the home and in society. In the Basque Country, feminists engage in conscious political action in order to gain access to new areas of activity, such as ritual and festival.
Photo: Iñaki Ugarte

Feminism is really based on the sameness that is questioned by the concept of cultural, social, and political difference. Borrowing a phrase from Marilyn Strathern, there is an "awkward relationship" between feminism and gender theory.

From Women's Studies to Gender Studies

One of the repercussions of attributing a privileged status to the female researcher with regard to the women she studies is the risk of marginalization (Moore, 1988:5–7). The segregation of women scholars who study women within their own particular discipline can create a ghetto. Rather than interlocking with the theoretical base of their field and promoting change in the analytical models used across the discipline, the danger is that women scholars in "women's studies" form a subgroup that excludes men and has no influence over areas of study in which men participate.

This has been one of the difficulties with Gender Studies from the outset: since its inception gender has been related to women, and female scholars have therefore found it hard to convince their male counterparts of its vital importance in any social study. The evolution of gender theory is partly responsible: if the study of women was initially important for bringing women into view in the social sciences, it ultimately slowed down the process of incorporating feminist theory into the mainstream of the social sciences. Nevertheless, the work done in the seventies that led to the fine-tuning of the term "gender" in the eighties was critical. As we have seen in the previous section, at first inequality was explained by gender difference perceived to be rooted in biological difference between men and women. The realization of difference between those who were biologically similar led to the discovery that the biological and natural dimension was not a straightforward, factual given, but rather a social and cultural construct.

In this period two lines of thought that had been explored individually began to converge in the analysis of gender:

1. The symbolic-structuralist approach, which looked at the way biological difference was constructed symbolically through cultural categories
2. The Marxist approach, which analyzed ways in which gender categories were linked to processes of production and inequality

This is where the distinction between "Women's Studies" and "Gender Studies" becomes important. The breakthrough really came when the concept of gender became common currency. Gender is a category that refers to the cultural construct of what it means to be a man or a woman in a given society. Commenting on the Western study of women, Izquierdo reiterates the point that the object of study called "women" is not by any means universal and does not embrace all human females, but rather is restricted to those who experienced the bourgeois revolution and the aspiration to freedom and equality (1998:15–16). Two Basque anthropologists, Mari Luz Esteban and Carmen Díez (1999), see in this three key points that form the basis to the development of feminist theory:

1. Action: the conceptualization of women as political subjects who do things
2. Temporal and spatial dimension: the limitation of time and space to countries where the bourgeois revolution has triumphed
3. Militancy: the assumption of a call for greater equality both in theory and practice

Gender refers not only to cultural factors but at the same time to the social relations and power structures between men and women in a given society. "Gender" moves us away from a purely female focus to one that contemplates both men and women and looks at the way in which the relations between them structure society in terms of history, politics, economics, and culture. Gender then becomes an intrinsic variable of social study: one that is inherent in any social structure and cannot be ignored.

Lesson one

Summary

To sum up this section, we can distinguish certain phases in the evolution of gender theory:

1. "Women's studies": a result of the recognition of the neglect or distortion of women's activities in the social sciences and an attempt to correct male bias in the representation of women
   a. This first phase assumes the universal subordination of women and focuses on similarity and shared experience
2. "Gender Studies": a response to the questioning of the universal category "woman" in recognition of differences existing among women as well as between men and women:
   a. Cross-cultural differences revealing the term "woman" to be a historical and geographical construct, differing across time, space, and culture
   b. Socioeconomic, ethnic, and sexual differences: the contemplation of other variables such as class, race, ethnicity, and sexual orientation

---

c. The shift in emphasis is also conditioned by an awareness of the danger of "women's issues" being segregated or marginalized in the social sciences and the need to apply gender theory transversally to all areas of study
d. The categories "men" and "women" are constructed in relation to one another, and both must be taken into account in any area of study that pretends to contemplate human relations in society

Suggested Reading

Henrietta Moore, Chap. 1, "Feminism and Anthropology: The Story of a Relationship," in Feminism and Anthropology (1988), 1–11.

Marilyn Strathern, "An Awkward Relationship: The Case of Feminism and Anthropology," Signs (1987) 12(2):276–92.

Bibliography

English Bibliography

Edwin Ardener, "The Problem Revisited," in S. Ardener, ed., Perceiving Women (London: Dent, 1975), 19–27.

Marilyn Boxer, "For and About Women: The Theory and Practice of Women's Studies in the United States," in N. Keohane, M. Rosaldo, and B. Gelpi, eds., Feminist Theory: A Critique of Ideology (Brighton: Harvester Press, 1982), 237–71.

Janet Saltzman Chafetz, Gender Equity: An Integrated Theory of Stability and Change (Newbury Park–London–New Delhi: Sage, 1990).

Teresa del Valle, "Introduction," in T. del Valle, ed., Gendered Anthropology (London and New York: Routledge, 1993), 1–16.

Olivia Harris and Kate Young, Anthropology and Feminism (1974).

Henrietta Moore, Chap. 1, "Feminism and Anthropology: The Story of a Relationship," in Feminism and Anthropology (1988), 1–11.

Judith Shapiro, "Anthropology and the Study of Gender," in E. Langland and W. Gove, eds., A Feminist Perspective in the Academy (Chicago: University of Chicago Press, 1981), 110–29.

Spanish Bibliography

Teresa del Valle, "Introducción," in T. del Valle, ed., Perspectivas desde la antropología social (Barcelona: Ariel, 2000), 9–24.

Mari Luz Esteban and Carmen Díez, "Introducción," in Antropología Feminista: Desafíos teóricos y metodológicos (Donostia–San Sebastián: Ankulegi, 1999), 9–28.

María Jesús Izquierdo, El malestar en la desigualdad (Madrid: Feminismos, Cátedra, 1998).

Written lesson for submission

Explain the meaning of "feminism and difference" and outline its implications for theory and problems posed for practical feminism.

2 · The nature–culture debate

To pursue gender theory further, a fundamental distinction must be made between sex and gender, and this in turn will lead us into the dialectic of nature and culture. In the social sciences, "sex" has come to mean the biological difference between males and females. "Gender" is used to mean the sociocultural construction of what is understood by or expected of males and females in a given society or culture, what it is that makes them "men" or "women" (Chafetz, 1990:28).

While biological differences are on the whole constant across time and space, the cultural construction of what is understood by the categories of "man" or "woman" vary considerably through history and across cultures. The way gender operates in a particular culture may be seen to be a result of

1. A symbolic construction
2. A social relationship

In both cases, the analysis of gender relations is seen to be crucial to an understanding of social organization in general and female subordination in particular. We will look at gender as a symbolic construct in this section and concentrate on gender as a social construct in the next.

Human Universals/Cultural Particulars

One of the first problems to be tackled is the huge cross-cultural variation in categories of "man" and "woman" but at the same time, the coincidence in many different cultures of certain basic notions about gender. This apparent contradiction is expressed by Sherry Ortner in her now-classic essay: "Is female to male as nature is to

Closer to nature
Through reproduction, women have been seen as being closer to nature than men, who are associated with production.
Collection Asunción Maisterrena

culture?" (1974). She expresses it as the need to explain both "human universals" and "cultural particulars" (64). With relation to women, one of the universal facts is that of women's secondary status in society. Nonetheless, "the specific cultural conceptions and symbolizations of women are extraordinarily diverse and even mutually contradictory." Ortner also states that women's relative power varies as well across cultures and through history.[1]

Let us take a closer look at Ortner's article (suggested reading for this chapter) since it proved to be groundbreaking in the analysis of women's subordination, paving the way for a new approach to gender symbolism (see Moore, 1988:14–15).

---

1. Ortner takes universal female subordination as a point of departure and sets out to look for an explanation for it; she finds that biological determinism is not a valid reason and that there is no physiological explanation for this; therefore the explanation must lie elsewhere.
2. She reasons that biological differences between men and women are only significant within a culturally defined value system; thus sexual asymmetry must be located in cultural ideologies and symbols (Ortner 1974:71).
3. The next question is: what could be common to all cultures that makes them value women to a lesser degree than men? The answer: something that every culture devalues—nature (72).
4. Ortner finds that all cultures distinguish between human society and the natural world. "Culture" attempts to harness nature and channel its forces for its own use; it seeks to strike a balance between the raw state of the environment and the human need for cultivation and control of the elements.
5. "Culture" is seen to be superior to nature because it controls and transcends nature.
6. Men are associated with "culture" and by extension with superiority, domination, and control; women are associated with "nature" and therefore with being controlled.

Now, the main arguments for asserting that women are associated with nature or seen to be closer to nature than men can be grouped into two blocks:

1. First, woman's physiology, being specially adapted to reproduction, gives the impression of her being closer to nature. Men resort to cultural, artificial means of creation such as technology, which in turn

reproduce culture itself, whereas women's creativity comes from within them and both derives from and is fulfilled through nature by conceiving, gestating, and giving birth (Ortner, 1974:77; Moore, 1988:15).

2. Second, women's social activity is seen to be closer to nature because their part in the reproductive process has tended to restrict them to certain social roles that are in turn perceived to be closer to nature. That is to say, women have been associated not only with giving birth to children but also with the subsequent care involved in rearing them. Children are seen to be closer to nature in many societies since they are not considered to have become "culturally created persons." Thus women are doubly associated with nature, and this link to reproduction and child-raising is found to restrict them to the domestic domain and to family concerns.

The nature–culture dichotomy is found to be at the heart of the separation between the private and public arena that is crucial to explaining the gender divisions and stratifications in society. Women are associated with nature, with reproduction, with child-raising, with family relations, and ultimately with "particularistic or socially fragmenting concerns" in the private, domestic domain (Moore, 1988:15). Men are associated with culture, with artificial means of creation, with the extra-domestic, public, and political domains identified with social life and the public interest.

As Moore points out (1988:15) it is important to remember that Ortner is not saying that women are really any closer to nature than men; rather she is looking at the way this idea is presented in different societies in such a way that women appear to be closer to nature.

Pollution and Inferiority

One of the most analyzed areas of female inferiority is that of "pollution," which takes into account different beliefs and practices regarding the female body and its functions, especially in connection with childbirth and menstruation, and examines how the taboos and restrictions that spring from these construct sexual ideologies that in turn influence the structure of the sociocultural world, the categorization of people, and in this case the subordination of women. The idea is that at certain times—or, in some cultures, always—women are conceived to be polluting through their natural bodily functions, and this has been proposed by some scholars as a symbolic explanation of their inferiority.

Problems with the Nature–Culture Dichotomy

Criticisms have been expressed of the nature–culture / female–male opposition, such as those in the suggested reading by Carol MacCormack (1980) or that of Nicole-Claude Mathieu (1978). Nevertheless, the impact of Ortner's thesis cannot be underestimated for pointing the way toward an understanding of the cultural construction of gender and the symbolic significance (rather than the biological basis) of the categories of "man" and "woman."

The main problems revolve around the following questions:

1. The female association with nature does not always tally with the male association with culture. Men—through sex—can be equally associated with nature, nonhuman attributes, animality.
2. The need to consider who believes women closer to nature—do they? For whom is this belief valid?
3. It is not just sexual relationships that matter in the construction of gender in terms of male–female

opposition: other gendered relations are also important (brother/sister, mother/son, father/daughter) in what it means to be a woman or a man.

4. Ethnocentricity of analytical categories: the very notions of "nature" and "culture" are culturally specific and vary widely, nor do they necessarily signify the same as our Western tradition understands them to do—i.e., the concepts of superiority of culture over nature and of civilization as man's subjection of the wild (through industrialization, modern science, technology).

Lesson two

Summary

1. The progression from Women's Studies leads to a refinement of definitions and differentiation between sex (the biological differences between males and females) and gender (the sociocultural construction of what is understood by being male or female in a given society).
   a. While biological similarities are more or less stable, cultural constructions vary immensely throughout history and across groups, societies, and cultures.
   b. The gendering of society operates on two levels:
      i. Symbolic construction
      ii. Social relationships
   c. Gender permeates social organization and is the basis of social differences and hierarchy in general, inequality between males and females in particular.
2. Despite cultural variation, the finding that female subordination is virtually consistent across human

groups prompts the question of where that hierarchical order stems from. It is proposed that the differentiation is rooted in the distinction between "nature" and "culture":

a. Women are associated with the natural world through their reproductive function, which restricts them to the roles of child-bearing and -rearing and housekeeping, whereas men are identified with culture, understood here as the human manipulation of natural forces to meet their needs.
b. Given men's lack of a natural reproductive potential, they turn to the development of technology directed at subordinating nature for human use.
c. Thus culture in this sense is seen as superior to nature as a brute force or raw element and is associated with domination and control, both of nature and of women, conceptually situated in the natural world.
d. Attributing values to culture over nature leads to other divisions in society such as the public and private domains, or to the assignment of negative values to female reproductive functions.

3. Certain problems are found with the nature–culture distinction concerning the difficulty of drawing such dichotomies, the assumption that the social actors assume the differentiations as valid for themselves, and the possibility that ethnocentric concepts of what is meant by nature and culture may distort the thesis.

Suggested Reading

Sherry Ortner, "Is Female to Male as Nature is to Culture?," in M. Rosaldo and L. Lamphere, eds., Women, Culture and Society (Stanford: Stanford University Press, 1974), 67–78.

Carol MacCormack, "Nature, Culture and Gender: A Critique," in C. MacCormack and M. Strathern, eds., Nature, Culture and Gender (Cambridge: Cambridge University Press, 1980, 1–24.

Bibliography

Edwin Ardener, "Belief and the Problem of Women," in S. Ardener, ed., Perceiving Women (London: Dent, 1975), 1–17.

Nicole-Claude Mathieu, "Man–Culture and Woman–Nature?," in Women's Studies (1978), 155–65.

Henrietta Moore, Chap. 2, "Gender and Status," in Feminism and Anthropology (1988), 12–41.

Written lesson for submission

Evaluate the nature–culture debate, showing that you understand the dichotomy and outlining its main strengths and weaknesses.

3 · Gender and status

Moving from a symbolic explanation of women's subordination in terms of the identification of women with nature that is valued as inferior to culture, associated with men, we encounter another school of thought, not necessarily in opposition to this symbolic approach but potentially complementary, which prefers to look at gender as a social relationship in terms of what men and women do in society, rather than the cultural values or ideologies attached to them, their actions, and their behavior. The focus on what men and women do leads us to the sexual division of labor, and this in turn draws us into the division of social life into "domestic" and "public" spheres.

In this section we will address both the symbolic and the sociological aspects of the domestic/public division, and later (Chapter 4) we will apply the theories to the Basque case. Our concern with Basque Gender Studies implies that we have a dual mission in this book: first to address the question of the universality of women's subordination to men, and second to analyze the particularities of that subordination in Basque society. Accordingly, we will look first at the debate surrounding the issue of whether women are always subordinate to men—through history and throughout the world—and later in the book we will turn our attention to the way in which this subordination works in Basque society.

From Nature–Culture to Domestic–Public

Hot on the heels of the nature–culture debate is the domestic–public distinction, which many have seen as a model of universal application for explaining women's subordination. Ortner holds that women are "closer to nature" because they are more closely connected to the domestic sphere than to the public realm. Despite the criticism this model has received, it has remained a predominant feature of social and gender analysis, as it enables the evaluation of the cultural construct of "women" in relation to the social organization of women's activities.

Michelle Rosaldo, in the introduction to her joint book with Louise Lamphere, provides one of the first explanations of the domestic/public models and a declaration of its virtually universal application. Following Ortner, she sees the negative association of women with the domestic domain as being directly linked to the female reproductive role: i.e., as mother and child care provider. Rosaldo attributes a hierarchical value to the public and private, reflecting the nature–culture order. That is to say, the domestic, nature-related sphere is seen as inferior to the public, culture-related realm. It will be useful to consider her definition of these categories (Rosaldo, 1974:23 and 1980:398; Moore 1988:22):

Domestic: those institutions and activities organized around mother-child groups
Public: activities, institutions, and forms of association that link, rank, organize, or subsume particular mother-child groups

As with any dichotomy, this division poses certain problems:

1. The categorical separation of the domestic and public spheres must be considered, since they overlap and it is difficult to make a rigid division between them (see Rosaldo, 1980).
2. The two spheres are interrelated.

Nature inferior to culture
Women's sphere of knowledge has traditionally been associated with nature, in the realm of childcare or healing for example, and generally valued less than the typically male domains of science, technology and culture. Collection Asunción Maisterrena

---

3. Culturally specific concepts of family, home, motherhood, and fatherhood must be taken into account when theorizing about these realms.

Women, Children, and Families

The main reason why the universality of the domestic/public opposition seems plausible is that it is based on "a defined mother-child unit which seems 'naturally' universal" (Moore 1988:23). Although there will be cultural variations in forms of family and types of gender role, "women everywhere give birth to children" (ibid.) and hence mother-child units can be perceived as the basic building blocks of society.

However, nice and simple as this equation seems at first sight, it has to be taken along with the general debate over the forms of the family. Our Western concept of the family is one in which the home, the household, and the domestic arena are seen to coincide and to be a haven for intimacy, emotional bonding, and child rearing and nurturing. This is set against the notion of the public realm of work, business, and politics where market relations characterized by "competition, negotiation and contract" (Moore, 23) prevail. The family, thus conceived, cannot be maintained to be universal in any sense, and we find ourselves face to face with the same problems listed above for the domestic/public distinction made in the first place.

"Women everywhere give birth to children" reiterates Moore (29), "but this fact receives varying degrees of cultural recognition and elaboration." What it means to give birth and be a mother varies from culture to culture, and it cannot be assumed that all societies share the same ideas about motherhood, fertility, nurturance, and reproduction as our own Western societies. Moore concludes that "even the most natural of functions 'mothering' is a culturally defined activity." Hence, the assumption that women's subordinate status is linked to their role as mothers has to be treated with caution since we can easily fall into the mistake of transferring our own Western notions of family and sociosexual relations onto other cultures.

Gender Roles: The Social Construction of Gender

The Marxist anthropologist Eleanor Leacock criticizes the assumption that women are universally subordinated to men on the basis of its failure both to situate itself firmly in a historical context and to consider the effects of colonization and the rise of a world capitalist economy.

Moore (1988:31) summarizes Leacock's arguments for us. She starts by rejecting two of the feminist premises we have just seen elaborated:

1. "That women's status is directly related to the functions of giving birth and rearing children"
2. "That the 'domestic'/'public' distinction is a cross-culturally valid framework for the analysis of gendered relations"

Leacock draws on Friedrich Engels's *Origin of the Family, Private Property, and the State*[2] in maintaining that the evolution of private ownership of the means of production lies at the root of women's inferior status to men and is responsible for both the institution of monogamous marriage and the creation of the family as an autonomous economic unit.

She argues that primitive "pre-class" societies were egalitarian: men and women were independent beings, autonomous individuals who held positions in society that, though different, were attributed equal value and prestige. Nevertheless, others have disagreed with the generalization of primitive equality and argued for the possibility of variation (for example, Karen Sacks, 1974, "Engels revisited: Women, the organization of production and private property" in Rosaldo and Lamphere [eds.], *Women, Culture and Society*, 207–22).

The thrust of Leacock's argument cuts across male-biased ethnographies that explained women's status in relation to their role as mothers and their restriction to the domestic sphere that that implies. Instead she postulates that in all societies women are vital contributors to the economy and their status depends not on symbolic valuations but rather on their degree of control of

Mothering as a culturally defined activity
Basque women's centrality to the family and role in childcare is acted out in folk ritual and dance, as in this representation of the *Iñude eta artzaiak* ("Wet nurses and shepherds")
Photo: Iñaki Ugarte

resources, labor, and production. She specifies these three areas thus:

1. Access to the resources
2. The conditions of their work
3. The distribution of the products of their labor

On this theme, she rejects the domestic/public dichotomy as valid for smaller agricultural or self-sufficient societies (such as the Iroquois she analyses in her article, 1978:253) where "household management" is one and the same with the management of the public economy and political affairs. Later we will assess whether the status of Basque women in traditional rural society can be considered in the same terms.

Finally, Leacock—like many more who have addressed this issue—demonstrates that colonization, capitalism, and latterly globalization have transformed gender relations in societies across the world. The introduction of wage labor is seen to increase women's dependence on men where previously they exerted greater control in the processes of production.

A Bit of Both

Nowadays, the consensus is that sociological explanations of the position of men and women in relation to the means of production are not in themselves sufficient to explain gender relations in a given society. The symbolic valuations are also important and the two must be taken together.

However, an extra complication arises with this picture that derives from the realization that the two do not always sit nicely together. Female control of resources does not invariably result in a higher status for women. Ironically, it is often the case that although men are represented as being dominant, in many societies women nevertheless possess a certain amount of political or economic power that does not seem to marry with the way they are portrayed as dependent and subordinate. This apparent contradiction requires further explanation in terms of gender ideologies.

Moore (1988:369) tells us that consequently "a number of feminist scholars have attempted to combine symbolic and sociological approaches to the study of gender, because of a realization that ideas about women and men are neither wholly independent of, nor directly derived from, economic relations of production." The aim is to try to connect the culturally conditioned gender ideologies to the actual social relations in which men and women live out their daily lives.

Cultural conceptions of gender begin to emerge not as the direct result of social or productive relationships, but as "ritualized" or symbolic statements or stereotypes constructed—in the context of these social and economic relations—on the basis of what men and women expect from each other in political terms. Referring to her own work in Kenya, Moore (1988:37) concludes: "Cultural ideas about gender do not directly reflect the social and economic positions of women and men, although it is true that they originate within the context of those conditions. This is because gender stereotypes are developed and used in the strategies which individuals of both sexes employ to advance their interests in various social contexts."

Lesson three

Summary

1. In this section we have considered the school of thought that favors gender as a social relationship, in

terms of what men and women do in society, rather than as a symbolic construct:
   a. The initial focus is on the sexual division of labor between the domestic and public spheres.
   b. A hierarchy is established in which the domestic, nature-related realm is inferior to the public, culture-related sphere.
2. The two main problems with this analysis both recur constantly in our survey of gender theories:
   a. First is the difficulty of establishing dichotomies when in fact the divisions are not clear-cut and moreover the two realms are interrelated.
   b. Second is the danger of falling into ethnocentrism since "domestic" and "public" are both culturally specific constructs.
3. The problem with establishing a domestic/public distinction that is cross-culturally valid leads to an emphasis on the historical context and in particular to the rise of the world capitalist economy:
   a. Rather than the female reproductive functions being at the core of their subordination, this line of inquiry identifies private ownership of the means of production as the root of women's inequality, with monogamous marriage and the creation of the family as an economic unit evolving from there.
4. Both sociological explanations stress the control of resources, labor, and production as fundamental, and symbolic analysis can be complementary in locating the functioning of gender difference in society.

Suggested Reading

Eleanor Leacock, "Women's Status in Egalitarian Society: Implications for Social Evolution," in Current Anthropology (1978) 19(2):247–75.

Karen Sacks, "Engels Revisited: Women, the Organization of Production, and Private Property," in M. Rosaldo and L. Lamphere, Women, Culture and Society (Stanford: Stanford University Press, 1974), 207–22.

Bibliography

Henrietta Moore, Chap. 2, "Gender and Status," in Feminism and Anthropology (1988), 12–41.

Michelle Rosaldo, "Women, Culture and Society: A Theoretical Overview," in M. Rosaldo and L. Lamphere, Women, Culture and Society (Stanford: Stanford University Press, 1974), 17–42.

———, "The Use and Abuse of Anthropology: Reflections on Feminism and Cross-Cultural Understanding," Signs (1980) 5(3):389–417.

Written lesson for submission

Explain the sociological explanation for women's lower status in society and evaluate in relation to the cultural orientation of symbolic analysis.

4 · The current status of gender studies

Gender Studies today is the result of a process of evolution during which theories have been thrashed out and concepts refined. The most recent developments include the notion of personhood, the interplay of variables such as ethnicity, economic status and ideology in the construction of gender difference, and the multiple interactions betwen women and men at different levels of the social system that have different repercussions in terms of the gendered balance of power.

Women as persons

The social sciences as a whole have reevaluated the objects of their study and transformed them into subjects in their own right, with their own models or world-views and their own field of influence on social action. Gender studies has followed this trend toward the perception of women as persons or individuals in their own right, looking into the cultural construction of self or person through a gendered perspective. Taking women to be persons means reviewing the assumptions of the domestic/public division and women's attendant power, autonomy, and authority in society. At all events, it means regarding women to be individuals with power in their own right, whatever their relationship to men.

Once again there is the danger that in a cross-cultural study we will fall into the old error of using Western assumptions about personhood or individuality that mar our comprehension. "Individual" or "person," warns Marilyn Strathern (1981) in her work on the Hagen of Papua New Guinea, "is best seen as a particular cultural type (of person) rather than as a self-evident

The Basque Case
One of the most significant figures in Basque Gender Studies today is Teresa del Valle, professor of social anthropology at the University of the Basque Country and pioneer of research on women in Euskal Herria.
Photo: Elena Asins

analytical category itself." What we have to remember is that gender constructs are related to concepts of self, personhood, and autonomy but that these concepts themselves are culturally specific and are related to particular social values. That is to say, we must take into account the different factors influencing the choices and strategies of individual social actors in given contexts. It is in these areas that feminist scholarship is making some of the most significant advances in the connection between "symbolic or cultural aspects of social life and the social and economic conditions under which life is lived" (Moore 1988:41).

The complementary consideration of the symbolic and the socioeconomic realms of experience inevitably leads to the question of power, which we will look at more closely in Part 3. Here we will pose Moore's question about the evaluation of women's power in the domestic and public domains: "The question is an old one: if we want to see women as effective social adults in their own right, is it enough to say that they have power within a specifically female domain, or must we argue that they have power in those areas of social life which have so often been presented as the public, political domain of men?" (ibid. 39)

In an article that considers the contemporary status of Gender Studies, Verena Stolcke gives a few pointers as to the current theoretical problems faced (1996):

1. Awareness of the added dimension of race, initially posed by black women in the US who have criticized the lack of sensitivity of their white counterparts to their particular form of oppression. Stolcke deals with this issue in greater depth in an aptly titled essay, "Is Sex to Gender as Race Is to Ethnicity" (1993).

2. Awareness of socioeconomic and ideological factors producing differences that override similarities of sex.
3. The need to address not just the influence of these added variables but also the way their intersection produces shared experiences among women living in an increasingly globalized world but at the same time reinforces differences that are apparently insurmountable.

Gender Systems

One of the most important developments in the conceptualization of gender is that of systems. Moving us on from a more static, unitary vision of "women," through the realization that "women" as cultural constructs exist as such only in relation to culturally constructed "men," the idea of systems enables us to embrace the complexities and contradictions of these categories, acknowledging the importance of their interaction well as their infinite variation according to the social system within which they are inserted.

Janet Saltzman Chafetz (1990:28–29) refers to the term "gender system" as the "socio-cultural status quo" that "includes systems of gender stratification and differentiation as well as the gender division of labor, gender social definitions, and power inequities between the genders."

The analysis of gender systems can therefore help us to understand the way in which the asymmetrical relations between men and women in society work. Let us consider Chafetz's definitions of the factors included in the term "gender system" to get a clearer picture of what is meant:

By "gender stratification" Chafetz means the degree of gender equality or inequality in a given society or sector of that society. It contemplates male/female disadvantage in terms of: "the extent to which males and females who are otherwise social equals (e.g., in terms of age, social class, race/ethnicity, and religion) are equal in their access to the scarce and valued resources of their society." (ibid. 29)

This refers us back to the social construct of gender through a consideration of people's access to social, economic, and political resources. Chafetz numbers among scarce and valued resources: "material goods, services provided by others, leisure, prestige-conferring roles, health care and nutrition, personal autonomy, physical safety, opportunities for physical enrichment and gratification, and opportunities for education and training." (ibid. 29)

Money should also be included among these as a resource that may be employed to access virtually all the above and that makes a good marker of gender stratification in modern complex societies, although to a lesser degree in simple societies. Even in more complex societies money is not the sole factor determining access to resources of value and should be considered alongside other means of apportioning power and authority.

Furthermore, it should be noted that gender stratification will vary in different sectors of society where factors of social class and race/ethnicity or religion may influence inequality.

"Gender differentiation" is another facet of gender stratification or inequality, or rather it is a further step into understanding how that inequality works. It involves "engenderment," which is "the process by which males and females come to be gender differentiated" (ibid. 30). Certain differences between males and females as individuals are projected onto males and females as collectives and attributed positive or negative values. These differences are categorized as gender differences. The concern here is the way in which a statement of difference is converted into a factor of inequality and particularly the way "female traits come to be devalued relative to male ones" (ibid. 30).

To this effect, and in accordance with Stolcke, Susana Narotzky (1995:36–39) sees gender as one more way of creating difference that interacts with other factors of differentiation (race, class, age, etc.) to compound a system of inequalities in society.

The Basque Case

Some of the ways in which asymmetrical gender relations are constructed in any given society are applied to the Basque case by Teresa del Valle in the suggested reading for this section, which provides an overview on "The Current Status of the Anthropology of Women" (1989). In this article, del Valle engages with the theories we have been discussing and looks at the way cultural constructs combine with features of the social structure, contextualized in a particular time and place. Innovative features of the article are her construction of symbolic and cultural categories of "women" and "men" through the use of stereotypes that are part of the process of engenderment, used as if they were diametrically opposed in a simplistic, binary relation even when we know full well that these categories are complex and varied. Stereotypes are "characteristics that are applied in a fixed mode as representative of a person, a group, a collectivity" (ibid. 132). The characteristics attributed to women or men in a particular society, often backed up by references to biology or nature, are expressed as the norm, as a sweeping rule for all, obscuring differences and exceptions. The stereotyped conception of women and men feeds into the stereotyp-

The good mother stereotype
The importance of the role of mother is generally emphasized in Basque culture, and especially in traditional rural society where the etxekoandrea or "woman of the house" has frequently been considered to be practically in charge of her children's upbringing and spiritually responsible for them through her participation in rites of passage, particularly those related to birth and death.
Collection Asunción Maisterrena.

---

ing of gender roles, laying down certain "appropriate" functions on the basis of the received ideas about what women and men are like: "For example, the dichotomized roles of male salaried workers/female housewives are often sustained by the perception of men as adventurers, oriented towards the exterior, with public projection, whereas women are perceived as private, defensive of the interior and of closed spaces, and preoccupied with minutiae and intranscendental matters." (ibid. 132)

Del Valle stresses the need to distinguish between stereotypes and attributes. Attributes are qualities that are ideally characteristic of a woman or man in a given society. They are used to construct stereotypes in which the said quality is fixed, distorted, and frequently demeaned. In the Basque case, she gives the example of cleanliness as being a culturally valued attribute that is assigned to women but that can be distorted by the negative associations with an obsession for housework, competition with other women, or the general low value attached to domestic work. It is a stereotype that becomes a limitation on women: "For example a characteristic attributed to Basque women is that of being clean, something which is valued. However, presenting her as always obsessed with house cleaning and with clean laundry, and making this an element in her competition with other women, is to stereotype an attribute and convert it into a fixed characteristic of all Basque women that is charged with pejorative connotations." (ibid. 132–33)

This is our point of departure in Part 2, where we will look at the ideal traditionally established for Basque women and how elements of that model prevail despite far-reaching changes that have meant a departure, in real terms, from the ideal.

As well as looking at the social structure, del Valle gives us certain other indicators for studying gender in the Basque context. She emphasizes the historical, religious, economic, and political contexts, and in Part 3 we will examine the way power relations are mythified through reference to a prehistorical goddess religion and matriarchal order that carry over into certain symbolic interpretations involving real consequences for women in the past and continuing to be evoked in the present.

Del Valle also stresses the importance of socialization processes, so in Part 4 we will explore different aspects of women's participation in cultural transmission—a vital function in a minority culture like the Basque one where women (particularly in their role as mothers) are a vital link in passing on the Basque language, customs, and traditions. This is also true in the case of the Basque emigrants, where women again play a crucial part in the continuity of Basque references among the diasporic community. The defense of the Basque nation in terms of political militancy will also be taken up there.

Rituals, games, and competitions constitute other important elements in Basque life in which gender relations are colorfully played out. These will be the topic of Part 5, where we analyze the maintenance or disruption and reconfiguration of gender relations in certain Basque rituals, carnivals, and festivals and consider the confluence of gender with space.

Finally, in Part 6, we will look at the evolution of the feminist movement in Spain and the Basque Country, taking up del Valle's recommendation to investigate the "new spaces" of gender relations—those areas or actions that fly against the established norm and that contest the dominant stereotype of women and men, breaking new ground and building new ways of being a woman, or a man. Del Valle proposes bringing the marginal in from the periphery, placing it at center stage, and by doing so shaking off the tendency to consider as "abnormal" that which is merely different from the norm. Thus, if we look at alternative living arrangements, sexual orientations, or ritual practices, we can not only challenge the preconceptions that attempt to define and fix meaning and prevent change, but we also can keep our finger on the pulse of that change: "In the majority of cases, the value system that is generally accepted is that which corresponds to what the society regards as ideal or most acceptable, which then equals what is 'normal.' In depicting such a system and determining its supports it is likely that all other behaviors constitute or fall into the category of abnormality, of marginality. Its influence may well extend beyond the definition of abnormality, of marginality as a social concept; it may even cause health practitioners to consider persons manifesting such behavior as abnormal, marginal deviates." (ibid. 144)

As well as the achievements and challenges still facing the Basque feminist movement, we will finish by considering new areas of interest in Gender Studies, such as health and sexuality, immigration and multiculturalism. The emerging models will give us pointers for ongoing research in gender, whether in the Basque context or beyond, and will contribute to the project of a more equal society for all.

Lesson four

Summary

1. Culturally specific concepts of personhood, self, and autonomy should also be taken into account when considering what it means to be a woman or a man in a particular society.
2. The concept of gender should be taken together with factors of race, class, and other variables of social differentiation that may intersect in the production of inequality.
3. The concept of gender systems enables the contemplation of the multiple intersections that contribute

to maintaining unequal gender relations in society. Gender systems embrace:

a. Gender stratification: the degree of gender inequality of a society measured by the different access to valuable resources between males and females who are otherwise social equals
b. Gender differentiation: the process by which gender difference is translated into a factor of inequality through the ascription of positive or negative values

4. Once gender is accepted as depending on the social relations between men and women in a given context, then the categories of "women" and "men" are shown to be not single, universal, nor timeless but both multiple and locally, culturally, and historically specific. Furthermore, they are inevitably dependent upon each other, and therefore the social construction and situation of both men and women must be understood in relation to one another.

Suggested Reading

Teresa del Valle, "The Current Status of the Anthropology of Women: Models and Paradigms," in W. A. Douglass, ed., Essays in Basque Social Anthropology and History, Basque Studies Program Occasional Papers Series no.4 (Reno: University of Nevada Press, 1989).

Henrietta Moore, "The Differences Within and the Differences Between," in T. del Valle, ed., Gendered Anthropology (London: Routledge, 1993), 192–204.

Bibliography

English Bibliography

Marilyn Strathern, "Self-Interest and the Social Good: Some Implications of Hagen Gender Imagery," in S.

Ortner and H. Whitehead, eds., Sexual Meanings (1981), 166–91.
Verena Stolcke, "Is Sex to Gender as Race Is to Ethnicity?" in T. del Valle (ed.), Gendered Anthropology (London: Routledge, 1993), 17–37.
Spanish Bibliography
Susana Narotzky, Mujer, Mujeres, Género: Una aproximación al estudio de las mujeres en las Ciencias Sociales (Madrid: Consejo Superior de Investigaciones Científicas, 1995).
Verena Stolcke, "Antropología del Género: El cómo y el porqué de las mujeres," in J. Prat and A. Martínez, eds., Ensayos de Antropología Cultural (Barcelona: Ariel, 1996), 335–43.

Written lesson for submission

In what way can the notion of "gender systems" help us better understand the roots of inequality between women and men in any given society? How will "systems analysis" aid our approach to gender relations in the Basque context?

Key words

SEX: the biological difference (chromosomal, hormonal, morphological) between males and females.
GENDER: the social definition attached to one's biological sex that creates a cultural concept of men and women, masculine and feminine.
FEMINISM: the advocacy of women's rights on the grounds of the equality of the sexes.
ANDROCENTRIC: showing male bias.
ENGENDERMENT: the process by which males and females come to be gender differentiated.

Part two. Basque women from farm to factory

5 · Women in traditional Basque society

Basque society as a whole underwent major changes in the twentieth century, changes that were related to the political climate, economic development, and social values, and that revolutionized women's lives in many ways. In this section, we will look at how women moved from the traditional ways of life in the farming and fishing communities of the Basque Country and joined the labor force in the factories and related outlets during the midcentury industrial boom. First we will consider what life was like in traditional society, examining the elaboration of an ideal that works to fix reality even as it is altered. We will see how labor was divided by gender in traditional rural and coastal society and then how this is modified by socioeconomic change, attracting both women and men to paid jobs in the urban, industrial environment. Finally, we will look at the areas of gender and technology in the context of the cooperatives of Mondragón, evaluating the benefits for women workers of democratic principles derived both from cooperative philosophy and Basque cultural values. We will posit both a cultural analysis of women's symbolic relation to work and a sociological explanation of their practical experience in the labor market.

Up till the eighties, there had been little work done on the place and participation of women in Basque society. The information available had to be gleaned from works on society in general, and these were typically studies of rural life. José Miguel Barandiaran (1889–1991), considered the founding father of Basque anthropology, continues to stand out as one of the main sources in this respect, along with Julio Caro Baroja (1914–1995), held as its first theorist. The information they give of the

Basque woman is primarily fixed in the rural context and linked to the institutions of family and religion. It is in this context that we will consider the position of women in traditional Basque society.

In all cultures there exists an ideal, a model or stereotype of the way both women and men should be. The fact that the ideal may be far removed from reality and fails to take into account the huge variety of types of women and men is irrelevant for the functioning of the ideal: it remains a model by which people are valued, judged, punished, or rewarded in society. It is used as a measure by which one stands or falls, a norm to which some aspire and against which others rebel. It is an indicator of cultural values and of change in those values where an old ideal is rejected and a call for alternative models is heard. Gender models operate a set of stereotypes that, as we have seen (Chapter 4), are based on beliefs or perceptions of differences between men and women, differences in psychological, biological, and behavioral traits that supposedly better equip women and men for specific roles. Often, the stereotypes are founded on apparently "natural" differences, nature acting to legitimate difference in a process of "naturalization."

The first and most comprehensive attempt to analyze the ideal representation of Basque women and compare it with the reality is to be found in the pioneering work *Mujer vasca: Imagen y realidad* (1985), the fruit of research carried out by a team directed by Teresa del Valle in the early eighties.[3] The team dedicated three years to study the contemporary social and cultural situation of women in the Basque Country, expanding on the information derived from the predominantly rural setting to include the coastal and urban communities of Euskal Herria, and bringing up to date the available knowledge that was focused on the past. We will come back to this book in the following chapters, as, though there is regretfully no English translation, it is an obligatory work of reference in Basque Gender Studies and an invaluable source of information on Basque women. In this section, we will follow the overview of the studies of Basque Women given in the first chapter of the book, which will help us look at the different ways women have been represented in Basque Studies in the past (ibid. 22–61).

The Ideal

First, let us see how the image of the ideal Basque woman is borne out in the work of the different authors discussed, first of all José Miguel Barandiaran and Julio Caro Baroja, whose work paves the way for all subsequent studies, and later William Douglass, Sandra Ott, and others such as Davydd Greenwood, whose work we will consider when we look at the issue of change in traditional Basque society. The twenty volumes of Barandiaran's complete works (*Obras Completas*) provide us with a wealth of ethnographical information on a broad spectrum of traditional Basque life, whereas Caro Baroja's work has a more analytical edge. Nevertheless, with regard to Basque women, both paint a picture of women in the rural world, focusing on their role in relation to the family and religion, and also in the realm of mythology and witchcraft, though in this section we will concentrate on the former and look at the latter in Part 3. Other activities Barandiaran mentions for women are: *hilandera* (seamstress), *serora* (church warden), *adivinadora* (fortune teller), *partera* (midwife), *maestra* (teacher), and *curandera* (healer). He refers to the fishwives of the coast as well, though he tells us little more about these coastal women, his sphere of study being largely the rural world.

Following in the footsteps of Barandiaran and Caro Baroja, William Douglass[4] was the first American anthropologist to carry out extensive field work in the Basque Country, and to him we owe the first analyses of traditional rural society from a social anthropological perspective. In Echalar and Murelaga (1975), Douglass reveals aspects of gender relations concerning conflict and change that had not previously been considered within the baserri and moves from ethnographic description to a more thorough interpretation. In Death in Murelaga (1969) he gives particular attention to the ritual role of women at death and in funeral rites. In a similar vein, the work of Sandra Ott (1981) in the French Basque village of Sainte-Engrâce provides a wealth of detail about women's and men's roles in pastoral life.[5]

In her thesis on "The Basque mother in her psychological context: a study of personality in culture" (my translation), Charlotte Joanne Crawford (1982) establishes a model based on certain sociocultural factors related largely to family structure and socialization strategies and then sets out to establish a dynamic relation between these factors and the personality of Basque women. Although it is not in our interests to enter into a discussion of personality studies here, the authors of Mujer vasca (39) question the usefulness of applying a psychoanalytical frame of analysis to sociocultural phenomena. Nonetheless, the elements on which Crawford builds her model of women in Basque culture are common to those that emerge in the portrait painted by Barandiaran and Caro Baroja of the archetypical Basque woman:

The ideal Basque woman
The ideal Basque woman was to be a good mother, hard worker and efficient wife. The rural woman worked both in the house and out, but her main area of control was the kitchen.
Collection Asunción Maisterrena

---

1. The importance of her role as mother
2. Her administration of domestic finances
3. Nondiscrimination in terms of inheritances
4. Her shared responsibility in the baserri or Basque farmhouse

The Rural Tradition

The woman of the farmhouse or baserri is known in Basque as etxekoandrea (literally "the woman of the house") and the man is etxekojauna ("the man of the house"). The attributes of the Basque housewife are being a good mother, hard worker, helpful neighbor, sober, willing to serve, good organizer and administrator, clean and healthy. Negatively sanctioned traits are nosiness, vanity, and ostentation.

A good mother. The importance of the role of mother is generally emphasized in Basque culture, and she is seen performing functions in relation to this role. In the works mentioned, the etxekoandrea is portrayed mostly in her participation in rites of passage, especially those related to birth and death (see Part 5):

At birth: women are the midwives and attend each other in birth; women look after the newborn, bathing and caring for the baby, taking them to be baptized; female relatives and neighbors visit the mother; in contrast, the father has a more public function of announcing the birth to the community.

At death: women are responsible for maintaining the links with the ancestors and in this sense are responsible for the well-being both of the living and the dead, those who live or have lived in the household; the men represent the family vis-à-vis the auzoa (neighborhood) and the village.

The etxekoandere is also seen to be important in the transmission of the Basque language and culture, passing on the heritage to successive generations and thus keeping it alive.

A hard worker. Although we will speak more of the division of labor below, let us just point out here that male and female roles on the baserri or farm are differentiated. The woman was held mainly responsible for the domestic domain, and her focus was toward the organization of the household and child care. She was seen to be the mainstay of the farm, mediator and main reference for the family. At the same time, she had a part to play in the farm work, albeit under the man's direction, and her hard work was valued both in the home and on the land. The men's realm of activity and influence was the public sphere and involved a social role that they maintained into old age. Apart from work, women are seen in festive and ritual activities, particularly those that take place in the family where they have the role of organizer. Women's social sphere was reduced to their relations with their female neighbors, people of their own age group, or the priest.

An efficient wife. In the work of Barandiaran, we see women mostly in interaction with their children and are told nothing about the affective relations between women and men. Nevertheless, there is information to be gleaned about marriage, and Julio Caro Baroja elaborates on this theme. He emphasizes the woman's place in the socioeconomic unit of the household and the family, in which the institution of marriage has an important economic role to play in the relations established between the households of each spouse and especially in terms of inheritance (Mujer vasca: 29).

Marriage was considered to be the desirable state for both women and men, singleness being negatively viewed except in the case of the serora, a type of church warden who had a certain independence and influence and was an agent of change through introducing new elements in religious rituals.

Within marriage, a woman was valued in terms of work, economic responsibility, the exercise of power, obligations toward the senior couple, her husband, and

The traditional Basque housewife
In traditional rural society the Basque woman was required to live at close quarters with her husband's family and required to be a dutiful daughter-in-law.
Photo: Iñaki Ugarte

---

children. Douglass considers women-influenced decision-making to the extent that men could not make financial transactions without their consent. Nevertheless, despite a certain power that the woman appears to exercise within the family and farm, it is not acceptable for her to rule over her husband, such behavior being negatively sanctioned.

Finally, as has often been the case, adultery by a woman was punished but pardoned in a man.

A dutiful daughter-in-law. Douglass points to the presence of conflict within harmonious household relations, especially on farms with an inheriting male whose wife is theoretically in charge over domestic life but comes into conflict with her mother-in-law, who is supposed to desist from her previous rule of the roost yet finds it hard to do so. In extreme cases where the inheriting son or etxekojaun is unable to solve the situation, the farmhouse is divided into two independent units with the corresponding division of human and economic resources. Often, to avoid the diminishing returns that this would suppose for the farm, differences between women were frequently suppressed and not allowed to surface.

Coastal Society

Until fairly recently, comparatively little work has been done on women of the coast. According to the information available, the coastal women responded to a different stereotype from that operative for the rural women. Typically they had a greater public presence than their rural counterparts, it being their job to sell the fish the men went out to catch, and this contributed to a stereotype of the Basque fisherwoman as decisive, enterprising, and authoritative with a clear role in the family economy.

The public role of coastal women in marketing the fish caught by the men propels her into a realm of social activity that gives rise to a stereotype of the fisherwoman as outspoken, competent in speaking out in public and expressing her own ideas and opinions, standing up for herself.

Lesson five

Summary

1. The ideal of the Basque woman is based on an archetype of the rural woman that transpires from the work of Barandiaran and Caro Baroja and

---

overshadows the contemporary reality until the publication of Mujer vasca in the eighties.
2. The ideal of the Basque rural woman stresses her role as mother, wife, and daughter-in-law who, moreover, must be a hard worker and good administrator.
3. The stereotype of coastal women differed from that of their rural counterparts, projecting a more public role with greater autonomy and independence.

Suggested Reading

Charlotte Joanne Crawford, "The Position of Women in a Basque Fishing Community," in W. A. Douglass, R. W. Etulain, and W. H. Jacobsen, Jr., eds., Anglo-American Contributions to Basque Studies: Essays in Honour of Jon Bilbao (Reno: Desert Research Institute, 1977), 145–52.

Bibliography

English Bibliography

William A. Douglass, Death in Murelaga: Funerary Ritual in a Spanish Basque Village (Seattle and London: University of Washington Press, 1969).

———, Echalar and Murelaga: Opportunity and Rural Exodus in Two Spanish Basque Villages (New York: St. Martin's Press, 1975).

Sandra Ott, The Circle of Mountains: A Basque Shepherding Community (Reno: University of Nevada Press, 1st ed. 1981, 2d ed. 1993).

Spanish Bibliography

José Miguel Barandiaran, Obras completas (Bilbao: La Gran Enciclopedia Vasca, 1972).

Julio Caro Baroja, De la vida rural vasca (Estudios Vascos, IV) (San Sebastián: Txertoa, 1974).

———, Baile, familia y trabajo (Estudios Vascos, VII) (San Sebastián: Txertoa, 1976).

Joanne Crawford, "La madre vasca y su contexto psicológico: Un estudio de la personalidad" (Ph.D. diss., University of Barcelona, 1982).
Teresa del Valle, et al., *Mujer vasca: Imagen y realidad* (Barcelona: Anthropos, 1985) (Chap. 1: "Visión general de los estudios sobre la mujer vasca"/Overview of studies of Basque women).

Written lesson for submission

Show how stereotypes function in the projection of an ideal for Basque rural women and say how this is different for coastal women.

6 · The gender division of labor

In the first section on gender theory we saw the differentiation of gender roles, the distinction between the public and domestic domains, and the generalized association of men with the former and women with the latter. We also saw the argument for taking into account women's access to and control of resources, the means of production, and the share of profits. In this section we will look more closely at how the gender division of labor works in the Basque case, continuing first of all with our discussion of traditional life patterns.

What Women and Men Do

In Basque society, as in most others, men and women do different kinds of work and certain cultural norms distinguish women's and men's tasks. Douglass emphasizes the complementarity of functions performed by the etxekojaun and etxekoandrea producing equality between the sexes in family partnerships such as husband and wife or brother and sister. He believes there is no double morality in this arrangement, though del Valle et al. consider there is insufficient data to make this claim for Basque society as a whole.

Chafetz (1990:31) points out that the cross-cultural differences defining male and female activities are most obvious when comparing societies with different forms of economies and technologies (e.g., foraging, pastoral, horticultural, agrarian, industrial): "For instance, in one society or societal type (e.g. horticultural) women may be responsible for growing most or all of the food, while in another (e.g. most agrarian societies) men may be, and in yet others (e.g. rice-growing agrarian societies) both are involved in food growing but their specific tasks differ."

In the Basque case, a chronological view of men's and women's tasks through history, charting the development of society from a subsistence agricultural and pastoral society to a complex industrial one, will reveal changes in the gender division of labor. Moreover, as well as the vertical, historical approach, we need to look at the picture on the horizontal plane, taking into account the different areas of activity occurring within the Basque Country and the gender-differentiated tasks associated with them. It will be helpful here to divide Euskal Herria broadly into three main areas of economic activity (though, like most analytically useful divisions, these categories may overlap and cannot be assumed to be water-tight): rural/agricultural, coastal/fishing, and urban/industrial.

Apart from important differences, Chafetz signals that there are also fundamental cross-cultural uniformities in the gender division of labor:

1. Women everywhere bear a greater responsibility than men in the work of child care, food preparation, and home keeping. Men may take on differing degrees of responsibility in this realm, from none to a significant amount, but the degree of women's responsibility is uniformly high.
2. Men everywhere take part in a number of extradomestic tasks related to economic, political, religious, educational, and cultural areas of activity. The level of women's participation may go from none to a significant amount, but men's participation is uniformly high.

Or in Chafetz's words (1990:31): "Women tend to shoulder the bulk of responsibilities associated with children and the household, and vary in the extent to which they participate in other types of work; men are universally involved in extradomestic work tasks, and vary in the extent of their domestic and child-rearing work."

The gender division of labor is thus a variable and one to be taken into account when assessing the gender inequality of a society. The first step is to ascertain the extent to which men's and women's activities—both in and out of the domestic domain—are gender segregated. The second step is to discover how the gender division of labor leads to gender inequality. What is it that makes the different tasks done by men and women come to be valued differently? How does it happen that the work done by men is often considered to be superior and thus receives higher rewards than women's work, which tends to be deemed inferior and is undervalued and underpaid?

In our examination of the gender division of labor in Basque society let us first examine the traditional sectors of rural and coastal life and then, in the next section, look at the changes brought about by the rural urban exodus, industrial revolution, and urban expansion.

The Division of Labor in Traditional Basque Society

An analysis of the sexual division of labor in traditional Basque society reveals interesting differences between the agricultural, pastoral and fishing sectors. Women are found to have been responsible for the domestic realm across the board, but take their place alongside the men to work the land, though the responsibility for the livestock, especially the sheep, falls to the men. In the coastal societies, fishing is a male activity, but the

The changing face of women's work
Butchers, bakers and candlestick makers; presidents, bankers and captains of tankers.
Illustration by Seymour Chwast.

commercialization of the catch is the women's. Let us take a closer look.

Farming. In the traditional rural way of life, there are three spheres of activity to consider:

1. The domestic domain: etxekoandere is in charge of household organization and caring for the children
2. The farm: etxekojaun is responsible for the land and livestock
3. The auzoa or neighborhood: female activities are connected to rites of passage, assisting neighbors in birth and death; male activities are more public, responsible for making announcements of birth and death

The Basque baserri or farm was a small holding, traditionally organized as a self-sufficient unit that functioned to meet the needs of the household who lived and worked on the land. A small vegetable garden provided food for the family and any surplus was sold at the local market. Main crops were corn and turnip for the livestock, and potatoes and other roots, beans, and greens for the house. The animals were housed in the baserri in winter and grazed on the farm lands or common mountain pastures in the summer. Given the mountainous terrain and small size of the properties, there was little arable land for crops and the fields needed intensive fertilizing to produce annually. Hence, the manure gathered from winter stabling was important for feeding the lands for crops and the meadows for pasture. Sheep were the principle livestock kept, suited to the mountains and valued for meat and milk for cheese. Oxen were kept as beasts of burden, along with a donkey or mule, and used to pull the plough, hay carts, and other farm implements. A pig was killed each year and cured to provide meat, ham, bacon, and sausages for the winter; poultry gave eggs and meat.

Work on the land was divided between the etxekoak, the members of the household, which typically comprised three generations. The senior couple handed over ownership and management of the farm to one of their sons or daughters, but continued to live on the farm, though technically retired from work. The junior couple, the inheriting son or daughter with their spouse, together formed the central core of the household's labor force and were aided by their own children as they grew up, as well as by any unmarried siblings who remained in the baserri.

The workload was also shared with neighbors of the auzoa on a reciprocal basis and in an arrangement that established an order of interaction with one's "first" neighbors.

Following through the seasons, we can get an overview of male and female participation in the agricultural work:[6]

Spring: The preparation of the land, involving turning the soil for planting and the raking and fertilizing of pasture lands, was performed by the junior couple.

Spring planting was done by the married couple together, sometimes with the assistance of a male relative or a male first neighbor.

Summer: Hay-making: all the able members of the household, male and female, participated in cutting and turning the grass for hay. Vegetable gardening: women's work.

Autumn: The women gathered fruit and nuts from their own land and the common lands, mainly walnuts, chestnuts, and hazelnuts, as well as apples for eating or making into cider; apples formed part of the goods that were reciprocally exchanged between neighbors (women

Women in coastal society
On the coast, women worked on shore while the men went out to sea. As in this picture from the quay of Bermeo, they helped bring in the catch and were responsible for selling the fish, as well as performing other tasks such as making baskets or mending the nets.
Photo: Gari Garaialde

---

were expected to take a bag of apples to their first neighbors whenever visiting); the men hunted wild boar and pigeons that they either sold to local restaurants or used for household consumption.

Fern cutting: The gathering of ferns for animal bedding and ultimately the making of manure was also a way of clearing and tending the land and was a predominantly male activity carried out at the end of summer, usually in September; it involved first-neighbor reciprocity among men, and the etxekojaun would invite one or more male first neighbors to assist and would then be obliged to return the service.

Maize harvest: A task for both men and women in October and one in which first neighbors participated, all gathering in the barn in the evenings to husk the corn and drink wine together.

Winter: Pig-killing: winter work for all. The men were in charge of slaughtering and butchering, and in each case the male head of the household invited two others to help him, either kin or neighbors. Traditionally the slaughtering took place before dawn, the butchering took two to three hours and then they would stop for a big meal or *almuerzo*. Then the women would take over and spend three days making the black puddings with the blood collected when the pig's throat was cut, cleaning the intestines for sausage skins and making the sausages, cooking meat, making paté, curing hams and bacon.

Sandra Ott (see below) found the women referred to the pig-killing season as a "bad month" because of the blood, stench, and unpleasant tasks they had to perform.

Shepherding. When it comes to shepherding, the work is performed largely by men and in this sense, Ott's fascinating study gives us unparalleled insight into the organization of a shepherding community. She signals the following activities:

1. Men were mainly responsible for herding, feeding, and (in spring and summer) milking the ewes and making cheese.
2. Traditionally women were allowed to assist in herding and feeding but not in the milking, which was considered an exclusively male task (as was the cheese-making, which, as we shall see later, in some communities had specific sexual connotations); Sandra Ott records for Sainte-Engrâce that women

regarded the milking of ewes, though not of cows, as a filthy and disgusting thing to have to do (1993:33).

3. The tending of the sheep in the summer mountain pasture was also an exclusively all-male task; the women were invited up to the shepherds' hut or olha on the first day when the flocks were taken up to the heights, but they performed no domestic tasks; they partook in a meal prepared by the men but were forbidden entry to the hut, where they were repulsed by the wood smoke and the cooking conditions inside.
4. Sheep shearing: a male task but one in which close male relatives are asked for assistance rather than neighbors.
5. Slaughtering lambs in spring and ewes in the autumn also falls to the men.

What is of particular interest for our concerns is the distribution of roles in the olha, a term used both for the shepherds' syndicate (which groups together several shepherds and their flocks for the purpose of sharing the summer work of mountain pasturing, milking, and cheese-making) and the hut itself where the shepherds stay during their time in the mountains. Traditionally, six men worked together at any one time, performing a series of tasks in a system of rotation that followed a hierarchical order in which those associated with the hut and domestic tasks were given female names. Thus, at the top of the hierarchy we find that the man in charge of housekeeping, cooking, and, most importantly, cheese-making was known as etxekandere or "woman of the house." His assistant, responsible for menial domestic chores, was the neskato or "female servant," right at the bottom of the ladder.[7] The other roles that concerned tasks outside the domestic space of the hut

> were designated as male and divided between the master shepherd and his assistant, the guardian of the nonmilking ewes and the guardian of the lambs.
>
> In their mountain huts, the shepherds re-created the domestic and ideologically female domain of the house. In the carefully balanced division of labor, feminine roles were played by shepherds working within the hut, whereas masculine roles were played by those who worked outside the hut among the sheep....
>
> Even as outside the house is the domain of the female etxekandere in the valley, the hut was—and is still is—the domain of a male etxekandere playing an ideological "feminine" role. (1993:151–52) as outside the house is the domain of the female.

An interesting dimension of the assumption of "female" roles by the shepherds is the association between the production of cheese and the conception and care of children. As well as there being an ideological connection between the way a child is conceived and the way a cheese is made, which leads to an evaluation of masculinity and particularly virility in terms of being a good cheese-maker, the analogy is carried over into looking after new cheeses, which are said to be like newborn babies and require special care and attention early in life. The symbolic assumption by the shepherds of both the male and female aspects of procreation through cheese-making and child care through the turning and salting of the fresh cheese set out to dry, does not seem to undermine their masculinity in any way, which is reinforced by their cheese-making ability. In the same way, Ott observes that feminine references are applied to the looking after of the sheep as well, requiring the "patience of a woman towards her children," giving them affection and attention (ibid. 171). This appropriation of female attributes in the construction of a positive male model is illuminating and poses possibilities for enhancing the usually inferior status of "women's" work as well as for altering the often negative attitude to men who work in professions ascribed as "feminine."

Fishing. Moving from the mountains to the sea, we have seen that although Barandiaran and Caro Baroja contemplated the coast in their work, there have been relatively fewer studies done on the coastal communities and consequently we have less information about the women from fishing villages. Studies in Spanish are indicated in the bibliography, but we have little to go by in English and even less that specifically focuses on women in either language. Juan Antonio Rubio-Ardanaz's work on maritime anthropology in general and on the fishing community of Santurtzi (Bizkaia) in particular provides some of the most up-to-date insights, complements former work such as that of Felipe Barandiaran (1982), and paves the way for more recent studies like that of Pio Perez (2001),[8] who nonetheless reiterates the general absence of women and family in the studies conducted.

Overall, the traditional division of labor in these communities worked along the lines of the men going out to sea to fish and the women staying behind. It is generally agreed that the conditions of life were hard on both men and women. The men faced not only the hardships out at sea but the separation and loneliness that went with it, while the women also had their share of suffering, bearing dual responsibilities in the private and public domains. Women were in charge of running the household and caring for the children single-handedly and at the same time worked outside the home in the harbor, preparing and mending the nets,

Strength and independence
Coastal women have been renowned for their strength and independence, developed in the long absences of the men at sea. Their own engagement with the sea is reflected in their participation in rowing, a sport popular in the coastal communities where there is fierce competition. Here a group of bateleras prepare to row their small boat called a batel.
Photo: Iñaki Edroso.

---

fetching and carrying the fish from the boats to the place where it was to be weighed and dispatched for sale, and then selling the fish. As Rubio-Ardanaz points out (1994:117)[9] unlike the subsistence economy of the baserri, which covered most of its basic needs without recourse to the market, fishing relied on a monetary economy since it needed to sell the fish to purchase other foodstuffs and basic necessities. As well as the commercial activity that surrounded fishing, the production of baskets to transport the fish was a craft in which both women and men were employed.

The women watched for the arrival of the boats early in the morning and would run down to meet them with the baskets on their heads to bring in the fish and put it up for sale. It was then auctioned off for distribution and sale at a market stall or fish dealers or, as in the case of sardine fishing to which Ardanaz refers, to *sardineras* who would then sell it on the streets.

Owing to the nature of their work, both fishermen and women had greater mobility and a wider social network than their rural counterparts. The women would travel to other villages to sell the fish, meeting other women and also selling their wares and thus expanding their area of social interaction. Activities such as mending the nets was also a communal chore, performed in groups led by a "maestra" (literally, teacher) who directed the work.

Lesson six

Summary

1. The sexual division of labor varies over time and place. In the Basque Country we can plot changes from an agricultural, pastoral, and fishing economy to an industrial, and currently postindustrial, society. At the same time, in any one sphere of activity we can expect to find a gendered segregation of work in which women have greater domestic responsibilities and men have a higher level of participation in extra-domestic activities, which are more highly valued than those performed by women.
2. Some authors argue for the egalitarian division of labor in the traditional Basque rural world. There is

evidence that women and men shared the tasks outside the house, but on the whole, women were chiefly responsible for the domestic domain and men for the land and livestock.

3. Shepherding is seen to be a predominantly male activity, but there is an interesting parallel between the female world of child rearing and the male realm of shepherding and cheese-making in which feminine values are carried over and incorporated into a culturally specific model of masculinity.
4. In the fishing communities, the men go to sea and the women are in charge of selling the catch brought in by the menfolk. Here, both the commercial and the social aspects of economic activity stand out. Interaction between buyers and sellers is important, as is the teamwork of mending the nets. At the same time, the women are in charge of managing the family and home, especially while the men are away.

Suggested Reading

William Douglass, "The Baserria," in Echalar and Murelaga, 23–32.

Sandra Ott, "The Seasonal Cycle" (31–38) and "Rotation and Serial Replacement in the Olha: Past and Present" (151–56), in The Circle of Mountains, A Basque Shepherding Community (Reno: University of Nevada Press, 1993).

Bibliography

English Bibliography

As in the section Women in Traditional Basque Society above.

Spanish Bibliography

Felipe Barandiaran, "La comunidad de pescadores de bajura de Pasajes San Juan (ayer y hoy)," Estudio antropológico (Oiartzun: Litografía Danona, 1982).

Juan Antonio Rubio-Ardanaz, "La Antropología marítima subdisciplina de la Antropología sociocultural: Teoría y temas para una aproximación a la comunidad pescadora de Santurtzi" (Bilbao: Universidad de Deusto, 1994).

Written lesson for submission

Traditional Basque society exhibits an egalitarian gender division of labor in the rural and fishing contexts. Discuss.

7 · Women and change

In assessing women's role in the transformation of traditional Basque society, it is interesting to observe whether they are receptors of changes occurring in the broader social and economic context or whether they are agents provoking changes to suit their own interests. It is evident that against the backdrop of deterioration and decline both in the rural and coastal sectors, set off by the growth in industry and the accompanying urbanization, women respond in different ways to new opportunities for incorporation in the labor market.

In the rural world. In Douglass's comparative work on two rural Basque communities, Echalar and Murelaga, which we mentioned above, women are portrayed as agents of change in the traditional socioeconomic organization of the farm. Many women were found to have left the farm in search of alternatives, and here we see them in working environments or social contexts beyond the baserri, working in hotels, laboring in factories, and even smuggling goods across the border or acting as lookouts or as messengers. They are also depicted in the public arena where they had hitherto been inconspicuous, meeting in a bar for instance.

The nature of the areas from which they originate influences the options taken by young women leaving the farms. In the village of Echalar, situated in the north of Nafarroa, near the Spanish/French border, Douglass found it was the girls who were most critical of village life and those who most wanted to leave. Their proximity to the coast provided opportunities of taking seasonal work in the hotels and restaurants in the French

Autonomy and authority
Fishing women spent long periods of time alone while the men were out at sea and had to run the house and family single-handed, developing both autonomy and authority.
Photo: Iñaki Edroso.

Basque resort of St Jean de Luz, and then, having learnt French, several went on to serve as maids in Paris:

> Migration from Echalar is most prominent amongst the young unmarried women. They leave to serve in tourist complexes or in some cases as domestics in wealthy Parisian homes. They are exposed to a way of life which differs markedly from that of the village. The nature of their work brings them into contact with people of another culture and forces them to learn the language. Their work also brings them into contact with a whole range of modern ideas and conveniences. (Douglass, 1975:123)

In the case of Echalar, Douglass found that the experiences of life beyond the baserri provoke a critical attitude in women toward the traditional way of life of the farm. The women who have worked away from home are more reticent to marry a farmer and return to the farming life. However, the experience of men was quite the contrary. Men leaving Echalar went either to the American West or to the French Alps, but failed to integrate into local culture since they tended to live with other Basques and had little exposure to the French or American people and their language. The nature of their work, sheepherding in the Far West or wood-cutting in the Alps, was the main factor contributing to their isolation and difficulty of integration. These men were found to spend their time daydreaming of their homes and only wanted to return to their villages: "The young female returnee is impressed and frustrated by the "backwardness" of local existence. The young man seeks his fulfilment in terms of approval by his fellow-villagers whereas the young woman is alienated from village way of life through her foreign experiences." (ibid. 123)

Nonetheless, the circumstances were discovered to be quite different in the rural village of Murelaga, situated in the interior of Bizkaia in a setting similar to that described for Echalar. Fewer women left the village of Murelaga and those that did went to work in the factories of nearby industrial centers. They were more willing to marry and stay on in the village, and marriage to an émigré who had returned home was considered especially desirable in terms of economic and social status. We will return to Basque women and emigration in Part 4, where we look at the women who chose to stay abroad and the place they occupied in the communities into which they integrated, but here we will consider other aspects of change concerning women in their home environments. A couple of other examples that emerge from Douglass's work concern the change in women's responsibilities. On the one hand, where they go into wage employment off the farm, they enjoy greater financial independence, and we find a woman paying for own wedding, which would formerly have been unheard of. On the other hand, modernization and professionalization lead to a shift in roles, for example, in health care, where traditional female duties such as assisting each other in birth pass to the doctors and midwives.

Davydd J. Greenwood also examines change within the traditional rural way of life in his study *Unrewarding Wealth: The Commercialization and Collapse of Agriculture in a Spanish Basque Town* (1976). Here he looks at the progressive abandonment of the farming life in Hondarribia. He plots the changes induced by both men and women who move to work in the factories or in business in the urban industrial centers but considers that women's reluctance to marry within the *baserri* is a critical factor in the crisis in this sector. As we have seen, marriage was a vital institution for the socioeconomic organization of the Basque farm. Greenwood considers it the way to access property, labor, and capital (123). Thus when women refuse to marry and stay on the farm they threaten the whole system upon which the farm functions.

Miren Etxezarreta, whose book on the Basque farm *El caserío vasco* (1977) also demonstrates the effect on the evolution of the *baserri* of women's desire to move on, perceives a correlation between the negative evaluation of their work on the *baserri* and a positive view of working at home and with the children in the town. On the whole, there is change in expectations and aspirations. Greenwood finds that women come to formulate their own desires more explicitly and focus on themselves in terms of dress and personal presentation as well as in their wish to pursue an independent lifestyle beyond the confines of the old ways of the farm.

The authors of Mujer vasca (1985:274) confirm this situation and remark that the woman's refusal to continue in the baserri reveals the confrontation between the ideal and the reality, showing the "complex problematic of a life often hidden under the veil of idealization" (my translation). We could add that at the dawning of the twenty-first century, this continues to be a problem for many rural men who want to stay on their farms but find it hard to convince a woman to join them. This has prompted some to head for the sunny climes of the Caribbean or Latin America where many women are willing to enter a marriage relationship with a European as a passport to leave behind the poverty and hardship of their own lives. Needless to say, not all these arrangements are straightforward and many bring their own problems, which are a new subject of concern in Euskal Herria today.

In fishing. In the fishing environment, it would seem at first sight that women are the receptors rather than the agents of change. In the coastal community discussed by Barandiaran (1978), women's work was dependent on the men's fishing activity, so evidently precarious an occupation that where it failed or diminished, her work was immediately affected. The large-scale commercialization and mechanization of the fishing industry has inevitably pushed women out of their traditional roles while over-fishing has reduced the stock and there are more regulations on types and sizes of fish that may be caught and sold. As a result, the Basque fishing fleet as a whole has been considerably depleted in recent years. In addition, tighter laws on health and hygiene have placed restrictions on the selling of fish, hitting hard the fishwives who sold their wares on a small scale, directly to the customer on the street. Such has been the fate of the *sardineras* of Santurtzi described by Rubio-Ardanaz (1994) who have virtually disappeared, their numbers dropping from over a hundred in the sixties and seventies, to only eleven in the nineties. Those who continue are mostly women over sixty years of age whose popularity built up over the years, evidenced in the nicknames by which they are fondly known, and that enables them to still make a living from a fairly unprofitable business.

In another article on the subject, Rubio-Ardanaz (1993:34) observes that while the *sardinera* has all but vanished from the streets of Santurtzi, the image of this particular Basque fishwife has grown in symbolic status. The historical figure of these women is projected in photographs, drawings, and names in public places and entrance halls that evoke their contribution to the traditional identity of a community facing change.

Commenting on the eradication of female economic activity in Pasajes, Barandiaran observes that while their work had been the propeller of an enterprising and outward-going spirit and gave them a great capacity for change, once the work disappeared, these characteristics died out with it. This would seem to be the reverse from the case of rural women who acquired greater autonomy and ambition as they left their traditional roles, and at all events this observation needs backing up and testing out. We must draw attention to the presence of women in unprecedented places, for example on the boats and out at sea fishing alongside the men. This is still uncommon, yet in Hondarribia there is at least one female boat owner.

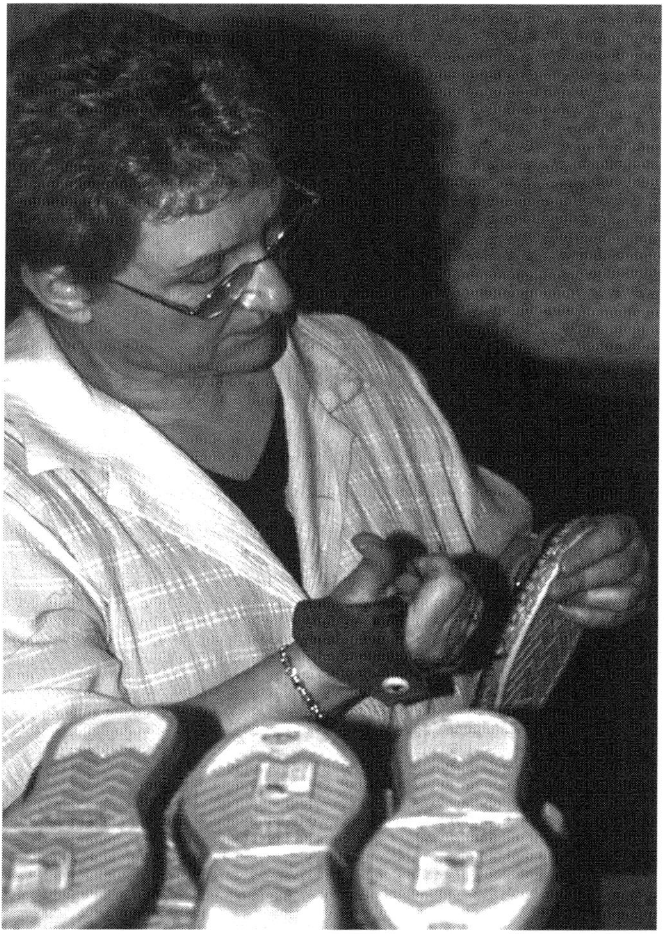

Craft, commerce and production
As well as attending to their duties at home, women have also been occupied in commerce and crafts, such as the sewing of these traditional Basque espadrilles.
Photo: Alain Pagoaga

Women in the Modern World

The changes in Basque society during the twentieth century can be seen to produce changes in the gender division of labor and in women's roles, attitudes, and aspirations, but as we have observed, women are also active agents in accelerating change. Thus women break with the traditional divisions of labor in rural life and emerge into modern industrial society where job distribution is different, though does not necessarily offer equal opportunities to women and men. However, in the context of twentieth-century Spain, the incorporation of women into paid labor in the Basque Country was not at all straightforward, and with the help of two articles by Carmen Díez (1999 a & b) we will situate ourselves in the historical context of the Franco regime (1936–1975) when it was virtually forbidden for women—especially if they were married—to go out to work (see Part 4).

Although Spain and particularly the industrializing regions of Euskal Herria and Cataluña experienced socioeconomic change linked to industrial development during the period 1950–1975, women's situation did not begin to alter significantly until after Franco's death in 1975. Judging by the figures for female economic activity, it was only from the second half of the seventies that a notable increase occurred in women's presence in the labor market, principally married women who had thereto been virtually absent from the workforce.

Women had been banned not only from the workplace but also from education, which had obvious implications for their later assimilation in the labor market. It is shocking to read that in 1970, when the Basic General Education Law was passed to ensure that primary education became available to all, 75 percent of Spanish women had only primary education and 12 percent had no schooling at all (which leaves an appallingly low 13 percent who had reached secondary school). Given these low figures, it is amazing to find that things could change so dramatically in the space of just over a decade, so that by 1982 no fewer than 82 percent of women between the ages of 15 and 19 had completed secondary education. Focusing on the repercussions of change in the Basque Country, the figures for the CAPV[10] show that the number of economically active, nonsingle women between the ages of 25 and 44 almost doubled in the period of 1985–1996 (rising from 37 to 66 percent), though many lacked a stable job and many potential workers were unemployed. Looking at education, Díez finds that 53 percent of Basque university students are now women, though there are still tendencies for a gendered division in the choice of subjects studied.

It is generally agreed that the incorporation of Basque women in the workplace is the most important change in the last quarter century and has had the greatest impact on their lives. The authors of Mujer vasca (1985:274–82) affirm this for the Basque women in their study. They point out that women not only began to take paid jobs when they were single rather than sit and wait to get married, but they also kept them after they were married. From the eighties, the studies of women in the urban environment have steadily increased and reveal a contradiction between women's aspirations and the roles traditionally assigned to them. Two significant studies from the eighties include one on the "Situation of Women in Euskadi," carried out for the Basque Government in 1982, and another titled "Sociological study of women between 20 and 60 years old in the Greater Bilbao area" by Alberdi, Ortiz de Zarata, and Peña. These pieces of research find that the traditional sexual division of labor is transmitted through

What women and men do
Women are also to be found in the caring professions and in the business of preparing and serving food, as in this Basque cider house.
Photo: Alain Pagoaga.

the institution of the family and reinforced through education. The main findings are:

1. That women assume the roles of wife and mother, often curtailing her career or cutting down her work outside the home to dedicate herself to the family, accepting a greater economic dependence on her partner
2. That women do not value the work they do within the home, reflecting the values of the broader society, which places value on paid work done outside the home
3. That in the workplace women do jobs traditionally assigned to women in the domestic sphere such as primary school teaching, administration, health, and other auxiliary and subordinate tasks
4. That women are absent on the whole from directorate positions

The interrelation between gender relations, the home, and the workplace is explored in another article by Carmen Díez (1995) that addresses the different socioeconomic contexts of a rural and urban environment. Comparing women's work in a rural area in the south of Nafarroa with that in the urban district of Donostialdea, she looks at aspects of the socioeconomic climate that affect women's degree of independence both through assimilation in the workplace and through new forms of socialization such as women's associations created with the specific aim of getting women out of the home. She also contemplates the changes in values with regard to the evaluation of women's and men's work as well as attitudes to women working outside the home or men participating in the domestic chores in the home.

Just as we saw in the influence of the political and economic context of the Franco years, we must also consider the implications of the postindustrial economic crisis affecting Euskal Herria from the eighties and requiring a transformation of the economy from an emphasis on heavy industry and manufacturing to the development of new technologies and services. These changes are to be taken into account along with higher levels of education, greater accessibility to nontraditional female employment, improved legislation providing for maternity leave, and better child care facilities. As we discover in the next chapter on women in technology, we will find, however, that despite the huge advances made in equal rights policies and various campaigns to promote women in their work and to lighten their burden at home, when we look at gender inequality at the beginning of the twenty-first century, we find we are still dealing with some of the very same issues.

Lesson seven

Summary

1. In the traditional rural world of the baserri, women are found to be decisive in bringing about change in their communities through their positive experiences of life beyond the farm, the benefits of paid work, and the increased freedom they enjoy. Their reluctance to marry and stay on the baserri is considered a factor crucial in the modification of an old system that not only ceases to be economically viable but also remains socially unacceptable, at least to women.
2. In the coastal communities, given the larger degree of independence exercised by fishwives, there is not

the same evidence of women propelling change. Rather economic changes affecting the fishing industry are seen to deprive them of the traditional activity of selling fish in the street, or at least changing the conditions under which they carry out their trade.

3. In the urban centers, women are found to enter paid employment in factories, shops, and offices. The political situation and socioeconomic climate prevailing before and after the Franco regime must be taken into account to understand the radical changes in women's situation in the workplace, but local factors are also important. The change in values with regard to women's and men's work and women's place in the home are noted to have changed greatly, but obstacles still remain for women with regard to entering male-dominated occupations, ascending to positions of responsibility, and combining paid work with domestic duties.

Suggested Reading

M. Carmen Díez Mintegui, "Female Labour, Participation and Gender Relationships: Analysis of Rural and Urban Environments," in RIEV (Revista Internacional de los Estudios Vascos), vol. XL, no. 2, 271–87.

Bibliography

English Bibliography

William Douglass, "Social and Economic History: The Settings," in Echalar and Murelaga, 109–35.

Davydd Greenwood, Unrewarding Wealth: The Commercialization and Collapse of Agriculture in a Spanish Basque Town (Cambridge: Cambridge University Press, 1976).

Spanish Bibliography

I. Alberdi, A. B. Ortiz de Zarate, and I. Peña Otero, "Estudio sociológico de la mujer de 20–60 años en el área de Gran Bilbao: Qué piensa, qué siente y como actúa" (unpublished manuscript).

Araldi Azterketa Elkartea, Emakumearen egoera Euskadin: Situación de la mujer en Euskadi (Departamento de Cultura, Gobierno Vasco, 1982).

M. Carmen Díez Mintegui, "Sistemas de género, desigualdad e identidad nacional," in P. Albite, coord., Sociedad vasca y construcción nacional (Donostia: Tercera Prensa–Hirugarren Prentsa, 1999a), 147–74.

———, "Historia de las mujeres en Euskal Herria," in (ed.) Euskal Borroka feminista aurrera (1999b), 105–17.

Miren Etxezarreta, El caserío vasco (Bilbao: Fundación C. de Iturriaga y M. Dañobeitia, Ed. Elespuru Hnos., 1977).

Juan Antonio Rubio-Ardanaz, "Las sardineras de Santurce: Desplazamiento de la mujer en un modo de distribución tradicional del pescado," in Narria: Estudios de artes y costumbres populares, nos. 61–62, Museo de Artes Tradicionales Populares, Facultad de Filosofía y Letras (Madrid: Universidad Autónoma de Cantoblanco, 1993).

Written lesson for submission

Outline the main factors of change for women's work in the past few decades.

8 · Gender, science, and technology

Women in science and technology is an area where some of the most groundbreaking work is currently being undertaken in Gender Studies, and the Basque Country, one of the leading regions in Spain in these industries, is producing some insightful new research (Part 6). As more women are entering the traditionally male fields of science and technology, more information also is becoming available about gender stratification and the obstacles facing women who want to move up in their profession.

Women in the Cooperatives of Mondragón

In this section, we will look at the success of a particular project in the Basque context that sets out to procure greater social equality through the institution of a worker-run industrial cooperative in Arrasate-Mondragón (Gipuzkoa) and judge how effective it is in achieving gender equality.

Arrasate in Basque (Mondragón in Spanish) is a location in Gipuzkoa that has attracted interest from various quarters thanks to its pioneering and successful experience in worker-owned and -managed industrial cooperatives. It is the subject of various studies that on the whole praise its successful democratic structure and process. Two studies of interest on the producer cooperatives of Mondragón are Sally Hacker's Pleasure, Power and Technology (1989) and Sharryn Kasmir's The "Myth" of Mondragón: Cooperatives, Politics and Working Class Life in a Basque Town (1997). It is the work of Hacker on women cooperative workers and the relation between gender and technology that will principally inform this section.

As in other parts of urban Gipuzkoa and Bizkaia, industrial centers of the Basque Country like Arrasate received a huge influx of immigrant labor from other parts of the Spanish State during the industrial boom of the sixties, and their presence has added an extra dimension to the thinking of Basque identity or the construction of a Basque or Spanish female subject. Since the Mondragón group of cooperatives was founded and headquartered in the province of Gipuzkoa, characterized by the decentralization of industry and often considered the heart of "Basqueness" in terms of language and culture (Hacker 1989:129), it has come to be a symbol of Basque-style business based on principles of solidarity and hard work as opposed to the non-Basque oligarchical enterprises behind the once powerful steel works of Bilbao—Altos Hornos de Vizcaya—which, Kasmir tells us, were backed by investors in Madrid and abroad. Marianne Heiberg, in her book The Making of the Basque Nation (1989:225), states that "cooperativism was the Basque nationalist mode of production."

Hacker sets out to test the hypothesis that the egalitarian principles of Basque culture and the democratic foundations of cooperativism unite in the case of Mondragón to produce more equitable participation of men and women in the workplace. It is argued that the Mondragón system is rooted in the antihierarchical values and behavior said to characterize Basque culture, where class difference and social status are relatively insignificant, one's circle of friends and family are more important than moving up the career ladder, and social life in the streets and bars privileges word-of-mouth communication and direct contact. Against this cultural background, Hacker found relations between the sexes to be open, socially expressed, and less individualized, and found women to be active in all aspects

Women as agents or receptors of change
Women have been key agents of change in the modernisation of Basque society, leading the way out of the traditional division of labour in the rural and coastal areas and taking up new urban lifestyles with a portion of paid work and leisure. Here a group of women who moved into the town from the country enjoy a social time which their mothers could only have dreamed of.
Collection Asunción Maisterrena.

---

of political activity as well as in feminist militancy: "Basque culture seemed to me among the least gender-differentiated of modern societies in appearance, style and presentation of self." (114)

Basque feminists, however, disagree with this image and point to the restrictions placed on them in public walks of life, in the matriarchal myths of Basque culture, and in the ritualized asymmetry of dance and festival (see Part 5). Drawing on the evidence gathered in *Mujer vasca*, Hacker concludes that the reality does not coincide with the image and that despite the egalitarian roots of Basque culture, patriarchal structures reinforced by institutions such as the Catholic Church maintain public/private divisions and hierarchical systems.

Similarly, the evidence of equality in the cooperatives did not come up to her expectations. She had thought that a Basque reputation for nonelitist engineering that combines theory with application would have made the cooperatives more participatory than she in fact found. While the Mondragón cooperative system does offer better and more equal opportunities for women than other more traditional sectors of the workplace, the author still believes it falls short of a gender-balanced democratic environment: "Mondragón is known as a system of democratically structured producer cooperatives yet the condition of women workers there is only somewhat better, relative to men, than in capitalist or already existing socialist organizations." (1986:120)

Cooperativist and egalitarian elements of Basque culture come into conflict with more authoritarian attitudes transmitted through the professional-technical approach over manufacturing technology and working-class culture (129). The emergence of a new management class is criticized as alien from workers, especially women workers. Gender stratification is built into manufacturing technology and its administrative structure and as a result, the organization and administration of work in the cooperatives is no different in this respect from that of other industrial societies. The cooperatives seek balance between workplace democracy and market demands and wish to strengthen cooperative participation, but in practice this is only for men and fails to change patterns of family and work.

Looking at opportunities for women in terms of employment, position, and pay, Hacker finds that women vary from a minority (20 percent) to a majority (70 percent) of the workforce, depending on the nature of the cooperative, but finds more men at the higher of three pay levels and in management, with women's presence increasing only gradually. More women are in clerical posts than in production, where they are generally found performing unskilled, low-paid tasks.

Although the cooperatives' orientation toward heavy industry might lead us to expect a lower percentage of women workers, Hacker found that the percentage was in fact slightly higher (28 percent) than the average for the Basque Country as a whole (25 percent). She attributed this on the one hand to the occupational structure, since working relations are found to be less hierarchical and more relaxed in the co-ops, and on the other to higher pay. Women in co-ops receive higher pay than their counterparts in private firms because the lower levels of the cooperative structure, where more women are employed, are better paid than in the private sector (though the higher levels receive less than their private counterparts).

Hacker focuses on "Auzo Lagun," a married women's co-op that provides services for the other co-ops (meals, cleaning) and manufactures heavy equipment for their work. Ironically, she found the only male in the co-op was the director. It has an interesting history, formed in 1969 in defiance of a Spanish law that forbade married woman to work in most private firms up until 1970 and in co-ops till 1973. Women met with initial resistance from men who felt that women belonged at home but changed their minds once they saw that the extra money helped improve their own standard of living. The women said they enjoyed cooperative work more than

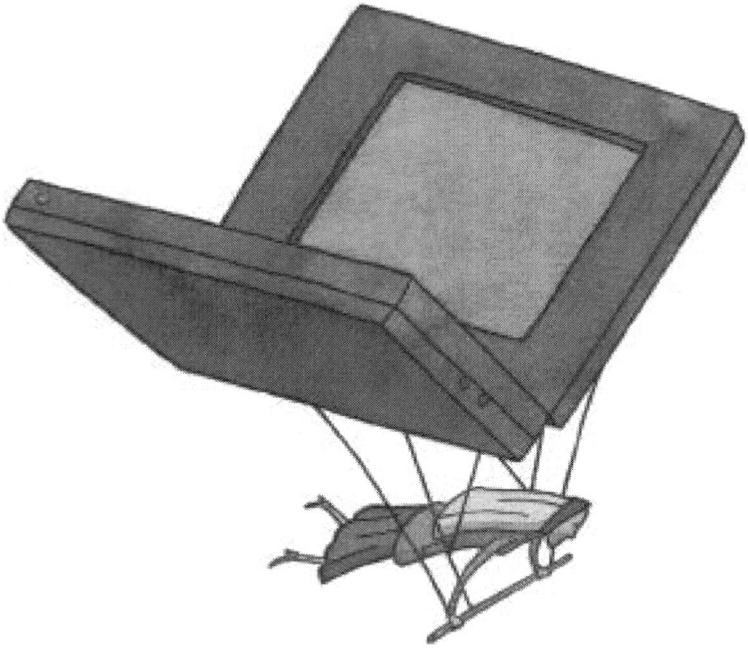

Liberating tools
The workplace is dominated by machines that demand uniform, portable skills. This works both ways. Ability and expertise that can be used for any employer also give people new freedom.
Illustration by Ingo Fast.

staying at home since it gave them greater freedom and autonomy, sociability, and a feeling of community.

Hacker cites three main impediments to gender equality in the Mondragón system. First, as in all industrial societies, women, whether wage earners or not, still maintain major responsibility for the home; in fact, she holds that the economic success of the cooperatives—like that of society as a whole—depends on women's unpaid labor in the home. Furthermore, she believes that care of children and other dependents has not been sufficiently supported by the cooperatives. Second, the capitalist market devalues collective social goals, and finally, the technical world is still overwhelmingly masculine and men control decisions about technology.

Combining Work and Family Life

One of the current areas of concern in equal opportunity is the conciliation of women's working and family life, the management of one's paid and unpaid work, and the sharing of responsibilities with male partners. Assessing the changes in women's situation in the last century, Díez (1999b:109) asks whether economic activity and education are sufficient indicators of progress and suggests that we also need to look more closely at the gendered division of labor, particularly the distribution of domestic work and the articulation between paid and nonpaid activities that is necessary for the reproduction of social life as a whole. Hacker suggests that despite changes, the social norm continues to be based on the patriarchal structure of family that emphasizes women's responsibility and separates it from male control of scientific and technical knowledge and skill. She believes it is the acceptance of these gendered spheres that prevents the development of alternative gender systems.

In the cooperatives, men at the upper levels are more likely to be married than at the lower, but the reverse is true for women, for whom marriage and children represent an impediment to promotion, not just because of internal prejudices but also for the practical difficulties and the onus on the woman to bear the brunt of child care. Some couples even work shifts to share child care or take advantage of child care provided in the cooperatives' nurseries. The women of Auzo Lagun, for example, work four-hour shifts to manage family/child care as well as work, but absenteeism for sickness (care of a family member) is still the biggest problem. Parental leave is available to both sexes but tends to be taken far more by women, though this is something that is beginning to change with more favorable conditions now offered in the Basque Country.

Feminist activism and day-to-day resistance challenge the contradictions arising between the ideological principles of participatory democracy that stand men and women on an equal footing and the hierarchical organizations in place in practice, which locate power in specialist technical knowledge not available to all (133).

Devaluing Social Goals

Social transformation requires that the work that many women do unpaid should be contemplated at a community level. This involves focusing on the person rather than the traditional family household as the basic economic unit (137). The practice of paying the man a wage to support his dependents maintains their dependency. The distribution of resources to the family as a unit reinforces its patriarchal structure: "When the community is perceived as the collective of its members, not patriarchal households or families, women will enter the workplace decision-making as men engage in daily life decisions about the care and rearing of children." (138)

Hacker concludes that feminist goals should be taken on board with other revolutionary social processes; for example: participatory and degendered technology; community responsibility for childcare; gender and race liberation; democratic and participatory organizations that do not depend on women's unpaid labor in home and community.

Technology and Masculinity

Hacker shows how technology has been inextricably linked with modes of masculinity, furthered bolstered in the Basque case by the influence of the Catholic Church and the Spanish State with its military institutions. She shows that these institutions promoted authoritarian gendered relations, suppressed women's sexuality while applauding men's, and cut off family concerns from those of work and politics. However, she does not argue a case of imposed values, gender inequality already being inherent in Basque society. Although Basque culture is supposed to be more egalitarian than the Spanish, gender difference is found to be a central structural principle throughout the Spanish State (del Valle et al. 1985; Hacker 1986:122).

The education system, even in the cooperatives' own polytechnical schools, is pinpointed as responsible for the reproduction of patriarchal forms in fields like engineering where professional knowledge is increasingly valued and comes into conflict with the participatory and democratic approach of the cooperatives.

Hacker then finds that there is no clear equation between feminism and social movements like cooperativism that fails to focus sufficiently on gender. She suggests that the major obstacles to democratic participation lie in the gendered structure of design and technology, including models of technological and managerial manufacturing. Technical and professional knowledge and skill are concentrated among a few men in administrative positions. The higher value placed on these as against domestic skills, for example, requires a thorough examination of the roots of that evaluation. Why, she asks, are technical skills, closely linked to military institutions, valued over domestic skills connected to life-sustaining activities of families and communities?

The challenge, then, is to encourage greater particpation of women in technical and engineering fields, which in itself requires a change in emphasis at all levels of education. This in itself is not sufficient. As we have seen, it is not enough just to "add women and stir." Since the women who do access the areas of science and technology are frequently relegated to the least prestigious areas of work, and since few are found in the top directive positions, other strategies need to be designed to implicate society in the responsibility of reproduction (in its widest sense) by supporting women in the coordination of home and work, to democratize technocratic administration and demystify the masculinity of technical skills and knowledge.

Feminist Science

By way of conclusion to this section, attention must be drawn to a pioneering group of Basque women scientists and technologists from different fields (physics, mathematics, biology, chemistry, and engineering) who are involved in the analysis of science from a feminist point of view. This group, known as "Ke Taldea," was formed in 1998 and since then has met on an informal basis to discuss books on different aspects of gender and science or general scientific works that are then analyzed from a

Rural women unite
As well as leaving to work beyond the baserri, the women who choose to stay behind on the farms have also experienced the benefits which come from uniting in defense of their rights and in pursuit of their best interests. Here a group of women participate in a seminar on female farmers organized by the agricultural workers' union, EHNE.
Photo: Gari Garaialde

---

gendered perspective. Some members of the group, namely Enkarni Gómez and Lourdes Dominguez, are part of the teaching team on a master's course at the University of the Basque Country entitled "Equality for Women and Men," on which they are responsible for "Feminist Science," and have participated in national and international conferences including the European Commission's conference on "Women and Science: Networking the Network" (1999). They have presented papers with intriguing titles such as "For a Woman to

---

Be a Good Engineer, She Must Be a Good Girl. Now Let's Deconstruct That" (my translation of Spanish title) or "Toward a Degenderized Science or a Nonunivocal Science." The importance of the innovating work of women like these has been presented in a recent issue of Emakunde's quarterly magazine.[11]

Lesson eight

Summary

1. Although women are moving increasingly into the workplace and making their mark on traditionally masculine areas such as science and technology, it is evident that there are still several obstacles in the path to their participation and promotion.
2. In the industrial cooperatives of Mondragón (Gipuzkoa), the successful functioning of a democratic system of organization and ownership that is, moreover, symbolically embedded in Basque cultural values of solidarity and equality is expected to contribute to a more-egalitarian gender system. However, researchers have found that, though better than in the traditional private sector of industry, working conditions and opportunities for women are still inferior in comparison to men.
3. Three main causes are found for the ongoing situation of disadvantage: the difficulties women face in combining their work with family responsibilities; society's focus on households rather than individuals, which reinforces an unequal gendered division of labor biased toward men at work and women in the home; the masculine gendering of science and technology, institutionalized in Spain by church, state, and military.

Suggested Reading

Sally Hacker, Pleasure, Power and Technology (Boston: Unwin Hyman, 1989) (Chap. 6, "Women Workers in the Mondragón System of Producer Cooperatives," 95–119; Chap. 7, "Gender and Technology in the Mondragón System," 120–39).

Bibliography

Marianne Heiberg, The Making of the Basque Nation (1989).

Sharryn Kasmir, The "Myth" of Mondragón: Cooperatives, Politics and Working Class Life in a Basque Town (Albany, N.Y.: SUNY Press, 1997).

Written lesson for submission

What is the outlook for women in technology and other traditionally male-biased professions? Does the nature of Basque culture contribute to a more egalitarian gender system and more democratic participation in the cooperative system of Arrasate than more traditional forms of industrial enterprise?

Key words

GENDER DIVISION OF LABOR: the way male and female activities are segregated at a particular time and place.

GENDER INEQUALITY AT WORK: throughout history and across cultures, women are found performing more domestic activities than men, and more men are found in the public, extra-domestic domain, where their work is more highly valued than work done in the home.

SOCIAL CHANGE: changes in society affect the gender division of labor, breaking down the segregation of male and female roles and producing a shift in the values attached to the different activities.

Part Three. Power, matriarchy, and myth

9 · Concepts of power

It is said that Basque women are powerful women, at the head of their households, in charge of finances, exercising authority over their family, and responsible for decision-making in the domestic sphere. This image sets them apart from their Spanish or French counterparts and is a source of pride for the Basques as a whole. The notion of Basque women's power is also boosted by the theory, put forward by some scholars, that Basque society was originally a matriarchal order and evolved around a goddess religion that rendered cult to the mythical figure of Mari. The fact that this thesis is based largely on myth, together with the evidence of contemporary reality, belies the otherwise attractive idea of a Basque matriarchy. Feminist critics have challenged the assumptions of the matriarchalists and questioned the real power of Basque women today.

Power is a crucial concept in Gender Studies, being central to the establishment and maintenance of gender systems of inequality. Nevertheless, it is not an easy one and it is imperative that, before going on, we discuss what we mean by power and understand how it works. In the first chapter of this section, we will address different concepts of power as developed in gender theory and as applied in the Basque case. We will look at different ways of theorizing and analyzing power, explore power relations within gender systems, and home in on concepts of power in the Basque context.

In the rest of the section, we will apply the theory to the Basque case, exploring the matriarchal thesis and the myths from which it is derived, looking at their

Cultural concepts of power and strength
Basque culture has different concepts of power, amongst which physical strength or indarra stands out and is celebrated in rural sports such as wood chopping, stone lifting, or tug of war.
Photo: Gari Garaialde

---

evolution and their problematization in the phenomenon of witchcraft.

Different Ways of Theorizing and Analyzing Power

Although there are cultural differences, we have seen that gender inequality occurs universally. As we examine the cultural particuliarities of the Basque case, we must also question why, in spite of differences of time and place, the balance of power is almost always weighted in favor of men. With this in mind, let us take a look at the different ways theorists conceptualize power in their attempt to better understand how gender systems are built on the basis of unequal power relations in which men invariably get a fairer deal than women.

Wielders and compliers. "Power is defined in the Weberian sense as the ability of persons or groups to command compliance from other persons or groups, even in the face of opposition (Chafetz, 1990:32). Janet Saltzman Chafetz uses the terms "power wielders" for those exercising power over others and "compliers" for those who act in accordance with the stated or muted commands or wishes of the powerful. For the power wielders to be effective they must be in possession of something desirable to the compliers or needed by them. This could be something material such as money or goods, something more abstract such as safety and protection, or something even less tangible such as approval or love as a form of emotional capital.

The possession of whatever it is the complier wants or needs means that they yield to the demands of the powerful to obtain this and accept manipulation, bribes, or punishment from the power wielders.

Resistance and struggle. Michel Foucault (1980:109–33) elaborates a concept of power that, like Chafetz's, departs from the premise that the wielding of power is about simply imposing one's will, but takes us beyond a definition of power as a "thing" that can be possessed in greater or lesser quantities and argues that rather it is a force that is diffused through a web of social interaction and struggled over. He challenges the concept of power as monolithic, stemming from a single source and located in the control of factories or guns, and suggests that power is diffused through a complicated system of interrelationships.

Foucault argues that society does not divide neatly into the powerful and the powerless: that disadvantaged sectors of society—whether in terms of gender, economic means, or ethnicity—are not to be seen as helpless victims, for in fact they are actively engaged in a power struggle.

Power operates across different social divisions (gender, class, race, age, linguistic group, and so forth). Individuals have complex identities constructed in relation to these variables, which gives them different power potentials in different contexts.

Power always meets with resistance and at the same time depends upon it.

Decision-making. In a paper on power in the Basque context, "Women's Power in Basque Culture: Practice and Ideology" (1986) Teresa del Valle adopts a working definition of power in its widest sense as the capacity to make and effectively apply decisions with relation to people, situations, and resources. She also draws on Foucault's notion of power/knowledge when she states that power derives from having a knowledge of the "real situation" and the ability and drive to transform it.

The consideration of the decision-maker's power requires that we take into account the circumstances surrounding the making of the decision, at its point of conception or execution as well as at its point of reception or influence. On the one hand, we must assess the point of departure: the person who makes the decision, the context in which they do so, and the circumstances, values, or other interests that must enable them to choose but that also affect their choice. On the other, we must look at the point of influence of the decision made: how different choices are perceived as having different outcomes and how the decision made is seen to have a particular effect on the person or situation in question.

Furthermore, following Peggy Sanday (1981:113–14), the incorporation of the concept of power in the decision-making process can be categorized in terms of political, economic, or social power, according to the context:

1. Economic power: the potential for controlling the distribution of goods and services beyond the domestic sphere
2. Political power: the ability to exercise control or influence in group decisions, entailing leadership beyond the domestic sphere
3. Social power: the capacity to maximize the sociocultural values attached to certain areas of responsibility by making decisions in those fields

Sanday also points to "invisible" areas of female decision-making that undermine the traditionally assumed male supremacy at all levels. For example, she suggests there are decisions made in the domestic sphere that may influence the political and economic balance of power. Or women may "choose" to delegate their power. Or again they may develop other alternatives.

Authority, legitimacy, responsibility. Attached to the concept of power are the concepts of authority, legitimacy, and responsibility. Chafetz defines authority in a Weberian sense as "legitimated power" and legitimacy as "a perception on the part of both the power wielder and the complier that the former has the right to make binding decisions or issue commands, and the latter, the moral obligation to comply with them" (1990:33).

In gender terms, the issues to be tackled here are how male power is legitimated and thus converted into authority (and for that we will need to look at gender ideology) or how the process may be reversed in order to question legitimacy, remove authority, and undermine power.

Responsibility is another concept to be reckoned with, as the responsibilities assumed can either aid the effective application of decisions made or curb the freedom of action of the complier.

Uncovering Power Relations within Gender Systems

As we have seen, gender stratification refers to the degree of gender equality or inequality in any given sector of society, considering the extent to which socially equal males and females are also equal in their access to scarce and valued resources. If, as Chafetz maintains (1990:32), all systems of stratification are systems of power inequity, a system of gender stratification must then imply greater power for men. So then, if we are to uncover the way power works within a gender system, we must address the following questions:

1. What constitutes the basis of this greater dividend of male power?
2. How do men acquire their power resources?
3. How do they use their power to maintain the status quo?
4. Under what circumstances is their power reduced?

At the micro level of analysis, we can see that power exists wherever men—whether as husbands, as partners, or in other roles—extract compliance from women with whom they personally interact. Male authority is evidenced wherever those women feel it is their duty to comply with the decisions or commands of these men.

This micro level of power and authority needs to be explained by a further analysis of the roots of male power. How do men come to wield power in the first place? Where does that "right" to make decisions come

Strong women
Gendered concepts of power are changing as women have the opportunity to take part in activities that were once an exclusively male domain. In recent years, for example, Basque society has witnessed the emergence of women in sports involving a show of strength, such as this female *aizkolari* or wood cutter.
Photo: Iñaki Ugarte

from, and why do women concede it to be a right and comply with it?

By contrast, at the macro level, power and authority are found to reside in the elite roles of dominant social institutions that in modern industrial societies are primarily political and economic organizations, with religious, educational, and cultural organizations in a subsidiary role. In gender-stratified societies men predominate in these elite roles.

Concepts of Power in the Basque Context

When addressing the concept of power in the Basque context with reference to gender we need to analyze the relationship between the ideal and the reality. This is the subject of del Valle's article on women's power in Basque culture in which we are invited to look at the symbolic conceptualization of force and strength as they contribute to a particular cultural concept of power. Following on from this, we will then consider a gender ideology that attributes a dominant role to Basque women on the basis of a mythical matriarchy.

The reality, as investigated by Teresa del Valle and her team and later expounded in *Mujer vasca: Imagen and realidad* (The Basque woman: Image and reality), which we mentioned in Part 2, is that in the Basque context female power is mostly restricted to the home and family: "The Basque woman makes her decisions mainly in the domestic sphere, constrained by family roles" (del Valle 1985:7). Female roles are primarily those dictated by their position in the family as mother, wife, daughter, or sister, and each of these carries a limited decision-making capacity confined to certain situations and defined by specific social norms and cultural expectations. For example, the woman is expected to be the one who cares for the old and the sick in the family—whether her own or her political family—and while this responsibility may confer decision-making power, it essentially constrains, being an obligation to be fulfilled with little room for choice.

It is said that Basque women have great decision-making power in the domestic sphere and that it is they who rule the roost, but a closer look at the value attached to the decisions they make reveals once more that this power is not all it is made out to be. The decisions made are related to subsistence: arguably the most important, fundamental decisions for life, yet food, clothing, and the general running of the house are not areas of activity that carry great social worth. Women's prime domestic activity therefore does not receive social recognition.

Men's activities—even on the *baserri* (farm) where women were traditionally attributed a greater portion of power than in contemporary society—have always been considered of greater merit, especially in Basque society where a cultural onus is placed on physical strength, as exemplified in the rural sports that reflect past occupational activities such as wood-chopping (for timber or firewood), stone-lifting (in the quarries), or controlling strong animals as they pull the plough, shift rocks, and otherwise serve as beasts of burden. In the latter case, men receive merit for raising fine, strong animals that reflect their own strength.

Strength is similar to power in that it is understood as the capacity to exert or resist great force. In traditional Basque culture different concepts of strength are expressed by different words. The physical strength we have just referred to is known in Basque as *indarra*: the strength displayed by persons or animals in the type of activities mentioned, involving carrying, lifting, pulling, pushing. It is the strength necessary for hard, physical

Powerful women
Like this gigantic baserritarra or female farmer brought out for a festival, the matriarchal thesis portrays women as larger than life. Held up as a matriarch and attributed power and authority over her home and family, her influence is in fact restricted to the domestic realm and therefore limited in scope.
Photo: Alain Pagoaga

labor that has traditionally been most highly valued in Basque society and that is applauded in the competitions and displays of rural sports known in Iparralde[12] as Force Basque.

However, indarra is also used to refer to other innate biological strengths, the very energy of the human body, the sexual power of reproduction, the sheer pulse of life of a developing fetus. Sandra Ott (1993:29), in the study previously mentioned on the Basque shepherding community of Sainte-Engrâce, distinguishes between human and supernatural indarra. First she mentions that both men and women tend to have great physical strength or indarra, which is highly esteemed in the community. She also notes that importance is attached to eating both as a means to increasing indarra and as a social activity. She finds four main types of human indarra:

1. "the life-force acquired at conception"
2. "the procreative power which men and women acquire at puberty"
3. "the physical strength of the body, acquired by means of eating well and working hard"
4. "the jural power and authority acquired by the younger heads of the household through their premarital contract" (1993:87)

Indarra is not restricted to humans or animals. The natural elements (wind, rain, thunder) have indarra, and so does wine as it is fermented and acquires alcoholic content. Then indarra can also be the power of persuasion, the force of the "old religion" or the "old ways" that constrained and compelled people to be faithful in their attendance at mass and observation of the dictates of the church and generally to abide by the moral laws of the community.

Finally, apart from and over and above human indarra is the supernatural indarra of God—mystical, all-pervasive, spiritual.

In the complete works of José Miguel Barandiaran (1:63) we find the concepts of berezco and adur. Berezco is defined as a spontaneous, self-generating force that resides in or emanates from an independent object or being without the intervention of any outside agent. Adur is said to be a mysterious force that can carry positive or negative energy and act upon other persons or objects. Xamar (1992:48) tells us that in the old system of beliefs, every thing and every being had a likeness, linked to it by the magical power, adur. Whatever was done to the likeness was also felt by the person or thing. Several tales tell of people inflicting pain or death on a robber or wrongdoer by disfiguring an object that represented the guilty party, often twisting or burning candles or bending coins that were then thrown into the fire.

Lesson nine

Summary

1. Power is a complex concept that should not be approached as a "thing" nor as a one-way process. It involves at least two parties and works through a network of interrelationships. A useful way to conceptualize power is to think in terms of "wielders" who have something "compliers" want and hence they yield to them. The yielding is not always straightforward, and frequently there is resistance and struggle that thwarts attempts to impose power. The ability to make and carry out decisions is an indication of power, but it must be legitimated by the authority

invested in the perceived right of the wielder to make a decision as well as by the complier's recognition of their obligation to obey.

2. Women and men have an unequal portion of power in most societies, which is maintained by multiple threads of the economic, political, and social structure, in turn reinforced by dominant institutions in which men occupy elite roles. It is necessary to uncover the process by which men, at both the micro and the macro levels, cause women to comply with their wishes and women recognize men's right to do so.
3. Power must be analyzed in the historical and social context in which it is exercised, and specific cultural beliefs or notions about power should be sought out with a view to understanding the symbolic side of power. In the Basque context different concepts of power can be observed, but the most common form, indarra, is conceptually linked to strength and differentiated for women and men. Other, more ethereal, concepts of power, such as adur and berezco, relate to the world of superstition and magic.

Suggested Reading

Teresa del Valle, "Women's Power in Basque Culture: Practice and Ideology," unpublished paper (1986).

Bibliography

English Bibliography

Janet Saltzman Chafetz, Gender Equity: An Integrated Theory of Stability and Change (Newbury Park–London–New Delhi: Sage, 1990).

Michel Foucault, Power/Knowledge: Selected Interviews and Other Writings 1972–1977 (Brighton, UK: Harvester Press, 1980).

Peggy R. Sanday, Female Power and Male Dominance: On the Origins of Sexual Inequality (Cambridge: CUP, 1981).

Spanish Bibliography

Xamar, Desde el Orhi: Conocer el País del Euskara (Pamplona-Iruñea: Pamiela, 1992).

Written lesson for submission

How does the information we have about power in the Basque context help answer some of the questions posed about the production and maintenance of male power?

10 · The matriarchal thesis

Central to the cultural concept of female power in the Basque context is the assumption of a matriarchal tradition, rooted in the past (when women reigned mystically through goddess religions), and extended through myth into the present. In this section we will look at the way the matriarchal thesis has been developed for the Basque culture, considering the existence and evolution of matriarchies, the evidence of a Basque matriarchy, and the critique of the matriarchal thesis from the different authors, especially the team behind *Mujer vasca* (Chap. 1: 44–45), which analyzes the Basque matriarchy as a cultural construct, arising in a specific historical and political context

The Existence and Evolution of Matriarchies

In the seventies, a revival of interest in primitive matriarchies showed them to have been the subject of different works in the nineteenth century (revolving round Johann Jakob Bachofen's Mother Right), and a rush of articles and books came out in defence of an archaic age when women ruled (Bamberger, 1974:264). It is in the wake of this general revival that the Basque matriarchy was unearthed and held up as an example.

Matriarchy, according to Bachofen, is the dominion of the mother over family and state, by natural, biological right. In a matriarchal society the balance of power would be tipped toward women. They would exercise authority, make decisions, and wield influence over men. The gender balance of power would produce differences in the social, political, and economic structure of society. Primitive matriarchies were said to be characterized by a communal spirit of solidarity and sympathy and were essentially nature-oriented.

A matriarchal society was purportedly characterized by matrilineage, which refers to the reckoning of descent and the transmission of property through the female line. Matrilineal descent groups also tend to be matrilocal, which means that a couple establishes postmarital residence in the wife's mother's group. These circumstances tend to occur when the women of a community are responsible for agriculture and continue to tend their lands, while men are occupied hunting and fishing. However, a matrilocal-matrilineal arrangement does not necessarily mean that the women in that society exert political and economic control over men, since in most such instances men still control the group's corporate resources. Thus we may have a society where the mother is the head of the family and descent is reckoned through the female line, and which may be described as matriarchal on this basis, but it does not make it the female equivalent to a patriarchal system where political power through government is wielded by men. It may be useful to distinguish between a "domestic matriarchy" in which women are the heads of their household and control the domestic space, "political matriarchy" where women exercise political power in the public arena, and "symbolic matriarchy" where religious beliefs and practices reflect a matriarchal ideal.

In opposition to Bachofen's matriarchal model of the ancient world, Henry Sumner Maine proposed that human society was universally founded on patriarchy, rooted in man's natural superiority over women. Others see primitive matriarchies evolving into patriarchies, as is argued for the Basque case. While Bachofen reasons that marriage was promoted by women to regulate the unbridled sexuality that men subjected them to, and in

Mari and the mother-daughter relationship
The Basque goddess, Mari, was said to be particularly jealous of the mother-daughter relationship, ensuring that a mother's word was fulfilled to the point of punishing a curse on her daughter by whisking the girl away and taking her under her own wing or condemning her to wander the hills and mountains.
Photo: Alain Pagoaga.

so doing reinforced women's control of the family, the patriarchal model argues that monogamous unions evolve with the rise of private property in settled societies and are instigated by men, with a view to establishing their rights to land. In primitive societies, children belonged to their mothers' clan and received her name and goods, which was not problematic until ownership of property entered the equation. Men wanted to be able to pass property on to their own children, and owing to the difficulty in establishing paternity in seemingly "promiscuous societies" there was a move toward monogamy. By this argument, the institution of monogamous relationships brought a more important role for men in the reproduction of the family and transfer of wealth, and consequently women lost their former power.

However, the scant evidence for either position means that both incorporate a great deal of conjecture. Here we are less concerned with ascertaining the existence of matriarchy than with contemplating the construction of a model and its implications for both Basque culture and Basque women.

The Basque Matriarchy

A strong current in Basque anthropology, based mainly on the work of José Miguel Barandiaran and Julio Caro Baroja has propounded the thesis of a matriarchal society founded mostly on mythology and ethno-historical data. The main exponents of the matriarchal thesis in the Basque case are Andrés Ortiz Osés and Franz K. Mayr in their work *El matriarcalismo vasco* (1980); their ideas were taken up by Txema Hornilla in *La Ginecocracia vasca* (1981).

Ortiz and Mayr plot the evolution of Basque society from a prehistoric, native matriarchal system to a subsequently imposed patriarchal structure. They establish the existence of a pre-Indo-European, autochthonous, and ancient Basque matriarchal culture, peaking in the Paleolithic period. They argue that women exercised power through the control of resources and dominion of the magical-symbolic realm, through their religious role in the worship of the Earth Mother and their socioeconomic role in the hunting and gathering of food. They postulate a process of acculturation in the Neolithic period, under the influence of invading groups with patriarchal forms of social organization (such as the Indo-Germanic invasion from the Caucasus). They maintain that this influence continued under the Roman Empire and the introduction of the Christian religion but that the Basque peoples resisted, producing a conflict between the original matriarchy and a superimposed patriarchy. Their analysis departs from Jungian psychology and holds that the matriarchal base has not disappeared from the Basques' collective subconscious but rather continues to permeate their thinking. At the same time, they find traces of the matriarchy in the traditional rural world, incarnated in the idealized figure of the rural woman (Part 2).

The thesis of the Basque matriarchy rests on the figure of Mari, a Stone Age goddess, comparable to other goddesses of fertility found across Europe from Siberia to the Pyrenees.[13]

Problems with the Matriarchal Thesis

The arguments for primitive matriarchies have been contested by scholars such as Juan Aranzadi (1982), whose work was expanded on by the research team of *Mujer vasca: Imagen y realidad* (1985:44–54). The critique of the Basque matriarchal thesis revolves around three central issues. The first concerns the use of myths

The lady of the mountains
The goddess Mari was also given the name of the Lady of Anboto after this mountain of Bizkaia where she was said to have appeared on several occasions and in different forms.
Photo: Iñaki Ugarte

---

as a basis for building scientific theories, while the other two take up the androcentric and politically oriented interpretations of the material.

The first difficulty is then one of unsatisfactory evidence that leaves the matter open to individual interpretation and speculation. Joan Bamberger, in an article published in the seventies, "The Myth of Matriarchy: Why Men Rule in Primitive Society," opens with a skeptical comment on the popularity of the thesis despite the lack of solid evidence to support it.

Because no matriarchies persist anywhere at the present time, and because primary sources recounting them are totally lacking, both the existence and constitution of female-dominated societies can only be surmised. The absence of this documentation, however, has not been a deterrent to those scholars and popularists who view in the concept of primitive matriarchy a rationale for a new social order, one in which women can and should gain control of important political and economic roles. (1974:263).

In the Basque case, the use of mythology instead of archaeology as a foundation for explaining early social organization is dubious in accuracy and mixes frames of reference and levels of analysis. It is not that myth should be ignored, but that it should be read differently from history. Where myth is taken as historical fact, the interpretation is doomed to failure, but where it is recognized that myth "recounts a fragment of collective experience that necessarily exists outside time and space," it may be seen as part of a cultural history that does not coincide with chronological events or historical facts but instead presents a symbolic invention of reality aimed at explaining or legitimating a certain order or state of affairs (Bamberger, 1974:267). Joseba Zulaika, in *Basque Violence: Metaphor and Sacrament* (1988), opens with a reflection on history as myth, legend, and devotion in the town of Itziar (Gipuzkoa), showing that the myths of Mari, sightings of the Virgin Mary, and other apparitions are woven into the popular imagination and influence attitudes and interpretations of both past and present.

The second problem is the way the proponents of primitive matriarchies project an ideal of woman that is far from the notion of the modern liberated woman. It romanticizes motherhood and places women on a pedestal of moral virtue that inspires men to heroic and chivalrous deeds (ibid. 265). In this reading, it is a male notion of women's purity and perfection that empowers them to rule over the household and beyond. In the Basque context, we find a similar idealistic appraisal in which the archetype of the Great Mother is erected as a model for modern women, situating them in the context of the traditional values and social organization of Basque society in which females only appear as mothers and priestesses (see Part 2). Ortiz and Mayr interpret the Basque myths of the goddess Mari (see below) according to their own androcentric interpretation of "woman" and an idealized notion of motherhood in which the reproductive function of the female body is glorified as the generating principle of life. A moral evaluation is clear in the dichotomy established between Mari-mother and Mari-witch, along the lines of Mother=Good, Woman=Witch=Bad (del Valle et al. 1985:48).

Finally, in the Basque case, the argument for matriarchy has been used as an ideological and political vehicle for nationalism and as such has been criticized by Jon Juaristi (1987), writing on the invention of Basque tradition. It feeds into the mystification of Basque culture with its emphasis on the primitive past, stressing its timelessness and antiquity, and emphasizes its difference and superiority over others. In this sense, it fits nationalist ends, for the discourse portrays an official, foreign, and colonizing culture introducing patriarchy in opposition to an autochthonous, natural, matriarchal culture revolving around the community. The thesis suggests that the revitalization of matriarchal society (and autochthonous identity) is a viable way to resist external influences. At a time of political disenchantment, it encourages a return to the evocative power of the ancestral and intangible, the distant and permanent. In doing so, it refuses to accept present reality and denies the need for change.

If there is so much to be said against it, how is it that such a scientifically weak argument should be so strongly maintained? Teresa del Valle and her team believe it is because it has great appeal in the context of the Basque cultural and political situation. It reaffirms the ancestrality and mystique of Basque culture, setting it apart from and claiming superiority over more recent Iberian cultures. At the same time, it presents an ideological opposition between the Spanish central government and Basque nationalist parties, such that in the wider consciousness the figure of Mari, the Great Mother, has become a symbol for Basque collective identity.

The idea that women once ruled in the past is attractive to feminists who intuit that they could resume control in the present. The problems of the matriarchal model are glossed over in projecting a symbol of Basque female power.

Lesson ten

Summary

1. One line of argument holds that many early European societies were matriarchal in organization, descent was reckoned through the female line, and women exercised power in the family and in civil society. Others believe primitive societies were naturally patriarchal. It is thought that where matriarchy existed, the advent of agriculture and the importance of property in settled societies led to the installation of monogamy and patriarchal forms of organization.
2. Some authors have argued for the existence of a prehistoric, Stone Age matriarchy in the Basque Country, which was later replaced by patriarchal systems

superimposed by invading peoples, but which have not been able to erase the substrate matriarchal model.

3. The Basque matriarchal thesis is more appealing than it is reliable and has been used as an ideological vehicle to transmit notions of authenticity, cultural difference, and even superiority. It is criticized by scholars for its misinterpretation of myth, lack of scientific foundation, biased reading of the category "woman," and mystification for political ends. Nevertheless, myth is recognized as a cultural construct of symbolic significance.

Suggested Reading

J. Bamberger, "The Myth of Matriarchy: Why Men Rule in Primitive Society," in Women, Culture and Society (Stanford: Stanford University Press, 1974).

Joseba Zulaika, Basque Violence: Metaphor and Sacrament (Reno: University of Nevada Press, 1988) (Chap. 1: "History as Myth, Legend and Devotion," 1–15).

Bibliography

Spanish Bibliography

Juan Aranzadi, Milenarismo Vasco: Edad de oro, etnia y nativismo (Madrid: Taurus, 1981).

Teresa del Valle, et al., Mujer vasca: Imagen y realidad (Barcelona: Anthropos, 1985), 44–54.

Txema Hornilla, La ginecocracia vasca: Contribución a los estudios sobre el eusko-matriarcado (Bilbao: Ed. Geu Argitaldaria, 1981).

Jon Juaristi, El linaje de Aitor: La invención de la tradición vasca (Madrid, Taurus Ediciones, 1987).

Andrés Ortiz Osés and F. K. Mayr, El matriarcalismo vasco: Reinterpretación de la cultura vasca (Bilbao: Universidad de Deusto, 1980).

Written lesson for submission

What are the problems with arguing for the existence of a primitive matriarchy? What can myths tell us about gender and society?

11 · The myth of Mari

The anthropologist Carmen Díez, one of the original team of *Mujer vasca*, has reexamined the Basque myths of Mari and their different interpretations. In two illuminating articles, one entitled "Mari, un mito para la resistencia femenina" (Mari, a myth for feminist resistance) and the other simply "Mari" (1999; 2002), she provides a fresh vision that departs from attempting to demonstrate the existence of a Basque matriarchy or not, to comprehending the symbolic meanings encoded within the stories. Díez stresses the need to situate a myth or an interpretation of a myth in its historical context, at the same time as adopting a dynamic concept of culture that, contrary to an essentialist vision of a people's culture, understands that the social actors of any human group are immersed in a constant process of construction and reconstruction of their culture. Hence, rather than being timeless and unchanging, myths that have been invented in specific social contexts are reinvented at other times and with other meanings.

Examined from this angle, the picture that is built up of Mari, the central character of Basque myth that has been considered the cornerstone of the matriarchal thesis, emerges as complex and contradictory. Díez's work (2002) represents the most comprehensive analysis to date of the studies on Mari and shows how various writers have amalgamated different elements of Basque myth to make up a picture of an early goddess religion and a primitive matriarchal society. The pivotal figure in this picture is the Basque Earth goddess who appears in folktales in different guises and with different names, though from José Miguel Barandiaran she is known as

Mari.[14] Díez (1999:65) remarks on Barandiaran's elaboration of a hierarchy in which Mari is installed at the head, as Great Goddess, Great Mother, or Great Sorceress and is supreme, over and above all other beings and spirits, even though in the stories themselves she seems to share many similarities with them. Another aspect of Barandiaran's interpretation is his insistence on the religious dimension of Mari, the figurehead of a pre-Christian, autochthonous cult as well as of a matriarchal social order.

Ama Lur: Mother Earth

Primitive cults were characteristically nature cults through which early peoples sought out explanations for the mysterious phenomena they were unable to understand. The Basques were no exception, and in Barandiaran's elaboration the Earth is central both to ancient Basque life and mythology and to a cult of fertility.

Mari is known as Ama Lur or Mother Earth (in Basque, ama means mother, lur means Earth) and is closely linked to the Earth and earthly phenomena. She is the Earth, embodied in it, but at the same time she dwells in it and rules over it. This conceptualization is in keeping with the pre-Indo-European matriarchal cosmovision in which the Earth and Woman are considered to be one and the same. The world is conceived as a female body, indwelt by a magical force that permeates all things. The Earth is considered to be the origin of all things: giver of life, mother of both the Sun and the Moon, controller of the elements.

Mari is associated with the depths of the Earth where she is said to live, but when she emerges, she is often sighted in the heights or associated with mountains or trees that join Earth and sky. Mountains are believed to be especially powerful as they go down into the Earth but reach up into the sky.[15] In the folktales Mari is often sighted in some of the highest and most distinctive mountains in the Basque landscape (Amboto, Txindoki, Aralar, Aitzkorri), giving her the name "Lady of Amboto" and other titles. Trees' roots are also important because they penetrate deep into the earth, particularly those species that are indigenous to the Basque Country: oak (*haritza*), beech (*pagoa*), and ilex or evergreen holm oak (*artea*).

Mari inhabits a mysterious inner world in the heart of the Earth, which is connected to the outside by a labyrinth of caves and grottoes. Hence she is frequently said to appear at the mouth of caves, in ravines, or at other openings in the ground. Her underground kingdom is said to flow with rivers of milk and honey and be full of all sorts of treasures and marvels. But in this underworld also live the souls of the dead, whom Mari takes into her caves. Death is seen as transitional, not final but simply a return to one's origins, with a potential for rebirth under the fertilizing force of the Earth.

As well as the Earth, the elements of wind, fire, and water are closely linked to Mari. She may sometimes appear as a gust of wind, a breeze blowing through the trees, a burst of air rushing through an open window. Or, in association with fire, she may transform herself into a burning tree or sickle in the sky, symbolizing purification, but also death, as well as heat, passion, and love. In the guise of water she is also seen to have purifying and healing powers and to be vital for life and fertility.

Mari is often represented as a woman, flying over mountain peaks or resting in a cave, combing out her hair with a gold comb or winding thread around a ram's horns, or she may appear in animal form, as a billy goat,

Water spirits
In Basque mythology, the lamia was a creature with a woman's form except for webbed or cleft feet. She inhabited watery places and on the coast, was represented as a mermaid with a fish's tail. This sculpture of a lamia by Xabier Santxotena sits by a stream which runs alongside the sculpture park in Bozate (Nafarroa). Photo: Iñaki Ugarte

horse, young bull, snake, crow, or vulture. Or again, she may incorporate herself through metamorphosis into the landscape in the form of a rock, a stalagmite, a tree, a plant. Opinions differ as to whether what we see in the stories is the transformation of Mari into these animals and elements; or whether, since she is the Earth, she resides in all creatures; or again, whether they are subordinate to her and thus often confused with her. Barandiaran traces the transformation of Mari into animal form to the cave wall paintings of the Paleolithic hunters.

Attributes and Functions of Mari

We will now consider the prime attributes and functions that emerge from the behavior and characteristics of Mari in the body of myths and legends at our disposal and proceed to consider alternative interpretations from those suggested by the proponents of the matriarchal thesis. The authors of *Mujer vasca*, following Teresa del Valle (1983), stress that Mari is not a historical fact but rather a cultural construct, of which the most outstanding characteristics are her variety, versatility, and ambiguity (1985:25–26). As well as appearing in numerous forms, Mari acts unpredictably and inconsistently. She is good and bad, earthly and ephemeral, human and nonhuman. She is a creator and generator of life yet also represents death and destruction. She exerts both a positive (embracing) and negative (devouring) force. She punishes but also rewards. She demands respect and worship but at the same time encourages interaction as equals. Ruler of the elements, she can bring rain to water and fertilize the fields, or can punish with drought.[16]

Promise keeping and the power of the word. Mari ensures the fulfillment of promises and the given word, something that is highly valued in Basque society. Where Mari is concerned, a mother's word is particularly important. If a mother cursed her daughter—and the curses are usually in the form of wishing that the miscreant daughter be taken away—it was said that Mari would fulfill that wish and transport the girl away as her captive. Many stories revolve around this particular phenomena; some even say that Mari was thus taken from her own bad mother, who cursed her, saying, "May the devil take you," and with that the devil did indeed whisk her away and took her off to the mountains where she was later spotted by local people gathering wood.

Punishes wrong. The sins for which she punishes people are those that go against the values of matriarchy and its emphasis on solidarity, as opposed to the pronounced individualism of patriarchal society, capitalist exploitation, and ambition. Mari punishes those who fail to keep their word, steal, lie, brag or boast, as well as those who fail to proffer mutual aid to others. She punishes by simply provoking an uneasy conscience or anxiety, or she might remove goods stolen from or denied to others, or again (and more severely) by invoking storms.

Ruler of the elements. Mari causes and controls the weather and hence determines whether the harvest will be good or bad. Early agricultural peoples were dependent on her good will.

Destiny and wisdom. Mari is an Oracle and divines the future; in the mythology, people go to consult her and she is depicted spinning out destiny, winding and unwinding a ball of golden thread around ram's horns. She is an educator: she transmits knowledge to women, teaches the girls she takes to live with her, and trains them as her apprentices. They emerge in possession of great wealth. Mari is not then purely an Earth mother,

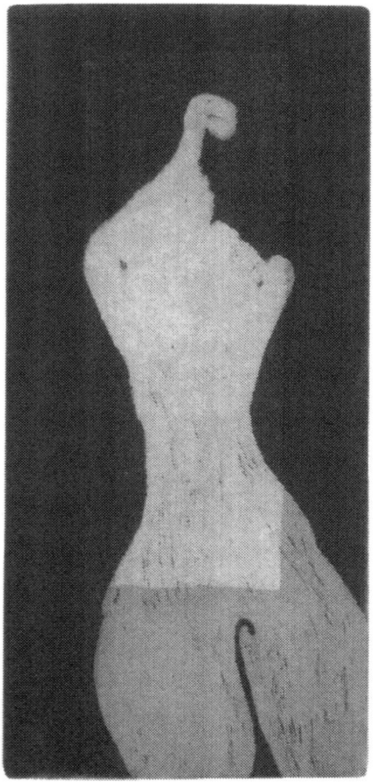

The goddess Mari
The Basque Stone Age goddess, known as Mari, manifested herself in many forms. Sometimes as a woman, sometimes as an animal or as one of the elements. Feminist anthropologists today have suggested we read the Mari myths as a representation of androgyny and the condensation of all manner of contradictions and tensions, real or imaginary. The legends are thus reinterpreted to provide answers to different human and social problems whether related with religion, medical practice, economic activity or sexuality.
Untitled print by Lola Sarratea.

goddess of nature; she is also linked to culture through the knowledge she imparts, her skill in agriculture, and her association with metallurgy, especially the transformation of ore into gold, which she often uses or gives as rewards (ibid. 26).

Demands worship. Mari demands worship of her followers and requires offerings (food, coins, clothes, candles) that people would take to her caves. Sacrifices were also made (especially of rams, sacred animals with special healing powers), or cow's entrails were left in the mouth of her cave.

Commands respect. Those who enter Mari's cave must not turn their backs on her but leave as they entered, with their faces turned toward her, and must remain standing in her presence, otherwise they may be turned to stone.

Nevertheless, she was to be addressed in the informal "you" form of Basque, which is known as hika and which has traditionally only been used by intimate friends or by parents to their children and by men to women and not vice versa. This has been interpreted by some authors as demonstrating not only the more-even distribution of power in a matriarchal society but also a particularly Basque notion of universal equality expressed in an ideally classless social system.

Pantheon of Lesser Gods or Spirits

In the hierarchical order of this prehistoric cosmovision, under Mari there appear a number of lesser gods, spirits or mythical beings, both female and male, animal and human, or a combination of the two. Those with greatest power after Mari are the Serpent and the Goat, male figures depicted as consorts of the goddess.

Maju or Sugaar (the Serpent):[17] The serpent is a characteristic matriarchal symbol and initially appears as a symbol of the goddess herself. The image of the snake conveys several of the qualities attributed to the matriarchal worldview, such as ambiguity, uniting good and evil, potentially poisonous but also life-saving. The serpent is also a cyclical symbol, representing the notion of the world as a continuous cycle through the processes of skin-shedding and metamorphosis. It is not till later that we find the patriarchal myths imbuing the serpent with strictly male and negative connotations, such as the biblical snake-devil of the Garden of Eden. Perhaps these postmatriarchal representations of the serpent account for the separating out of the figure of Mari and the snake in later mythology. The goddess appears with a serpent by her side, construed to be either her son or her lover. As a lover, the myths tell that Sugaar comes to Mari on Fridays, and thunder and lightning are said to result from their encounters.

Aker, the Goat and the Moon. Aker ("billy goat" in Basque) was the head of the lesser spirits. His powers included stirring up storms to punish, though he also had curative powers and was charged to protect livestock in his care. This old belief led to a tradition in the Basque farmhouses to always include a black billy goat among the flock of sheep and goats.

Friday was the traditional day for worshipping both Mari and Aker the goat, and this name gives rise to the term Akelarre, which has gone down into contemporary understanding as a witch's sabbath in which the goat is transformed into a devil figure and leader of the witches, but which—as we shall see in the next chapter—was originally a gathering for the adoration of the goddess, the goat, and the moon.

It seems that Friday was first the day of celebration of the moon. Ostirala, the Basque word for Friday, takes its root from ilargi, the word for moon. Mari was associated with the moon as well as the Earth, and again this is typical of matriarchal ideologies in which the cult of the moon is linked to the cult of the Great Goddess.

Throughout the ages and across different cultures, the moon is linked with fertility, menstruation, and conception, and hence Mari controls fertility and exerts control over plants and animals. Although many Basques today have scant knowledge of the origins of this belief, some share a belief in the fertilizing potential of the moon. The waxing moon (the fourth quarter) is male related while the waning moon is female related; this is said, for example, to affect the sex of babies conceived in the different phases of the moon. The waxing, male moon is associated with brute force and the waning, female moon with fruitfulness. It is said the crops should be sown in the waning moon because otherwise plants will grow strong but produce small fruits; wood to be burned should be cut in a waxing moon so that it will be harder and take longer to burn, but if the wood is for construction or carpentry it should be cut in a waning moon so that it will be more malleable and easier to cut or carve.

Lamiak and sorgiñak. As well as the male animal figures associated with Mari, there also appear in the myths a number of female attendant figures, the most common of which are the lamiak and the sorgiñak.

The lamia (lamiak in the plural form) is a woman with webbed or cleft feet, usually like a water bird's, as they tend to live in streams and rivers. On the coast, the stories tell of mermaid-like lamiak with a fish's tail. In the myths the lamiak appear as helpers to humans, carrying out domestic, agricultural, and construction tasks in exchange for food (typically bread, cider, and cuajada, a set yogurt made with sheep's milk). They are said to do spinning, wash the clothes, plough and sow the fields, and then perform a number of more spectacular works like the building of dolmens, bridges, castles, and churches. They work at night and must vanish with the dawn. If the farmers forget or omit to leave them food, the lamiak refuse to work and take their services elsewhere. In many stories young men fall in love with lamiak, whereupon their mothers or other womenfolk take it on themselves to prove to the boy that their loved one is not a human woman and their love cannot be.

The sorgiña, mythically related to fertility and life, was a kind of midwife who attended women in childbirth. This figure probably evolved into the figure of the rural midwife who looked after women in labor long before there were professional nurses. The sorgiña is also found working with Mari, taking away the possessions of those who lie, cheat, or conceal their wealth selfishly. The word sorgiña was later adopted as the Basque word for "witch" in keeping with a general patriarchal tendency to condemn positive magic-naturalist practices and label them as witchcraft.

Mari as a Myth for Our Times

José Miguel Barandiaran gathered stories about Mari during the first quarter of the twentieth century and hence it can be expected that the accounts reflect the context of Basque society at that time as well as his own perspective on traditional rural society as the archetype of Basqueness and the farmer's wife as the ideal woman. The mystical and the magical converge in the Basque farmhouse, or baserri, that Barandiaran saw as a sanctuary in which the etxekoandere or woman of the house was priestess. The Basque etxea, meeting place of living and dead, of life and procreation, of death and commemoration, connects with Mari's cave or underworld habitat. In this way, the Basque house is said to be

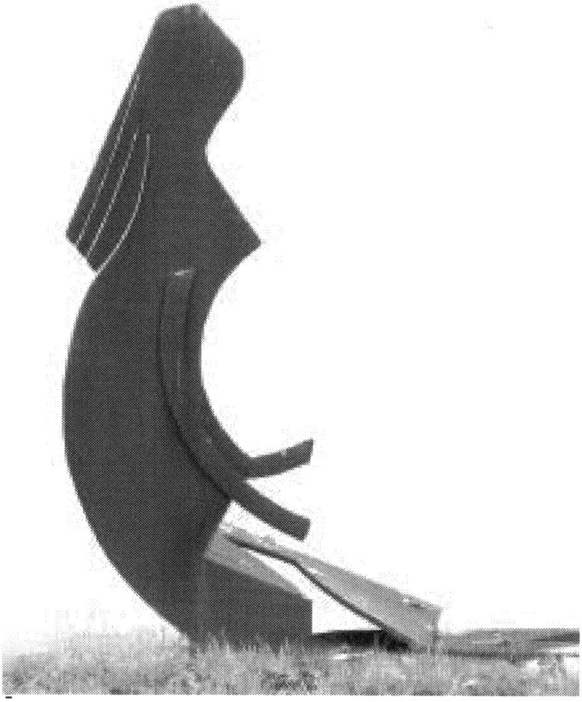

Mari's attendants
Blending with the landscape, the mythical lamia emerged from the water but worked on the land. The stories tell that as long as they were fed, and they were protected by the darkness, they helped farmers with their chores or busied themselves building bridges. Many an unwitting young man fell in love with these beautiful beings and in the tales, has to be dissuaded from an impossible union by the older women folk, who were wise to the lamia's other-worldliness.
Scuplture: Xabier Santxotena. Photo: Iñaki Ugarte.

a meeting point between Earth and Woman, between the inner and outer worlds, mediated via religious belief and practice. Barandiaran describes the characteristics of the traditional Basque house that he laments are being lost with the new ways of life: "The house is earth and shelter, temple and cemetery, material support, symbol and common place of all the family members, living and dead. It is also the community formed by the present inhabitants and ancestors."

The Basque house conferred certain duties and rights on its inhabitants, among which duties was to provide shelter and sustenance to those living under its roof, including all unmarried children; to render due cult to deceased relatives and make offerings to the ancestors; and to help one's neighbors. The rights were the right to form a stem family; to pass on the heritance undivided to a single inheritor; to occupy a family seat in church; to have a path linking the house to the cemetery; to receive assistance certain from one's neighbors. The importance of the land in traditional Basque society is also signaled as being reminiscent of the matriarchal bond with Nature. Importance was attached to preserving and passing on farmlands intact; attachment was to the farm unit rather than to family, and one was known by the name of one's *baserri* as much as by one's family name.

In the matriarchal household, the *etxekoandere* is the priestess and guardian of the hearth. Fire was connected with Mari, who often appeared in flames, and fire was linked with matriarchal societies in general, contrary to the patriarchal representation of male hunters discovering fire. Fires have been important in Basque tradition, believed to have magic powers linked to the Earth and Nature, to female fertilizing powers. For example, the burning of the biggest and best log felled on Christmas Eve was a practice kept for the protection and fertility of flocks; it was believed the charcoaled remains of the burnt wood had magical, protective powers and were used to mark the lintel under which the animals passed in and out. Well into the twentieth century, the etxekoandere was responsible for keeping alive the memory of those who had lived in the baserri by burning candles in the church.

If this was the interpretation Barandiaran proposed for the Mari myths in his day and age, Carmen Díez proposes a different emphasis for modern times: "Why not a reading or representation of Mari as something which contains all possible forms of contradictions and tensions, real or imaginary, and an interpretation of ...the different legends gathered as answers to human and social problems related with religion, medical practice, economic activity or sexuality?" (1999:70, my translation)

Díez suggests that the Mari myths can be reread as a representation of androgyny, "symbol of utopia and rebellion" in a particular social and historical context. The stories Barandiaran wrote down in the twenties should be reexamined not just as descriptions of a remote mythical past, but instead as expressions of a contemporary situation and a time of change. While Barandiaran's interpretation evoked the idealized rural past, the Basque Country was entering a period of change that would take society toward a conservative, capitalist, and industrial society in which women's freedom would be further curtailed. The prehistoric ambiguity of Mari—the union of feminine and masculine traits, the adoption of multiple forms, the ability to be everywhere, inside and outside of the home—is diametrically opposed to the modern world's segregation of the distinctly feminine and masculine, domestic and public, feeling and unfeeling. Díez proposes that we take the myth of Mari as an androgynous model of feminist resistance, in the "fight for a society in which differences, of sex or of another type, are not the basis on which unequal relations are maintained" (ibid. 71).

Lesson eleven

Summary

1. Myths should be taken as cultural constructions that are produced at specific moments in history and in particular socioeconomic contexts. Their interpretation can also vary in reflection of different interests or preoccupations at any given time or place.
2. Basque stories, myths, and legends are amalgamated to construct a picture of a prehistoric pagan goddess religion in which the figure of Mari emerges as Mother Earth. She appears in multiple forms, assumes numerous functions, and appears contradictory in many of her actions. She demonstrates ambiguity, uniting good and evil, life and death, creation and destruction, punishment and reward.
3. Given that the myth of Mari brings together male and female attributes and qualities, it is proposed that it be read as a model of androgyny and a metaphor for liberation in which sexual difference should cease to be the basis for inequality.

Required Reading

Luis de Barandiaran, ed., A View from the Witch's Cave: Folktales of the Pyrenees (Reno: University of Nevada Press, 1991).

Bibliography

Spanish Bibliography

Teresa del Valle, "La mujer vasca a través del análisis del espacio: Utilización y significado," LURRALDE, Ingeba (1983).

Carmen Díez Mintegui, "Mari, un mito para la resistencia feminista," Ankulegi 3, 63–72.

———,"Mari (Antropología)," electronic publication, www.eusko ikaskuntza, Bases de datos—Enciclopedia Auñamendi (2002).

Written lesson for submission

What aspects of the myth of Mari can be interpreted as a metaphor for feminine freedom and power?

12 · Magic and witchcraft

Over time, with the advent of Christianity and the consolidation of patriarchal systems, we find that the female figures related to prehistoric nature-oriented goddess religion and fertility cults are transformed into negative, pernicious characters and practices. This leads us into a consideration of magic and witchcraft, especially as the Basque Country was the scenario for a vehement witch-hunt in the sixteenth and seventeenth centuries and as the Spanish Inquisition has left us with copious records of the trials of the alleged offenders. In this section we will consider different theories of witchcraft from anthropology, theology, and social history, and then look at the witch-hunts in the Basque Country in the sixteenth and seventeenth centuries, paying particular attention to the cases of Zugarramurdi and Urdax and the trials of the Spanish Inquisition at Logroño.

Theories of witchcraft

Do witches exist? If we pose the question of whether witches do or did exist in the Basque Country, we find conflicting theories from anthropologists, theologians, historians, and other intellectuals, all giving their own interpretations of material from myth, tales, or historical data such as the confessions recorded by the Spanish Inquisition in the sixteenth and seventeenth centuries. Gustav Henningsen does just this in his work on the Basque witch-trials; his book *The Witch's Advocate: Basque Witchcraft and the Spanish Inquisition (1609–1614)* will be our point of reference for this section.

From anthropology. From the Enlightenment right up to the twentieth century, historians had generally agreed that the whole witch phenomenon was sheer illusion and that witches were innocent victims of a fanatical persecution. However, in 1921, anthropologist Margaret Murray revived the debate that had been laid to rest, proposing that witches were in fact part of a heathen fertility cult that had survived from pre-Christian times in remote regions of Western Europe. She reasoned that witchcraft was an organized religion in which the "devil" was no more than the horned god of the witches, Aker, the Goat of the Mari myths. She demonstrated that their weirder exploits were none other than ancient fertility rites.

Murray's thesis is appealing and nicely fits what we have seen to be the ancient cosmovision of the Great Goddess, the Earth Mother or Moon, closely linked to Nature and worshipped at the Akelarre. Nevertheless, we have to consider that, like the thesis of the Basque matriarchy, it is fabricated from myth that is manipulated to suit the writer's arguments. Another anthropologist, Lucy Mair, argues against Murray that there had to be more to witchcraft than ancient religious rites or else the concept of witches would never have come into existence. She argues that Murray ignores some of the more sinister accounts of witches' doings and neglects the fact that they overthrow the whole moral order of society.

From the church. Five years after Murray's controversial work was published, a Roman Catholic priest by the name of Montague Summers wrote The History of Witchcraft and Demonology. He agreed with Murray that the witches' confessions were to be taken seriously and that the sabbaths did take place, but refused her thesis of an ancient fertility rite and instead claimed the witches to be satanists involved in devil worship.

Women or witches?
Women dressed up in the clothes of the Middle Ages act as witches at a Medieval fair. The Basque Country was witness to vicious witch hunts in the past and both women and men were wrongly accused of heinous crimes. The stories concocted often under torture responded to pressure from the church, remnants of ancient pagan practises and social conflict.
Photo: Gari Garaialde

Summers goes too far the other way in his analysis, completely ignores the existence of folklore and the importance of folk belief, and claims that all those who invoked demons, worshipped the devil, or practiced black magic, as well as all fortune tellers, faith healers, and spiritualists, were the devil's accomplices and therefore witches. This view is consonant with the Catholic Church's overall position on witchcraft, which is invariably interpreted as involving the devil as conceived by Christian theology.

From social history. In his work *Las brujas y su mundo* (Witches and their world), first published in 1961, Caro Baroja considers two different sources for his analysis: the historical documents that exist for the witch-trials of Anboto, Zugarramurdi, Lapurdi, and Hondarribia, and local informants who express popular beliefs about witches. When he considers the case of the witch-trials, like Henningsen he believes it necessary to take into account the social and historical context in which they took place, acknowledging the influences of rivalries between local bands at the time.

Contemporary views of women, such as the opinion held by the Inquisitors, are found to be revealing in themselves. These men were scandalized by certain activities that were customary practice for women—among which were the duties of the *serora*, a church warden and housekeeper to the priest, often a widow or unmarried woman—and believed there was a witch in virtually every family.

According to the documents from the trials, the kinds of things for which witches were accused included metamorphosis, provoking storms, casting spells on crops and cattle or on people, vampirism and the eating of corpses (especially with child victims), and worship of and intercourse with the devil.

Caro Baroja believes many supposed witches were nature healers whose treatments had failed and who were accused of witchcraft by their unlucky and dissatisfied customers. This is the stereotype he gives of a Basque rural witch: "The rural witch, more often old than young, on the margins of society, feared and despised, seems to be a nervous woman, subject to major breakdowns, who possesses limited knowledge of curing, applying poultices and healing, who sometimes practices divination and may seek the comfort of the artificial paradises which the European flora can provide." (1984:314–15, my translation)

Caro Baroja looks into psychological analysis for clues as to witches' personality, finding they respond to an exaggeration of the personality that leads poor, rural, and middle-aged or older women to believe themselves different and superior to what they really are, and capable of incredible feats. He finds they often reach this state after being frustrated in love or somehow shamed, leaving them with a complex of impotence and dishonor against which they rebel by returning to illegitimate practices and powers. In Hondarribia, the cases were all brought against foreign women.

We still need to situate the psychological in the socioeconomic context where roles are attributed to women to discover what behavior is considered by the community to contravene the social norms. This is exactly what Gustav Henningsen does in his intriguing book The Witch's Advocate (1980), in which he stresses the need to study witchcraft in its social setting to understand what was going on. He looks at the kind of community in which witchcraft was said to have been practiced and the kind of people who were accused of being witches in that community. He finds that in rural communities, it was common to seek supernatural explanations for inexplicable natural phenomena, so that when disaster befell the community for no apparent reason, the calamity was attributed to the work of witches. For example, when a child or an animal died or the crops were diseased, the villagers—unable to identify the source of ill—blamed witches.

Henningsen explores the popular belief in witches in the sixteenth and seventeenth centuries and shows that, unlike the church's version, it has nothing to do with the devil, but rather with the supernatural powers attributed to the witches themselves. Folk belief held that the witches had special powers that enabled them to fly, to transform themselves into animals, and to injure people by touching or cursing them. They were thought to meet at night, often by a spring, and then to go out to do damage by destroying a neighbor's crop, killing a child, or afflicting an animal with sickness.

It is interesting to find that two target social groups came under suspicion of witchcraft in these communities:

1. The weaker members of the community: beggars, people with a disability, widows, orphans, the very old (i.e., all those who could be accused without risk, as they had little defense)
2. Those rejecting the moral order: the thieving, aggressive, spiteful, envious, fawning, or promiscuous

It seems that the accusations of witchcraft responded to a need to find a scapegoat when things went wrong in the community and that the obvious targets were the most vulnerable or the most antisocial.

Let us look more closely at what actually happened in Zugarramurdi and Urdax and examine how the people of these peaceful little villages came to be the center of a large-scale witch-trial.

Witch-Hunts in the Basque Country in the Sixteenth and Seventeenth Centuries

The Basque Country saw witch-hunts in the first two decades of the sixteenth century, but then things went quiet until a case of unprecedented proportions flared up in Logroño in 1610. This was simultaneous with a huge witch-hunt in Lapurdi in which the French judge, Pierre de Lancre, sent some eighty people to the stake. According to Xamar (1992:48), this Bordeaux-born judge was himself of Basque origins and was sent by the king to investigate accusations of witchcraft between two powerful and rivaling families in Donibane Lohitzun–St. Jean de Luz. De Lancre arrived in Lapurdi in 1608 and started to hunt down supposed witches. The results of his proceedings are published in the *Tableau de l'inconstance des mauvais anges et demons* (Account of the inconstancy of fallen angels and demons).

His attitude to those suspected of witchcraft was strongly colored by his opinion of the Basque Country and culture, which he viewed as infiltrated by the devil. While acknowledging that the land of Lapurdi was part of France and neighbor to Spain, he found the people to be neither French nor Spanish, considering their language, their dress, and their customs to be diabolically influenced. This might help answer the question posed by the authors of *Mujer vasca* as to why there were so many witches precisely in Euskal Herria (1985:32).

Pierre de Lancre interrogated 500 children and, on the basis of their answers, found 3,000 people from Lapurdi to be witches, though the figures for those said to have attended a witch's sabbath in Hendaye on one occasion soared to an astronomical 12,000. Even the priests came under de Lancre's suspicions, since they were found to practice Basque customs such as dancing and playing pelota. Several were put on trial and others fled south. As a result of this persecution, many were condemned to death, and according to the records some eighty people were actually burnt at the stake.

The Lapurdi witch-hunt on the French side of the border was followed by a major witch-trial in the Spanish town of Logroño in 1610. Most of those tried came from the two little villages of Zugarramurdi and Urdax, both rural communities situated in Nafarroa on the Spanish side of the Basque Country. The joint popu-

Shrouded in mystery
The misty woods and shady groves of Euskal Herria's lush countryside lend themselves to the elaboration of fantastic stories of strange apparitions, witches and mischievous deeds. Against the backdrop of an ancient nature-based goddess religion, fired by the vivid imagination of the Spanish Inquisitors out to uproot heresy, the mystical landscape of the Basque Country has set the scene for many a blood-curdling tale of witchcraft.
Photo: Iñaki Edroso

---

lation of the two villages numbered no more than 300 people, who formed part of the same parish with the main church at Urdax. The inhabitants of Zugarramurdi were peasant farmers and shepherds, while those of Urdax were mainly farm laborers employed on the land belonging to the monastery located there. Thus the people's livelihood rested on an agricultural economy, constantly threatened by the harsh climate, with the danger of hailstorms and frost ruining the crops.

The trouble started in December 1609 when a 20-year-old girl, Maria de Ximildegui, who had been living in the seaside town of Ciboure (Lapurdi) for a few years, returned to Zugarramurdi to work as a maid. She began to relate how she had been part of a witch's coven in Ciboure around the time of Pierre de Lancre's persecution, but affirmed that she had since reconverted to Christianity. During her time in the coven, she said that she had attended witches' sabbaths in Zugarramurdi and claimed to know who the local witches were. She began to name names, accusing 22-year-old Maria de Jureteguia, who protested her innocence until her family, convinced by the vivid accounts of Ximildegui, put pressure on the girl to confess. Jureteguia then admitted she had been a witch since she was a child and said her maternal aunt, Maria Chipia de Barrenechea, had been her tutor. Maria de Jureteguia was encouraged by the priest to make a public confession, and others who had also been denounced by Ximildegui followed suit.

It is likely the case would have rested there had it not been for the ambitions of the abbot of Urdax and the nature of the Spanish Inquisition. The Inquisition was a body charged with overseeing the purity of the Catholic faith. Its aim was not to eradicate heretics but rather to convert them to Catholicism. Those suspected of heresy were put on trial, but only those who refused to cooperate were sent to the stake. The trial was meant to arouse a sense of guilt in the accused, who were not informed of the charges against them until well into the trial. They were kept imprisoned for long periods of time until they were prepared to make their confession. Once the accused had acknowledged their guilt, they were to repent and cooperate with the Inquisitors, particularly by informing on their accomplices. Only then was a charge drawn up, defining the type of heresy of which they were accused. They could be interrogated under torture if there was any doubt as to their sincerity.

The accused were assigned a defense lawyer, who merely encouraged them to confess and beg for mercy, and the trial itself was little more than a ratification of the charge, during which the witnesses were reexamined to confirm their statements and make any necessary corrections. At the verdict, if there was circumstantial evidence but little proof, the accused was submitted to torture. If they withstood without confessing, the charge was considered insufficiently proved and they were let off with a renunciation of heresy and a light punishment. They were also tortured if they were thought to be protecting accomplices. The outcome of the trial was pronounced in a final auto de fe.

The Council of the Supreme and General Inquisition was the Inquisition's ministry and had its own secret intelligence service whose chief agents were mostly parish priests. It is likely that the Inquisition came to hear about the events in Zugarramurdi through Fray Leon, the abbot of Urdax, who was eager to apply for one of the privileged positions of Inquisitor. He wrote to the Inquisition to inform them that the northern strip of the Basque Country was susceptible to unholy influences since the mule trains traveling down through France could easily be bringing heretical books into Spain, as there was no Inquisitor to exert any kind of control in that region.

It is probable that he also informed the Inquisition of the events in Zugarramurdi, bringing inspectors in to find out what was going on. The outcome was a major trial in Logroño, at which a total of thirty-one alleged witches were tried, twenty-five of them from the villages

A figment of the imagination?
The witches which crowd Basque tales and legends are almost certainly a distortion of the myths of Mari, the lamias, and other attendants, taken up by the Church and used to fuel the charges of heresy to fit their own imagination.
Figure: courtesy of Jon Ander of Lurra.
Photo: Iñaki Ugarte

of Zugarramurdi and Urdax, a number constituting about a quarter of the adult population at the time. Among these, four stood out on charges of heinous crimes, including the murder of eighteen children and eleven adults, a number of bewitchings without fatal results, injuries to animals, and damage to crops. Of these four, there was an old lady of eighty-eight, by the name of Graciana de Barrenchea; a sixty-six-year-old shepherd, Miguel de Goiburu; and two sisters, Estevania and María de Yriarte, thirty-six and forty years old respectively.

One of the recurrent themes in these cases was the belief that witches avenged themselves on their enemies' children, hence the high number of infanticides. Goiburu confessed to having taken part in the murder of his niece, and of a widow's child, joining with other witches in biting and sucking the blood from the wounds. He also confessed to killing the eight-year-old son of a cattle dealer in Urdax who had performed an unsatisfactory deal. Barrenchea similarly confessed to killing the child of a woodcutter who had given her a thrashing for stealing his firewood and another whose parents had let their pig stray into her garden and ruin a pile of apples for cider. The Yriarte sisters acted directly on their victims. Estevania confessed to punishing a boy for eating a loaf with a throat inflammation, and María confessed to poisoning a man who had threatened with a knife for stealing his apples.

Witches as Social Outcasts and Scapegoats

Henningsen finds that these so-called witches were constantly quarreling with their neighbors and seen as unpopular in the community. They stole when they could get away with it and were beaten when caught. However, this merely proves they were bad neighbors, but in those days "bad neighbor" became synonymous with "witch." Any damage done, any natural disaster or inclemency of the weather, was attributed to the witches. Any misfortune was held to be the doing of evil folk, and people looked for culprits among their nearest enemies.

Although we do have the records of the trial in Logroño, and Henningsen provides an enthralling account of them, they are riddled with confusion and contradiction. Confessions made one day are retracted the next and the evidence is difficult to assess since it builds on a fantasy world that, in all probability, corresponds more to what the Inquisitors wanted to hear than to what might have been true. Nevertheless, the confessions provide an extensive description of the witch cult as it was supposed to be, however much fired by the Inquisitor's imagination.

The devil appears in the accounts as the witches' lord, sometimes embodied in human form, at other times as a billy goat (the aker of the Mari myths perhaps) or with animal attributes such as horns, an ass's tail, hands like a cockerel's feet and with a hawk's claws, feet like a gander. The witches' sabbath was called an akelarre, from the words aker (goat) and larre (meadow), referring to their meeting place, which in Zugarramurdi was at a cave that is quite a tourist attraction today.

The witches were said to fly to the meetings, after anointing themselves with an evil-smelling fluid. Once there, they greeted their devil-master and then began to dance around a fire to the music of pipe and drums. They were encouraged to pass through the fire to get used to the fires of hell. As well as the dancing, there was said to be sexual activity, between the devil and those of his choosing, and between other witches present. This was understood to be a fertility rite.

Another aspect was that of parodying the Catholic faith and Christian practice. On initiation to the cult, the novices had to forswear their Christian faith and commit themselves to the devil. On feast days, a black mass was celebrated in which an altar was erected, covered with a black cloth, and adorned with pictures of the devil, and communion was imitated with the black sole of a shoe for the host and a bitter gall to drink in place of wine.

One of the most appalling practices alleged was that of violating tombs to retrieve the bodies of witches buried and then feasting on the corpses. The bones and brains were said to be used to make poison, and the "yellow water" in which they were boiled was apparently deadly. Other witches' powders were also said to be made from toads, snakes, lizards, and other creatures or from puffballs and other fungi. These poisons were then supposedly used to inflict illness or death on people, animals, or crops, and when a witch wanted to perform some evil, they would go out in the company of the "devil" and other witches, sometimes transforming themselves into cats or dogs to do their dirty deeds.

Finally, toads were thought to be an important element of the witch cult. On initiation each witch received her own personal toad, which was understood to be her familiar spirit or imp. The toad was said to be the witch's guardian and adviser, ensuring that they got to the meetings on time. Moreover, the toads provided a poisonous substance from their excrement with which the witches made their "flying potion," enabling them to fly to the sabbaths. Given this detail, Henningsen suggests it is tempting to believe that what was held to be witchcraft was no more than a harmless drug cult, based on the use of a narcotic contained in toad's excrement and found to have a hallucinogenic effect that could have produced the sensation of flying. However, since there is no evidence for this, it remains pure speculation.

The question then remains: Did witches exist in the Basque Country? Was there a witch cult in Zugarramurdi? Henningsen concludes that the confessions made in Logroño were "probably lies from beginning to end," and though they were not extracted under torture, they do seem to respond to a picture the Inquisition formed for itself and elaborated on by amalgamating the disparate parts to create an impressive whole.

To return to the theories set out at the start of this section, we can present different interpretations for the practices, and though we lack evidence to draw any definitive conclusion, it seems reasonable to conjecture that the phenomena are probably a complex amalgam of different factors:

1. A remnant of the ancient heathen fertility cults built around a belief in the goddess Mari, in which Mother Earth and Nature were the principal forces and the object was to appease the elements and facilitate survival; along these lines, knowledge of herbal medicine, poisons, and their antidotes could have been interpreted as the manufacture of witch powders and the nature healers labeled as witch doctors
2. An anti-Christian cult fabricated by the Inquisition itself for their own purposes, taken up by ambitious ecclesiastics and perpetrated by overzealous parishioners
3. A mechanism of social control implemented by villagers offended by antisocial neighbors and in need of an explanation for inexplicable deaths or damage to their farms

Lesson twelve

Summary

1. Theories of witchcraft range from interpretations of them as ancient fertility cults to devil worship, to the persecution of social misfits. Attention to the historical context, the social attitudes prevailing, and the circumstances in which the accusations were made are vital for a correct interpretation of events.
2. There were major witch-hunts in both the French and Spanish Basque Country in the sixteenth and seventeenth centuries. Many were brought to trial and burnt at the stake. One of the most notorious was the Spanish Inquisition's trial of villagers of Zugarramurdi and Urdax.
3. There is no evidence of a witch cult, though it is not unlikely that there were pagan fertility rights or healing practices. Rather, it would seem to have been concocted by the Catholic Church and invented by villagers looking to turn social outcasts into scapegoats on whom to lay the blame of inexplicable misfortunes.

Suggested Reading

Gustav Henningsen, The Witch's Advocate: Basque Witchcraft and the Spanish Inquisition (1609–1614) (Reno: University of Nevada Press, 1980) (Chap. 4: "The Trial [First Part]").

Bibliography

Julio Caro Baroja, Las brujas y su mundo (Madrid: Alianza Editorial, 1984).

Xamar, Desde el Orhi: Conocer el País del Euskara (Pamplona-Iruñea: Pamiela, 1992).

Written lesson for submission

How do the themes of myth, marginality, and power apply to the analysis of witchcraft in the Basque Country?

Key Words

POWER: a process rather than a product, which to function requires that legitimacy be apportioned to the person wielding power by the one who complies and submits to their authority. The unequal gender relations in society respond to the complex power relations built through the economic, political, and socio-sociocultural network.

INDARRA: a culturally specfic concept of power from the Basque context, referring to physical strength.

MATRIARCHY: the dominion of mother over family and state, by natural, biological right. Women exercise authority, make decisions, and wield influence over men. Primitive matriarchies were said to be characterized by a communal spirit of solidarity and sympathy and were essentially nature-oriented.

MATRILINEAGE: the reckoning of descent and the transmission of property through the female line.

MATRILOCAL: a couple's establishing es their postmarital residence within the wife's mother's group.

PATRIARCHY: a system of society ruled by men, characterized by patrilineal descent (through the male line).

Part four. Family, society, and politics

13 · Making models

Returning to our initial definition of gender as the sociocultural construction of women and men, we will now turn our attention to how culturally specific gender models are made in relation to the Basque family, society, and politics. We will consider whether these standardized forms constrict women or whether women are able to move beyond them, break the mold, and cast their own model.

In the last chapter we saw the basis for the matriarchy thesis, which argues for a decisive and powerful role for Basque women as heads of the household and rulers of the domestic roost. Here we will look a little more closely at the social construction of Basque women in the framework of the family and examine what it means for them in real terms.

We will then go on to consider how the matriarchal model has been carried over into the Basque political arena. We have seen that the Basque stereotype of a strong female figure epitomized by the "matriarch" has been used as an identifier of Basqueness and employed as an element of ethnic differentiation. This is the model that has been taken up by the conservative Basque Nationalist Party or Partido Nacionalista Vasco, which we shall refer to by its abbreviation, PNV. In contrast stands a contentious model constructed in opposition to the archetypical matriarch. It is a model that unites the stereotype of feminist with that of radical nationalist in which the women are portrayed as deviating from the "norm" and tarred as troublemakers. In the Basque Country, where the cultural and political worlds frequently coincide, it is especially important to analyze the way political movements absorb gender ideologies, whether to confirm or contest them.

In the social sphere, we will contemplate the contribution of women to the transmission of key elements of the Basque culture, with special reference to the Basque language, Euskara. We will consider their importance in continuing certain cultural practices, at the same time as demonstrating adaptability and promoting change in keeping with the modernizing dynamic of contemporary society.

Finally we will consider the way women who have emigrated to other countries carry over Basque cultural values to their host country or whether, since they are removed from the immediate sociopolitical context of their homeland, the former models are challenged and new ones adopted.

Model Mothers

As Henrietta Moore points out (1988:25–30), in most societies the notion of "woman" is associated with that of "mother," though they are assigned different attributes in different cultures. The concept of "motherhood" has, on the whole, been associated with nature and with the domestic realm, while "fatherhood" has been deemed more of a social and practical construct linked to the public domain in terms of the father's need to provide for his wife and children by seeking sustenance beyond the family walls. While women's incursion into the labor market and their increasing contribution to the domestic economy has rendered unviable the model of the man as sole provider and protector of the family, the symbolic weighting of "motherhood" as a natural quality continues to prevail and, as we saw in Chapter 8, poses problems for the coordination of the domestic and public domains. Feminist critique has challenged the equation between women and mothers, signaling the diversity of roles that women exercise in addition to or apart from motherhood, as well as questioning the portrayal of motherhood itself. In her article on maternity, Carmen Díez (1995) shows that rather than being a universal, static concept with fixed qualities, "motherhood" is found in just the same way as the terms "woman" or "man" to be historically and culturally specific, differing through time and space and constructed through discourse along the lines of certain notions such as "motherly love" or what it means to be "a good mother."

In another article on systems of gender, inequality, and national identity, Díez (1999) refers specifically to the Spanish and Basque contexts and finds that the prevalent model that equates the concept of "woman" with the notion of "mother" and "wife" historically derives from Franco's times (1936–1975). She points out that as well as being a dictatorial political regime, "franquismo" involved a set of social influences ranging from the Catholic Church to education, transmitted through medical discourse, the business world, and other institutions, and which combined to symbolically cordon off public and private spaces in which men and women were assigned completely different roles and expected to comply with a different set of norms. The model of the ideal woman under Franco was that of a mother and wife dedicated exclusively to her family and home: "a sublimated image of the figure of wife and mother, centred in the world of the home, who in daily practice dedicates her life to the fulfilment of this role" (ibid. 1999:108, my translation). Nonetheless, while this was the social standard and anyone who failed to comply with it was dubbed a spinster or a prostitute, inevitably tremendous variety was observed among those who did fit the bill of "housewife." Differing economic positions meant that some women were able to enjoy the privileges of their class while others struggled to keep the household going and took on paid work in addition to their domestic chores. Predictably, the reality is always far more varied than the ideal.

As we saw in Part 2, in Franco's Spain, the low levels of female employment and education are proportional to the importance given to marriage and the role of the family in society. On the whole, women scarcely participated in the official labor market and their economic activity was highly restricted. However, this meant not that women enjoyed a high status within marriage but in fact quite the reverse. In his book *The Spaniards*, John Hooper comments that "towards the end of Franco's rule the only other European country in which there was a comparable degree of institutionalised discrimination against married women was Turkey and that on several counts the status of wives in Turkey was actually higher" (1987:196). Hooper gives us a detailed picture of married life during the regime that we will use as the basis for our discussion.

Permiso marital (marital permission): The institution of marriage was regulated by the Spanish Civil Code, which recalls the marriage vows in dictating that the husband's obligation was to protect his wife and hers to obey her husband. The concept of marital permission legally enforced the obligation to obey. It meant that without her husband's authorization a married woman was unable to undertake any kind of activity outside the home. She could not take a job, start a business, open an account, initiate legal proceedings, sign a contract, or buy and sell goods. A wife even needed her husband's permission before she could set out on a long journey.

Mothering is for life
Motherhood has been extolled in Basque culture as a lifelong ideal. Even in the modern world, where mothers also have paid jobs, grandmothers often take over the task of childcare.
Photo: Iñaki Ugarte.

---

property. A woman had no control over her own property once she entered into a marriage contract. The Spanish system distinguished between three categories of belongings: those the husband brought to the marriage, those brought by the wife, and then whatever both acquired during the marriage (these latter being known as bienes gananciales). While the husband was free to dispense with both his own and the acquired goods as he deemed fit, the woman needed his permission before she could sell, lend, or mortgage any of her own property or their shared goods, even if she had been responsible, in part or whole, for earning them. The inability to control her possessions was extended to her children, as the paternal authority (patria potestad) was assigned to the father, and the mother had no say without him.

Infringement. The breaking of these rules led to heavy sanctions. Having to obtain the husband's permission lo leave the home meant that a woman who did so without her spouse's authorization was committing the offense of desertion. As Hooper indicates, among other things this meant that battered wives could not seek shelter from their violent husbands with friends or family without infringing the law.

Adultery was considered a crime, punishable by sentences ranging from six months to six years, and this was true for both men and women. However, the criteria for considering it an offense or not followed a double morality that made it a crime for women whatever the circumstances, whereas for men it was considered a punishable offense only if committed in the family home, if he was living with his mistress, or if the adultery became known publicly.

Divorce. One of the other major restrictions of people's liberty under Franco was the abolition of divorce. A divorce law had been in place in Spain, passed under the Republic in 1932, but this was revoked in 1938 by the Nationalists while the Civil War was still going on. For the next forty years or so, the only way to end a marriage made in Spain was by an annulment granted by the Roman Catholic Church. The precepts for an annulment dictated that the marriage must have been unconsummated and "nonsacramental," which narrows the chances down to one of the partners being physically unable to have intercourse, being under age at the time of marriage, or not having given his or her genuine consent.

Nevertheless, despite these conditions, thousands of Spaniards managed to obtain a divorce through annulment during the Franco years. However, it was clear that those to whom annulments were conceded were rich, famous, and influential people. After 1971, it became easy to obtain an annulment as long as you had a large sum of money to deposit in the ecclesiastical court. This was facilitated by Pope Paul VI's decision to allow certain dioceses the power to annul the marriages of expatriates. Many of these courts were not as strict as the Spanish ones and were to be found in poorer countries of the world, for example in Africa, South America, or the Caribbean where the income was welcome. Corruption was rife. It was evident that officials of the Spanish ecclesiastical courts were collaborating, because the annulments procured abroad still had to be ratified back in Spain.

Failing the expensive and dubious option of an annulment, the only other alternative for unhappily married Spaniards under Franco was to obtain a legal separation. However, this process was also full of obstacles and even after lengthy legal wrangling, it was never certain that the separation would be granted at all. It was not enough for the lawyers and their clients to state that the marriage was over; moreover, they had to prove this on grounds of adultery. The judge and the court officials, among whom was a specially appointed defensor del vinculo (literally "defender of the [marriage] bond") set out to save the marriage and reconcile the parties. Given this predisposition of the courts to prevent rather than facilitate separation, the imperative of providing proof of the nonviability of the marriage was even more pressing. Blame had to be laid on one of the partners, and it had to be backed up by witnesses and statements, and sometimes even went so far as requiring the intervention of a private detective or the police who would be called to burst in to catch the "adulterer" in the act. This

Bedroom farce
The difficulties of obtaining a divorce during Franco's dictatorship led to some farcical situations where private detectives were hired to catch an adulterous spouse in the act. While the government argued that legal divorce would leave many women high and dry as their husbands left to join younger women, the majority of divorce suits filed were instigated by wives.
Dover Pictorial Archives.

seemingly farcical state of affairs had serious implications: on the chopping block was not only the individual's pride, but also the custody of the children and the prospect of alimony, both of which had to be forfeited by whoever was found guilty.

On top of all this, the process was extremely long and drawn out, usually taking two to three years but sometimes even up to eight. Like the annulments, legal separation was expensive too, and though for people on a low income there was the possibility of legal aid in theory, in practice the lawyers were reluctant to take up such unprofitable cases and they were postponed time after time. By the end of the dictatorship about half a million people had obtained a legal separation, though many more had been condemned to remain in unhappy marriages. In 1975 an official survey showed 71 percent of Spaniards to be firmly in favor of divorce.

Contraception and abortion. Like divorce, both contraception and abortion were banned under Franco. The Church's solution was to preach either coitus interruptus or outright abstinence and at the same time to encourage reproduction, to produce large Catholic families. However, inevitably, both contraception and abortion continued to be practiced. Condoms could be obtained in the red light districts or street markets, and once the Pill was invented it too became available, though it had to be prescribed for medical reasons (the regulating of menstrual disorders) rather than as a contraceptive. Nonetheless, the willingness of some doctors to write such prescriptions indicated a growing tolerance of contraception. By 1975, a report issued by the Instituto de Estudios Laborales y de la Seguridad Social and leaked to a newspaper, Cambio 16, found over half a million women to be using the Pill (Hooper 1987:189).

The greatest irony was that while abortion was prohibited, the ban on contraception meant that abortion among poor people became more of a necessity and was widely practiced in backstreet clinics, while those with resources went abroad to England or France to obtain abortions on demand (ibid. 191)

Alternative Family Arrangements

Díez (1999) plots a gradual change in women's circumstances in Spain and the Basque Country in the last quarter of the century, a change that she links to the end of the dictatorship and the introduction of a more liberal approach, industrialization and modernization, the increase in the number of women joining the labor market, and rising levels in education (see section "Women and Change" in Chapter 2). Another aspect to consider is the changing face of the Spanish and Basque family, evolving from the ideal traditional family that differs widely from the diversity of family arrangements practiced by domestic groups today. Hacker (1989:131) writes that the facts that celibacy is becoming more common, that people are leaving it later to get married, and that couples are choosing to have fewer children, or none at all, indicates a "structural and ideological shift on women's role in the family."

We have seen that in rural Basque society it was usual for the *baserri*, or farmhouse, to hold a multiple family arrangement, consisting of three generations of the family. Multiple families refer to families in which more than one nuclear unit is present, and in the Basque case it was usual to find the senior couple; the junior, inheriting couple along with any unmarried brothers or sisters of the heir; and the inheriting couple's children, all under one roof. We have also seen that in this arrangement the *etxekoandere*, or woman of the house, was expected to display a certain set of qualities and comply with a series of duties and obligations. At the same time she was considered the head of the domestic household, the controller of family finances, and the minder of religious rites and folklore for the good of the family. This image of the Basque rural woman, projected through literature, scholarship, and political discourse, overshadows all the other alternatives that can be found in reality, in both the past and the present. It leaves out coastal and urban women, as well as other kinds of rural women, and casts all Basque women in the same unitarian mold according to an idealized and essentialist vision of Basque culture.

Although a look at the figures for family types across Europe still places Spain in a bracket of the highest incidence of complex families (along with Portugal and Ireland), the norm is nevertheless in keeping with the European tendency for nuclear families. It is revealing that while Spain has a higher than average percentage of complex families, it has a lower than average proportion of both solitary households (i.e. persons living on their own) and nonfamily arrangements (i.e. people sharing accommodations, with no family ties). An increasing number of women also are choosing not to marry, either staying single or living with a partner without marrying, and with the comparative ease of obtaining divorce, more single-parent families or second marriages of divorcées. On the whole it would be true to say there is now more choice open to women both in terms of the way they choose to live with or without a stable partner and in relation to their option to work in addition to or instead of being uniquely a wife and mother. Having said this, one must note that greater social value still attaches to marriage and to building a typical nuclear family than to any other option, though attitudes are changing noticeably.[18]

Juan Cobarrubias, in an article that discusses the future of the Basque language, draws our attention to the demographic decline in the Basque Country, which he states is "one of the most dramatic population losses occurring in both Europe and the world" (1999:71). Spain is on a par with Italy with only a 1.2 birthrate per couple (compared with 2.0 for the United States), and this evidences a drastic turnabout from the days of the *familia numerosa* ("large family") of Franco's time when it was not uncommon to find families with a dozen or more children. For our purposes here, these data indicate the change in the ideology of the family, the freedom of choice, and the birth control available to women in present-day Spain, but for Cobarrubias the falling figures bode ill for the drive to promote and maintain a minority language spoken by a community that is failing to reproduce itself. This has implications for the transmission of both culture and language, traditionally considered to be the prerogative of women.

Lesson thirteen

Summary

1. The model of motherhood is particularly strong in Basque society, where despite change in the family the notion of a model mother still prevails. A conservative, idealized model of motherhood was imposed on Spanish and Basque women during the Franco years, translated into severe restrictions on women's freedom in marriage in which the husband had absolute control over his wife and children, property, and mobility. The impossibility or immense difficulty of obtaining a divorce meant that many were condemned to miserable marriages.
2. In the Basque case, the ideal woman was built around the archetypical farmer's wife, firmly situated in the traditional rural world and imbued with essentialist notions of Basque culture that ignored alternatives from other contexts of life.

---

3. After Franco's death, society as a whole experienced rapid change, and conditions changed radically for women. In contemporary Spain and the Basque Country, the traditional family model is changing and alternative arrangements are beginning to emerge.

Suggested Reading

Juan Cobarrubias, "Viability of the Basque Language in the Next Millennium," in W. A. Douglass et al., eds., *Basque Cultural Studies* (Reno: University of Nevada Press, 1999), excerpt "Demographic Spread," 69–77.

John Hooper, "Family Ties," in *The Spaniards: A Portrait of the New Spain* (London: Penguin, 1987), 196–201.

Bibliography

Carmen Díez, "Sobre la maternidad," in *Bitarte*, 3:81–93.

———, "Sistemas de género, desigualdad e identidad nacional," in P. Albite, coord., *Sociedad vasca y construcción nacional* (Donostia: Tercera Prensa–Hirugarren Prentsa, 1999a), 147–74.

———, "Historia de las mujeres en Euskal Herria," in (ed.) *Euskal Borroka Feminista Aurrera* (1999b), 105–17.

Written lesson for submission

Assess the nature and implications of change for women with regard to family arrangements from the Franco years to the present.

14 · Women and cultural transmission

The role of women, and especially mothers, in the passing on of cultural traits from one generation to the next is another aspect of the idealization of "motherhood." In the Basque case, the Basque language, Euskara, is the most salient feature of cultural transmission in which women are seen to play a key role, though one which is conceptually linked to their condition as mothers and carers of children, at home and school, and frequently undervalued. In recent years, women are moving into more public and prestigious areas of language, including both oral and written literature.

Motherhood and the Naturalization of Cultural Transmission

The movement for the promotion and protection of Euskara involves a wide range of institutions, educational establishments, and popular organizations, making it the most visible aspect of Basque cultural transmission. An extensive literature covers different aspects of the Basque language, and from it there emerges an emotive picture of the vital importance attached to Euskara as emblematic of the Basque people and their culture. With regard to women's role in language transmission, we only need to reflect on the term "mother tongue" as common currency in our vocabulary to recognize its importance. It is this aspect that has traditionally been emphasized for women, stressing the importance of their work from within the home on behalf of the Basque language. Linda White, whose doctoral thesis on Basque women writers in the twentieth century (1996) is a landmark in the literary history of the Basque Country from a gendered point of view, shows that by magnifying motherhood and placing women firmly in the domestic space, their activity beyond the home is silenced, ignored, or undervalued. In an illuminating article on "gendering and engendering Basque literature" (1999), White points to this symbolic tie between women and home that overshadows the evaluation of their contribution to literature: "The perpetuation of this link between women and the home invades their creative space as well, the world of the mind and the mind and the imagination. Even there, though they produce volumes, they cannot be viewed separately from their primary functions of wife and mother." (1999:135)

Teresa del Valle (1997) takes us back to the nature–culture debate to show how the passing on of a language from mother to child is closely associated with women's "natural" role of reproduction. Giving birth, bringing up children, and passing on a language are all seen as "natural" female roles. "In this way, the woman as transmitter keeps the language intimately related to the house, the domestic universe and the traditional world. The concept of procreation, of giving life, is inextricably linked to the vitality of the language. To transmit a language is to keep it alive." (1997:15, my translation)

Del Valle signals that because language learning is presented as something natural when related to women, it is devoid of social value. Both White and del Valle demonstrate that prestige is only acquired in this area when language learning leaves the "natural" domestic domain and enters the public arena, in which case it is assigned to men. Where women have made an incursion into literature, says White, they write within the "limitations of Basque society's domestic expectations by creating child-related and education-related materials" (1999:136). It is in the public world, where Euskara is institutionalized, where it enters the world of language planning and politics, of pedagogical techniques, the media and literature, that it generates the most interest and social significance. This world is, on the whole, dominated by men. An example is the overwhelming male membership of Euskaltzaindia, the Academy of the Basque Language, in which the first woman nominated was Miren Azkarate, taking the place of José Miguel Barandiaran on his death in 1991.

It is the case not only that women are absent from public linguistic activity, but also that where they are active their efforts are differently valued from those of men. For example, del Valle points to the work of women in primary education in the ikastolas, Basque language schools, where women are to be found both in teaching posts and as parents, where mothers may be visible militating in public meetings or protests. She suggests that since the ikastolas sprang from initially home-based, family-oriented organizations that have always favored a high level of parent-teacher coordination and emphasized the crucial part the mother has to play in children's linguistic acquisition, the scale of values that marks women's role as natural language transmitters is carried over and wrests prestige from their activity (ibid. 15). We might add that this is also a result of the low social rating generally attached to traditional female occupations such as nursery or primary school teaching, nursing, and other caring professions.

A contradiction, then, is inherent in the way women's importance is recognized in the continuity of the language and at the same time ignored in the areas where decisions are made about language planning and usage and undervalued in the construction of the Basque literary canon. Begoña Arregui (1988) signals the exclusion of the vast majority of women from education up until

Reproducing culture
The role of women in the promotion of Euskara has frequently been portrayed as limited to the undervalued work of school teachers and parents, participating in the maintenance of Basque traditions such as the Christmas Olentzero who these school children are singing about here.
Photo: Iñaki Ugarte

---

the seventies, as an obvious reason for their relatively low literary production.

Basque women writers today have the added difficulties attached to writing in a minority language that poses certain problems for the creation and evaluation of literature. However, the pervasive myth that "only a handful of women write and publish at all" (White 1999:143) is belied by the growing body of literature written by authors such as Itxaro Borda, Arantxa Iturbe, Mariasun Landa, Laura Mintegi, Lourdes Oñederra,

---

Jasone Osoro, and Arantxa Urretavizcaya. The presence of some of these women in university posts, or on the radio or television, as well as the recognition of their work through various literary awards, are helping to put Basque women writers on the map. A growing number of women also are writing in the daily or periodical press, and a new venture worthy of note is the recent launching of a women's monthly newspaper, *Andra*.

Typically, the studies with a gendered perspective on the promotion of the Basque culture, language, and nation have focused primarily on the contribution of women to Basque language schooling through the *ikastola* movement or in the teaching and promulgation of Euskara in other contexts. In connection with this we can place nationalist ethnolinguistic rituals, such as *Korrika*, which is a sponsored run to raise consciousness and awareness for Euskara. We will now go on to look at the participation of women in this run and their role in the transmission and diffusion of the language, and then turn our attention to an area where women have only recently made an incursion: the Basque world of oral poetry production and performance known as *bertsolaritza*.

Korrika

We are fortunate to have an English translation of Teresa del Valle's book *Korrika: Basque Ritual for Ethnic Identity* (1994), which provides us with an in-depth study of the run known as *Korrika*, organized biannually since 1980 by the Basque language coordinator AEK (*Alfabetatze Euskalduntze Koordinakunde*, or "Coordinator for Basque Literacy"). AEK grew out of a clandestine campaign for the recuperation of Euskara while it was still illegal during the Franco regime and developed into a network of language schools teaching Basque to adults throughout Euskal Herria. Although AEK is now government subsidized, it still relies heavily on fund-raising to supplement its income and keep fees to a minimum, and Korrika is its main activity in this sense. It is a run organized as a relay, in which different groups, associations, and businesses sponsor kilometers of the run, which follows a route through the seven Basque provinces nonstop for several days. As well as raising money, the express aim of the Korrika is to raise awareness of the Basque language and to represent symbolically its diffusion throughout Euskal Herria. Del Valle's study looks at the run from different angles that shed light on the ritualistic representation of Basque ethnic identity. As she contemplates the implications of different social sectors in the run, she observes the participation of women in Korrika and then considers how the nationalist and linguistic agenda takes on gender.

Being open to all, Korrika is a ritual that favors the free participation of women, but it nevertheless reflects the hierarchies operating in the assignment of tasks and the systems of prestige at work. As we have seen for linguistic and literary production, del Valle finds that naturalization influences the value system even in the field of popular participation. Over the years she has observed an increasing visibility of women in the Korrika, but on the whole their presence is related to their family responsibilities. Women mostly run in connection with their family roles: as mothers of children with whom they run, demonstrating their place in promoting schooling in Euskara. A symbolic representation of language transmission consists of the passing of a baton, or testigo, from mother to daughter or to women of different generations.

It has been observed that women's activities outside the home are related to their responsibilities within the

Passing on the language
The participation of women and children in the Korrika, a run to promote awareness of the Basque language, symbolically represents the cultural transmission which manifests itself visibly in the passing of a baton, or testigo, here held by a young runner in Korrika 2003.
Photo: Iñaki Ugarte

domestic group. If a woman holds a paid job outside the home that is not related to the teaching of Euskara, it is unlikely that she will find time to participate in the Korrika, unless it is with her children and on a holiday. Those women who do take part tend to be young people without children who have more free time, or else they do so when their children are at school. This is easier in smaller communities where everything is nearer to hand and requires less effort in terms of communication and organization; in the bigger towns and cities the women who take part are usually already members of women's groups and mostly young.

The main characteristics of Korrika, such as physical strength, cohesiveness, and action, are projected as male qualities. Nevertheless, women demonstrate their own strength and staying power, illustrating certain traditional Basque values (such as a sense of responsibility toward others and constancy in the tasks undertaken) that have been found to be more associated with women than men in the Basque context (del Valle et al. 1985: 152, 188–89, 292). This is evident in Korrika, where the toughness of the run and the difficulty of mountainous terrain do not deter the women. Observers also have the sense that this is a long-term undertaking and one in which the fruits of women's efforts, vulnerable to government language planning and policies, are not guaranteed to survive. The participants recognize that by running they are only doing a little bit—"bringing a grain of sand," as they say in Spanish—but that as they try to build, others may come and knock down their work and they will have to start over again. They show pride in running and doing it well. Even among older people who tire more easily, one can see a certain determination to finish the portion of the run they have set out to do. Those who carry the baton are particularly proud of their place and strive to complete their task well. If an older woman must delegate, she prefers to do so to her daughter, thus maintaining a sense of continuity.

While an emphasis on family and the mother-to-child transmission of Euskara is apparent, women are additionally involved with aspects of the organization of the run and may use it as a platform for airing other concerns, such as unemployment and the need for paid work. It must be said that more women are to be found at the grassroots level of the organization and fewer at the directive level, possibly connected to the historical fact that men devised the run or to the general tendency for men to hold positions of leadership. Recent years have seen a growing presence of women's groups and organizations, and we can watch women running in collectives rather than as individuals: women with their friends or work mates, with associations or feminist groups. Female members of nationalist groups also support amnesty or denounce the police presence in Euskadi, while others demonstrate women's concerns for issues other than motherhood and family. Work inevitably stands out as a cause to campaign for, and in the past the Coordinator for the Unemployed has chosen a woman to carry the baton, thereby challenging the male stereotype of the unemployed person. Pressure groups carry banners with their own slogans. Feminist groups champion women's rights, recently focusing on the condemnation of sexual violence, while ecological groups campaign against the building of roads and railways damaging to the environment.

In conclusion, while women are visibly active in Korrika, their participation continues to be framed within the symbolic universe of the domestic environment and the family, especially the mother–child relationship, naturalized language transmission, and socialization. However, ample evidence is also seen of women's capacity for innovation and change, taking initiatives in the organization of the event, moving into new fields of action, and showing a public, political, and collective face.

Bertsolaritza

The growing presence of women in the formerly male world of bertsolaritza is another example of the changing status of the female contribution to Basque language transmission. Bertsolaritza is a type of oral poetry, characterized by its spontaneity and improvisation. The bertsolari is a stand-up poet who performs in competition with others, inventing poems on a given theme and in accordance with certain rules of verse. Traditionally, the bertsolari was a man from a rural environment who possessed the innate gift of versifiying. Over the years, this mythical image has evolved and modernized, opening up to urban society and moving away from the notion of being a gift to being an art that can be learnt like any other. Gorka Aulestia, in an article entitled "The Basque Bertsolari in the New Millennium" (1999), outlines the state of the art of bertsolaritza today, showing it to have risen in favor in recent years, thanks to its evaluation independently of written poetry; the establishment of the Association of Berstolaris and schools of bertsolaritza; and the work of ikastolas and the incursion of young berstolaris with higher levels of education than before. He also signals the increasing involvement of women as one of the major areas of change that bertsolaritza has undergone in the last century.

In a paper on "Women Bertsolaris" Ana Franco plots the gradual incorporation of women into bertsolaritza.

She finds some evidence for women singing verses about everyday incidents while they carried out chores such as washing clothes at the communal washing place, but is unsure how they were later supplanted by men who came to the fore in improvised verse at a later date. Carmen Larrañaga (1997) provides insight into another aspect of female contributions to bertsolarismo in an illuminating article on the enclosed and silenced spaces of the home or convent that women have traditionally occupied and where they have written verses, called bertso jarriak, distinguishing them from the male world of spontaneous public performance.

It is not until the eighties that we find women appearing in public again, and we have to wait till the nineties to see the first woman to reach the finals at a national championship. This was Maddalen Lujanbio, who despite coming last of the eight finalists expressed her delight at being the first female finalist. Aulestia (1999:231–32) points out that several other young women had also reached the penultimate round and that their presence would have been unthinkable only a few years earlier. Andoni Egaña, the winning bertsolari, referred to the importance of women for the future of the art and signaled the progress made from the eighties, when women were no more than a topic about which to versify, to the nineties when they were a significant and active presence in the championship.

Bertsolaris have always voiced sociopolitical concerns, and this has been particularly true in the last decades when they have continually made critical comment on the Basque Country's political predicament, at times leading them into trouble, for example when their verses have been broadcast on Basque television. I would suggest that this aspect of their art has also facilitated the integration of women and contributed to the

Stand-up poets
The growing presence of women in the formerly male world of berstolaritza testifies to the new status of the female contribution to Basque language transmission as well as to the dynamics of a tradition which easily accommodates change. Not only Maddalen Lujanbio but other performers such as Oihane Enbeita, shown here with Unai Iturriaga, have reached the finals of bertsolari championships.
Photo: Gari Garaialde

welcoming attitude that has prevailed and produced a positive evaluation of women's presence as enrichment, rather than the reverse, which we shall see to be the case in other areas (Chapter 19).

Ana Franco (1994) and del Valle (1997:15) coincide in their observation that the women bertsolaris who progress in the art assume a masculine aesthetic and attitude, though I suspect that this is beginning to change. Perhaps to counter the initially "exotic" note that women brought to a performance or competition, female contenders are seen to distance themselves from a feminine stereotype in terms of dress and overall appearance, as well as in terms of their attitude on the stage, showing themselves to be sure of themselves and even arrogant. Franco puts forward these ideas but recommends further research and reflection on this theme. She also suggests that the increasing number of both women bertsolaris and supporters will bring about changes to this originally masculine universe, for example in a greater sensitiveness to sexism in the subject matters set and the language used.

Studies on the evolution of bertsolaritza from a gendered perspective will help us to plot the progress of this performed poetry and its capacity to reflect—or even redress—the gender balance of Basque society today.

Lesson fourteen

Summary

1. The ascription to women of the domestic space and the role as mother in Basque society has colored the evaluation of their contribution to promoting the Basque language through education, popular movements, and literature. It is only recently that women writers have come to be recognized, having been eclipsed in the past by the emphasis on women's role in linguistic and cultural transmission from the home.
2. Women's participation in popular events in support of the Basque language, such as the Korrika, continues to reflect the importance of their role in cultural

transmission in the family, but at the same time increasingly represents the incursion of women into other, public spheres of activity and questions the preconceived ideas that fix women to the home.
3. The performance of Basque oral poetry known as bertsolaritza is an area where we can observe the growing presence of women, who go beyond the stereotype of Basque women, not only breaking the mold of the male bertsolari but also challenging the gendered universe of this style of poetry.

Suggested Reading

Teresa del Valle, Korrika: Basque Ritual for Ethnic Identity (Reno: University of Nevada Press) (Chap. 6, "The Importance of Continuity and Its Different Interpretations," 1–37).

Linda White, "Mission for the Millennium: Gendering and Engendering Basque Literature for the Next Thousand Years," in W. A. Douglass et al., eds., Basque Cultural Studies (Reno: University of Nevada Press, 1999), 134–48.

Bibliography

English Bibliography

Gorka Aulestia, "The Basque Bertsolari in the New Millennium," in W. A. Douglass et al., eds., Basque Cultural Studies (Reno: University of Nevada Press, 1999), 227–44.

Spanish Bibliography

Begoña Arregui, "Evolución demográfica y cambio socio-económico: Modernización y mujer en el País Vasco" in T. del Valle, ed., La mujer y la palabra (Donostia-San Sebastián: La Primitiva Casa Baroja, 1988), 51–93.

Teresa del Valle, "El género en la construcción de la identidad nacionalista," in Ankulegi (1997) I:9–22; also in Foro Hispánico: Revista Hispánica de los Países Bajos (1999) 18:37–44.

Ana Franco, "Las mujeres bertsolaris" (master's thesis, "Estudios de la Mujer y Sistemas de Género," UPV-EHU).

Carmen Larrañaga, "Del bertsolarismo silenciado" in Jentilbaratz 6, Cuadernos de Folklore, Donostia–San Sebastián: Eusko Ikaskuntza Sociedad de Estudios Vascos (1997), 57–73.

Linda White, "Emakumeen Hitzak Euskeraz: Basque Women Writers of the Twentieth Century" (Ph.D. diss., University of Nevada, 1996).

Written lesson for submission

Plot the evolving contribution of women to Basque cultural transmission and discuss its evaluation.

15 · Women and nationalism

Because of the context to which the Basque culture is reproduced, the defense of Euskara or the choice to write in that language involve political choices. In the Basque Country, culture and politics are never far apart. Gender models are evidenced in the institutions and organizations of any society, and a nationalist project, like the Basque one, is reflected in a whole array of social, political, and economic institutions, from the family, the labor market, the educational establishment, and others. In her book on the presence of women in political parties in the Basque Country, Arantxa Elizondo (1999) gives us the most up-to-date vision of female political activity today. Here we will concentrate on the need, signaled by various authors, to discover the way gender difference is interpreted by different types of nationalism and how it is related to the model of nation to be built or developed. It is to be expected that, as with the vast majority of gender systems, we will find a dominant masculine ideology, but this will be shaped and molded by the ideology and practice linked to the particular concept of nation of the different tendencies.

In her article on gender and the construction of a nationalist identity (1997), Teresa del Valle points to the need to recognize the variable of gender in the history of Basque nationalism, something that has only begun to be recognized by a few feminist scholars in the fields of anthropology and history in the last twenty years. We will take this article as the backbone of our discussion on women and nationalism, as it provides an invaluable overview of the state of the art.

From history, del Valle cites the work of Mercedes Ugalde, who has written an important book called

Women in politics
Although still a minority in top positions, there are increasing numbers of women in high-powered political posts, such as Angeles Iztueta and Miren Azkarate (second and third from right), both members of the Basque Nationalist Party and councillors in the government of Juan José Ibarretxe (first right).
Photo: Gari Garaialde

Mujeres y Nacionalismo Vasco (Women and Basque nationalism), which plots the rise of the women's nationalist movement in the first third of the twentieth century.

In another article, Ugalde signals a dearth of studies on women and nationalism and points to a general ignorance among historians of gender theory and the notion of social relations between men and women that ought to be contemplated in the making and recording of history (1994:33). While the history of nationalism has attempted to absorb new categories of analysis such as nation-building, collective identity, and ethnicity, it has tended to overlook the category of gender. Alizia Stürtze is a historian who argues for the need to analyze the history of Basque women from a nationalist, gendered, and class perspective (1999). These authors show that leaving gender untouched reinforces the essentialist and antidemocratic nature of certain expressions of nationalism that nonetheless claim to be progressive and democratic.

In anthropology, del Valle finds a greater incidence of the theme of gender and nationalism, though it is rarely construed as such but rather is usually approached from other angles such as the concepts of maternity, family, and power. The symbol par excellence that is manipulated in the discourse of gender and nationalism is that of the Basque matriarch. As we have seen above (Part 3), feminist anthropology has criticized the matriarchal thesis and treated it as a myth while exposing the interplay between real power, the ideology of power, and symbolic power (del Valle et al. 1985). This line of critique looks at the symbolic aspects that intervene in the cultural construction of gendered beings—in this case, the use of woman as a symbol of the homeland, fatherland, or nation and the central symbol of woman as mother.

Ugalde (1994:40) shows that this double symbolism of woman as both homeland and mother has been taken up throughout history and is used to legitimate the prevalence of "nation" over the will of individual people by appealing to symbolic referents of nature, God, and history itself. In a way that engages with the nature–culture debate, the linking of woman–nation strengthens itself through the association of homeland with mother-goddess in both a divine and a natural way.

Del Valle (1997:11) observes that the feminist critique of nationalism has not been well received by either the conservative or the radical currents of Basque politics and believes the explanation lies in the fact that such a posture breaks down the vision of unity, the semblance of forming a whole that nationalism wishes to convey. The feminist critique of the matriarchy thesis has largely been ignored by nationalists who continue to see in it a strong marker of difference from non-Basques.[19] The resistance to unveiling the myth of the matriarchy entails the simultaneous veiling of contemporary studies in related areas such as the family where the emergence of new forms is apparent.

Basque nationalism uses the archetype of the Basque woman to represent all Basque women, drawing from a well of symbols that project an image of the ideal woman as mediator and transmitter of the Basque culture. It takes up the stereotype of the Basque matriarch: the traditional rural woman who, following Barandiarán, is situated in the sacred space of the farmhouse and enshrined therein as an ideal woman in an idealized domesticity. The etxekoandere, or woman of the house, is presented as the cohesive element that keeps the baserri running not only on a daily basis but down through the ages, and together they represent the essence of Basqueness (del Valle et al. 1985). The woman is the mediator between the past and the present, which meet at the crossroads represented by the baserri, and she enacts the meeting of these paths through various ritual practices, principally those related to death or those destined to keeping alive the memory of the departed:

We understand that Basque nationalism as a political ideology has fabricated a unilateral concept of the Basque woman, based on attributes of the rural woman in which elements of the woman as mother with a role in teaching and passing on the Basque language and culture stand out. Therefore, we consider that the fundamental objective of this image of the Basque woman is to preserve the structure of the family as a strongly stabilizing factor resisting any possible changes that might jeopardize her traditional role. (del Valle et al. 1985:61, my translation)

The work of both Joseba Zulaika (1988)[20] and Begoña Aretxaga (1988) stresses the role of the mother, rather than the father who remains invisible, when a member of the family (usually a son) joins Euskadi ta Askatasuna (Basque Land and Freedom, or ETA) and they have to deal with police, imprisonment, and death. Aretxaga's work on funerals in radical Basque nationalism shows how this traditional image of the Basque matriarch is updated in the contemporary context of the funerals of Basque radicals. Aretxaga examines the participation of women at the funerals of members of the radical Left and finds that the role of women in both conservative and radical nationalism continues to be that of the mother who stands at the head of the family and signifies its unification. She assumes the consequences of her children's political options, whether they face death or prison, and powerfully symbolizes not only the unification of the family but also the sense of belonging to the group. Given that the majority of the militants are men, Aretxaga suggests that the mother or female partner of the dead man ritually represents female indarra and fertility, ensuring the continuity of the group and signifying that the death has not been in vain but will be the seed of future freedom fighters.

Women in ETA

Despite the common appropriation of the Basque matriarch in nationalist discourse, in the opposition of conservative with radical nationalism, different sociocultural models of men and women emerge and challenge each other. Other works set out to uncover the variety of styles demonstrated by different women participating in other walks of political life and address the way they see themselves or are portrayed by the movement in which they militate or by the media or film industry. Miren Alcedo (1997) looks at the construction of gender through female participation in ETA and considers the possibility of revolutionizing women's rights and roles at the same time as waging war on other kinds of oppression. Cameron Watson (1999), on the other hand, analyzes the way Hollywood, for example, exploits the image of a female ex-ETA member to conjure up an imaginary image of Basque terrorism that equates sexual potency, passion, and irrationality with the danger and threat of terrorism.

Alcedo (1997:31) questions the possibility of elaborating the concept of gender from a revolutionary perspective within the context of an armed resistance group such as ETA. She observes the absence of women among the founders of ETA and only their gradual incorporation in the infrastructure during the 1960s, always in the rear guard, following behind the men. It is not until the eighties that women begin to take part in armed action. In her research, which led her to interview a number of women who militated in ETA, Alcedo finds a common concern for equality both within the organization and without. She opens her article with a quotation from Elixabete Garmendia et al. (1987) *Yoyes, desde su ventana*, a biographical portrait that gathers writings from the diary of Dolores González Catarain, a famous

Women in mourning
It is the mother figure which stands out at the funerals of Basque radicals. She stands at the head of the family and not only signifies the unification of the family but also the sense of belonging to the group. Here the parents of Lasa and Zabala, two young militants who were "disappeared" by paramilitaries in the eighties, receive their remains at the airport of Hondarribia.
Photo: Gari Garaialde

---

female militant of ETA, whose nom de guerre was Yoyes. Yoyes was one of ETA's historical leaders and after leaving the organization she was shot down in the square of her hometown by members of ETA, angry at her renunciation of the movement. The quotation expresses the driving question of how to fuse revolution with women's liberation and is representative of female militants' desire to incorporate the fight against sexual discrimination into the struggle for independence and a new social order. I here reproduce the quotation in my own translation: "I don't want to become the woman who is accepted because the men consider her in some way macho. How can I make my presence mean that other women might also take part? How can I make my presence attract other women instead of making them see me as some sort of crazy lady? How can I make these men understand that women's liberation is a revolutionary aim ...?"

Yoyes's words express different dimensions of the challenge women face inside ETA, and Alcedo examines how they are taken up by other women in the organization. She finds that women who join the group initially feel that they are constantly under observation, put to the test in (and subjected to) a male-dominated environment in which the women are treated with distrust or paternalism. They are the object of stereotyped and sexist jokes about women being clumsy, careless, or too talkative, and any mistake—which the women defend as a "human error" that a man or woman could easily commit in a new situation—is reprimanded in these terms. By contrast, if they do something well they receive excessive praise in a paternalistic fashion that would not be used on men in the same circumstances.

Once they have survived the first trial period, women and men are assigned the same sort of tasks, according to personal skills and ability rather than gender. However, this equality is not carried over into the wielding of power in the organization, with very few women making it to positions of leadership. Yoyes, one of those few, reflects in her diary in 1983, four years after leaving ETA, that the thought of triumphing as a women in a man's world was what had given her the impetus to reach the top, but once she was there she realized the consequences were not what she had expected. First, she felt that the energy that had taken her to the top had burnt out and she no longer had the drive to go on. Second, she became aware that—contrary to her desire to draw other women in with her, to achieve their recognition and respect—her success was a purely personal one and did not transcend the individual level. Finally, the place she had reached preempted the possibility of carrying on the struggle as a woman or on behalf of other women.

Alcedo finds that the pressure to prove themselves among men leads women to play down "feminine" traits and emulate masculine behavior, with the result that they often prove to be more "macho" than the men. The male militants say that in action, the women are tougher, more cold-blooded, more callous than they are themselves. Nevertheless, in the relationships established between women and men within the organization, traditional roles are resumed, with women assuming the major load of housework and child care. Men also have a tendency to take the blame for their female companions when brought to trial, rather than the other way round, with the intention of sparing the women from going to jail. Given the typical torturing of suspected ETA members under interrogation, evidence can be found of gender-specific techniques such as sexist insults, simulations of rape, and so on.

On the whole, Alcedo concludes, ETA has been a characteristically masculine organization in which men have been in control and in which the dominant values have been traditionally masculine in nature: independence, ambition, strength, and an assertion of difference from the opposite sex. This value system has meant that the presence of women has been problematic and only acknowledged when typically masculine attitudes have been adopted.

Women's literature
In the last few years, we are experiencing a proliferation of Basque women writers who are growing in prestige and changing the way women's contribution to Euskara is generally evaluated.
Photo: Iñaki Ugarte.

In a thought-provoking article on "Imagining ETA," Cameron Watson (1999) invites us to rethink our perceptions of "terrorists" in general and considers the way Hollywood, the media, and ETA itself exploit stereotypes that obscure the reality and confuse clear analysis. He looks at one particular film, The Jackal (1997), in which Bruce Willis plays the part of the hired assassin, called "the Jackal," and Richard Gere is an ex-IRA (Irish Republican Army) member who falls in love with Mathilda May in the role of ex-ETA member Isabella Zancona. Watson's analysis of Hollywood's representation of terrorism in this film reveals the promotion of a simplistic stereotype that opposes the fiery and passionate Irish and Basque terrorists, fighting for a cause, to the cold and calculating rationality of the Jackal. Both the IRA and the ETA militant have repented of their ways in this film, and the ex-etarra, Zancona, has even married into the American dream with husband, child, and nice house.

What is of interest for our present discussion is that a female member of ETA has been chosen and that it is her sexuality and passion that are heightened in the film. The mix of terrorism and danger with sexual attraction and adventure is a potent cocktail that simultaneously appeals and obscures. Watson finds that the role of Zancona, posing as a female object of desire, embodies Simone de Beauvoir's essential "Other," in which woman is totally alien to the rest of human experience and cannot be considered an equal, a fellow human being. By uniting the two stereotyped images of Woman and Terrorist, by situating terrorism in a sexually attractive female character, the danger, irrationality, and "otherness" of terrorism are accentuated (ibid. 99).

Radical Basque Women

Sharryn Kasmir's article "From the Margins" (1999) explores the representation of women in Basque popular music and calls for the repositioning of gender in Basque ethnic identity. She situates her study in the Gipuzkoan town of Arrasate-Mondragón, renowned for the owner-worker cooperatives based there and an obvious point to which workers from other parts of Spain migrated during the peak industrial period of the sixties (Chapter 8). She starts by focusing on a mural in a bar in which an alternative image of the Basque woman is portrayed, an image that eschews the traditional, folkloric identity located in the rural setting (carrying farm implements or performing a folk dance) and constructs in its place a mythic representation of a modern, urban, radical Basque woman, combining the emblems of radical nationalist organizations with the aesthetics of punk. The woman in the picture has punky spiked hair and is wearing a pin with the barbed wire insignia of the Gestoras pro-Amnistia, the organization campaigning for amnesty for ETA prisoners. In her outstretched hand she holds a tray laden with drinks and with abstract black shapes representing prisons and bombs.

The image represents not only women, but radical Basque youth as projected in the postindustrial economic crisis and unemployment of the eighties. The radical Basque youth emerged then as a sociopolitical subject, characterized by a punk aesthetic, radical nationalism, and left-wing politics. What is significant about the mural is that it chooses a woman as an icon of radical Basque youth and, as such, Kasmir considers her a "mythic" character: "She enacts for her viewers socially fraught contradictions between gender codes that privilege masculine agency and cultural values that prize radicalness as an expression of patriotism." (ibid. 179)

The woman in the picture also reflects the style of the female bartenders, daughters of immigrants who came from other parts of Spain in search of work back in the sixties. They do not come from Basque families and some of them do not even speak Basque, though they were born in the Basque Country and consider themselves Basque. Again, this tests the archetype of the ethnic Basque that reached its most extreme expression in the nineteenth century in the form of Sabino Arana, founder of the Partido Nacionalista Vasco (PNV) or Basque Nationalist Party. He pursued a racial definition of Basqueness that emphasized lineage and language.

Kasmir sets out to explore how the punk movement contributed to the creation of a nonethnic, nonessentialist Basque identity based on a vision of more equitable social relations, but finds that, in accordance with Jackie Urla's findings for hip-hop, there is little attention paid to breaking the mold of male bias. Although she shows some ways in which male imagery is contested, through an analysis of the music of Hertzainek, a successful all-male group popular from 1979 to their disbanding in 1993, she contends that on the whole, punk produced an overwhelmingly masculine identity. Her conclusions are as follows: "I suggest that punk presents a masculine version of Basqueness that attributes agency and cultural innovation to men, affirms the manliness of key political and social spaces, and writes a masculinist narrative of the nation." (ibid. 182)

Nevertheless, women were fans and participants in the punk movement and adopted punk dress and aggressive styles: "deploying a militant presentation of self, young women used their bodies to designate combativeness through a feminine subject." Their attitude forces the resignification of "militancy" in the Basque context and prompts us to rethink both gendered constructs of activism and gendered narratives of nation. Up till then, militancy was associated overwhelmingly with ETA and, as we have seen, ETA was characterized by a dominantly male membership, with masculine-coded symbols, activities, and modes of heroism. Begoña Aretxaga makes a similar observation about women, nationalism, and political subjectivity in Northern Ireland: "Such practices signify precisely because they are deployed within a shared universe, but, in so doing, they are capable of provoking a sliding of signifiers and

Women and rock
Rock singers like Sorkun who performs alongside Fermin Muguruza bring together the ideas of feminism and nationalism, both in their music and their political activity.
Photo: Gari Garaialde

---

thereby triggering new forms of representation and knowledge."(1997:20)

Thus though gender was not immediately taken up in the nationalist movements contemplated here, nor in their interconnection with subcultures such as the punk music movement described, the very participation of women, their adoption of styles, and their self-ascription of identities challenge the male image of rebellion previously projected. The industrial boom together with changes in women's circumstances contributed to the emergence of a new women's working class with an active social life. Where once the space of the street and bars had been considered the prerogative of men, women now joined in with their own *cuadrillas* or groups of friends, and through their participation in the punk movement they championed feminist causes, even though these were not taken up by the male punks. Women confronted male chauvinism and used a feminist discourse to challenge sexist language, biological-determinist assumptions of sex roles, and inequalities in domestic division of labor. They understood gender equality and sexual freedom to be important in the nationalist struggle and looked in particular to the African-American activist Angela Davis and Nicaraguan poet Gioconda Belli as references for framing their own feminist struggle in the nationalist and socialist movement. Kasmir concludes that while the punk movement privileged masculine models, its emphasis on breaking molds and contesting the norm provided women with the tools to question the gendering of both punk and nationalism.

Today, women of the nationalist left (known as *la izquierda abertzale*) are committed to the promotion of women's political participation. To this end, the women's group Egizan has organized numerous meetings for debate and discussion to bring together the ideas of feminism and nationalism, and the proceedings from the 1999 encounters are published under the title *Euskal borroka feminista aurrera* (On with the Basque feminist struggle). In 2001, the first assembly of the feminist nationalist left was held; the second was celebrated in January 2003, with about 300 women in attendance. The picture they paint of the situation is one of fewer women participating than men and for shorter periods of time, owing to the difficulties of combining the public life of politics with the private domain, which carries a greater load of domestic duties for women.

They also indicate that women leave the movement when disillusioned with the possibilities it offers them. Having analyzed their situation, the women at the assembly agreed that they need to implement measures to address what is identified as a structural problem and to increase the presence and participation of women.[21]

Lesson fifteen

Summary

1. Basque nationalism in both its conservative and radical expressions draws on the cultural stereotypes of the Basque woman as matriarch, associating the notion of mother with that of the homeland and reinforcing it through a naturalizing discourse.
2. The participation of women in radical armed groups like ETA poses questions about the behavior and expectations of females in warring environments where masculine traits of toughness and aggression prevail. It also brings up the issue of whether feminist goals can be successfully incorporated into a male-dominated revolutionary movement. Finally, the media's or Hollywood's projection of women as terrorists shows how stereotypes of sexuality and violence are exploited.
3. Although contemporary women are generally excluded from the discursive framework of Basque nationalism, which prefers idealized stereotypes of matriarchs to the challenges posed by women today, an active female sector participates in politics, music, and other popular movements, challenging the norm and proposing new ways of imagining and incorporating the politically active woman.

Required Reading

Sharryn Kasmir, "From the Margins: Punk Rock and the Repositioning of Ethnicity and Gender in Basque Identity," in W. A. Douglass et al., eds., Basque Cultural Studies, Occasional Papers Series, no. 5 (Reno: University of Nevada Press, 1999), 178–220.

Bibliography

English Bibliography

Begoña Aretxaga, Shattering Silence: Women, Nationalism and Political Subjectivity in Northern Ireland (Princeton: Princeton University Press, 1997).

Jackie Urla, "Basque Hip Hop? Language, Cultural Identity and Popular Music," unpublished manuscript (no date).

Cameron Watson, "Imagining ETA," in W. A. Douglass et al., eds., Basque Politics and Nationalism on the Eve of the Millennium, Occasional Papers Series, no. 6 (Reno: University of Nevada Press, 1999), 94–114.

Spanish Bibliography

Miren Alcedo, "Las mujeres de ETA: Construcción del género y militancia política," in Ankulegi 1:31–35.

Begoña Aretxaga, Los funerales en el nacionalismo radical vasco, Ensayo antropológico (Donostia: La Primitiva Casa Baroja, 1988).

Teresa del Valle, "El género en la construcción de la identidad nacionalista," in Ankulegi I:9–22 (1997); also in Foro Hispánico: Revista Hispánica de los Países Bajos (1999) 18:37–44.

Arantxa Elizondo, La presencia de las mujeres en los partidos políticos de la Comunidad Autónoma del País Vasco (Eusko Jaularitza-Gobierno Vasco, 1999).

Elixabete Garmendia Lasa et al., Yoyes desde su ventana (Irunea: Garrasi, 1987).

Alizia Stürtze, "Esquema para una aproximación a la historia de las mujeres en Euskal Herria," in Egizan, ed., Euskal Borroka Feminista Aurrera (1999), 119–26.

Mertxe Ugalde, "La historia de las mujeres y la historia del nacionalismo: una convergencia necesaria," in Revista de Extremadura (1994) 13:33–42.

———, Mujeres y Nacionalismo Vasco: Génesis y desarrollo de Emakume Abertzale Batza, 1906–1936 (Bilbao: Universidad del País Vasco, 1993).

Written lesson for submission

How has both conservative and radical nationalism projected women, and how have women contested this image?

16 · Women in the diaspora

In terms of constructing Basque or gender identities, or both, in different contexts across time and space, it is illuminating to look to a totally different setting for a moment and cast our eyes on the Basque communities established by immigrants who went out from Euskal Herria and settled in the American West. In Chapter 7 we saw how women had been a crucial factor of change when they left their home farm, or *baserri*, in search of paid employment in nearby towns where they experienced a different standard of living and a new way of life. In this section, we will look at the Basque women who went even further afield, emigrating to foreign climes, and we will consider their contribution to the consolidation of the Basque communities of the diaspora and to the maintenance of Basque values and traditions.

The emigration of Basques through the ages has been amply documented by different authors, and we have at our fingertips such classics as William Douglass and Jon Bilbao's *Amerikanuak: Basques in the New World* (1975) or much more recent collections of contemporary research such as the volume of articles from the 1998 conference on Basques in the Contemporary World, *The Basque Diaspora* (1999). While the emigration of Basque men is widely covered, women have been largely absent from the stories recorded, and it is only in the last few years that more information is coming to light through the work of scholars such as Jeronima Echeverría, Gloria Totoricagüena, and Begoña Pecharromán. A growing literature is also delving into gender and migration, which informs our contemplation of the Basque case but lies outside the scope of the present analysis.

Basque women in the diaspora
Emigrant Basque women have made an important contribution to building a new community in the host country at the same time as preserving and passing on elements of the old. Here Patty Miller, descendant of Basque immigrants and the director of the Basque Museum in Boise (Idaho) embraces children in typical Basque dress.
Photo: Begoña Pecharromán

Broadly speaking, throughout the ages the seafaring Basque people had a tendency to strike out across the water, and accordingly fishermen went in search of whales and cod as far away as Newfoundland and Labrador. The Spanish conquest and subsequent colonization of the Americas drew on Basque shipbuilders and sailors, and the Basque nobility rose quickly in the colonial administration and trade. After the different colonies had won their independence from Spain in the nineteenth century, the nature of emigration changed and attracted both farmers and shepherds in search of a livelihood, rather than the nobles who sought wealth and status. The main ports of call for the Basques were initially Latin American countries where the Hispanic heritage of the former colonies, not least the common use of the Spanish language, provided a point of contact and facilitated their integration. Nonetheless, large numbers of Basques also emigrated to the United States, particularly to the American West where there was opportunity and demand for sheep farmers. The peak period of this wave of Basque emigration to the States spans from the 1890s to the 1930s, and this is the time and the place we will be focusing on in the rest of this section.

The information we have on Basque immigration in the United States provides us with a picture that suggests that it was a predominantly male phenomenon. In her article "The Basque Hotelera" (1999[a]:239), Jeronima Echeverría suggests that this is probably due, on the one hand, to the fact that Basque men emigrated in larger numbers and in earlier periods than women and, on the other hand, to the significant contribution Basque shepherds made to the sheep industry in the American West, which made them the object of both literary and academic interest. The data for the 636

Basques arriving on New York City's Ellis Island in the five-year period between 1897 and 1902 indicates that 86 percent were men, and only 14 percent women. Moreover, of the men, 77 percent were single and 65 percent were between the ages of 16 and 30. In a talk delivered in Donostia–San Sebastián, Begoña Pecharromán gave these figures as she told of her field work among Basque women immigrants in the United States, the topic on which she is currently writing her doctoral thesis. She has recorded the life histories of Basque emigrant women, several of whom are now in their seventies and eighties, and the information she has gathered will complement the work done by Echeverría, Totoricagüena, and others.[22] Apart from her own findings, this anthropologist has also written a beautiful paper called "Searching for Miren," which recounts her search for Basque immigrant women through some of the classics like Douglass's rendition of Beltran Paris, sheepman of the American West; Robert Laxalt's Sweet Promised Land; or the more recent Deep Blue Memory by Laxalt's daughter, Monique Urza.

In her talk, Pecharromán started by raising two questions challenging the notion that emigration from the Basque Country was strictly a male affair. First, the fact that the majority of immigrants were men indicates that they must have had female support for their enterprise back home. The process of emigration was a costly one for most and meant an economic effort in saving for the voyage. She proposes that it was not an individual endeavor but rather a family undertaking that involved the women who stayed behind as well as the men who left. The second question concerns the contribution of the 14 percent of female immigrants to the process of migration and integration, suggesting that the relatively small number of women is not proportional to the scope of their influence in the host country nor in the building up of a new community at the same time that they preserved elements of the old. Jeronima Echeverría coincides with Pecharromán when she says that "until recently, popular and scholarly depictions of Basque settlement have de-emphasized the role of Basque women and focused on Basque men" (ibid. 239).

Women of the Basque Boardinghouses

Echeverría's article (1999a) gives us a synopsis of what she develops in her book Home Away from Home (1999b), the most extensive research published to date on Basque women in the United States. This work documents the history of Basque boardinghouses (known as hotelak or ostatuak in Basque), with a particular emphasis on the importance of individuals in the making of history and a special concern to bring out the formerly eclipsed contribution of women. She contends that the study of the boardinghouses in the American West reveals "the undeniable significance of Basque women in establishing a Basque-American culture and in putting down roots in the New World" (1999a:239). Their significance is directly linked to the importance attached to the ostatuak themselves for the immigrant Basque community, providing a point of contact for new arrivals, shepherds, and ranchers. The ostatu met practical needs for board and lodging, information and orientation, but in addition to providing a vital link in the chain of the transition from the homeland to the host country, it served a cultural and affective purpose in supplying a familiar Basque environment and offering a surrogate family in that "home away from home." Furthermore, the boardinghouses were a place where second- and third-generation migrants could get in touch with their ethnic roots.

Most of the boardinghouses were run by husband-and-wife teams who became etxeko aita and etxeko ama ("father of the house" and "mother of the house") to those who were far from home and needed companionship, advice, and practical help as much as a bed and board. The women were often left to run the ostatu single-handedly while the men continued to work in the sheep business and would be away for long periods, especially during the spring lambing and the summer sheepherding up on the high pastures. Echeverría draws a comparison between the hoteleras and the wives of the Basque fishermen who were used to looking after themselves and the family while the men were at sea (Chapter 6). In both cases, we find women who are more autonomous and independent, used to making decisions and exercising authority. She also finds that their role as etxeko ama to many who passed through meant that they had a wide-ranging influence on the burgeoning Basque-American community, and that some were looked up to as "matriarchs" in the sense that they continued to be called on as central advisers in the community even long after they had ceased to run their businesses.

Echeverría's work is significant for various reasons. In the first instance, it brings women to the forefront of the history of Basques in the American West—not, as she says, with the intention of eclipsing the men but simply to make the women visible. Second, by doing so, she contributes to our knowledge of Basque immigration, filling in other details of the picture painted of the lone sheepherder, and building up a sense of the broader community of women and men alongside him. Finally, given that time marches on and many of the first-generation Basque immigrants have been replaced by successive generations whose "Basqueness" is more

Integration and heritage
The children of Basque immigrants in the USA may assimilate totally to the American way of life, but still show an interest in their heritage and cultivate links with their relations back in the Basque Country.
Collection Asunción Maisterrena

diluted by their integration into American society, it is imperative to gather as much information as possible from the older generations, in order to gather the richest history possible.

Women and Identity Abroad

It is expected that recognition of women's contribution to history in the context of the Basque-American context will boost women's own evaluation of what they do. In an aptly titled article, "Shrinking World, Expanding Diaspora" (1999) Gloria Totoricagüena looks at the implications of globalization for Basque identity in the communities of the diaspora. Comparing the construction of identity in six countries with Basque immigrant communities, with regard to gender, Totoricagüena finds that there is a tendency for women to play down their part in their family's or community's migration history, attributing the "important" things to the men yet failing to acknowledge the transcendence of women's efforts to preserve and promote their home language, customs, and culture, both in their own homes and in the Basque centers set up in their communities. Nonetheless, like the women in Korrika (see Chapter 14), they are vital links in the chain of cultural and linguistic transmission.

Totoricagüena finds that Basque women often migrated as part of a family project and went to the place where the man had the highest chance of employment. In many cases, she gathers a negative impression of the migration experience from these women, who tell of their loneliness and isolation, their difficulty in integration because of the language barrier in English-speaking countries, and the resulting depression and low self-esteem. Against this backdrop, Basque centers became a crucial meeting point and support network for women who found in their shared ethnicity, history, and culture a common denominator that gave them strength, a new sense of self-worth, and a feeling of mutual comprehension and solidarity (1999:294). Although this first function of women's networking in the host country is no longer an imperative, it is still a critical part of the community life where second- and third-generation migrants build lasting friendships on the basis of shared ethnic roots, which moreover are given a certain continuity in the activities of the centers.

The work of the scholars mentioned has gone a long way to putting women on the map of Basque immigration. Further progress is to be expected through the founding of the Consortium for the Study of Basque

---

Women, directed by Linda White, Teresa del Valle, and Jeronima Echeverria.

Lesson sixteen

Summary

1. The Basques have a long tradition of emigration, but until the eighties it has been a story of seamen and shepherds, with little told from the perspective of the Basque women who emigrated too.
2. The role of women in the Basque boardinghouses of the American West was vital to aiding the immigrants' adjustment to the host country as well as providing a firm reference of the native country. Here we see the woman in another role of cultural transmission.
3. Against the negative experience of the loneliness that accompanied many women in their new surroundings, the formation of Basque centers provided a support network that was crucial for creating community and maintaining collective identity. Once again, we find women exercising an important role in passing on Basque culture to successive generations.

Suggested Reading

Jeronima Echeverría, "The Basque Hotelera: Implications for Broader Study," in W. A. Douglass et al., eds., The Basque Diaspora (1999a), 239–48.

Bibliography

William A. Douglass and Jon Bilbao, Amerikanuak: Basques in the New World (Reno: University of Nevada Press, 1975).

William A. Douglass et al., eds., The Basque Diaspora/La Diaspora Vasca, Basque Studies Program Occasional Papers Series, no.7 (Reno: University of Nevada Press).
Jeronima Echeverría, Home Away from Home: A History of Basque Boarding Houses (Reno: University of Nevada Press, 1999b).
Begoña Pecharromán, "Searching for Miren: Basque Women's Inner Strength," unpublished paper delivered at the Basque Museum, Boise, Idaho (1998).
Gloria Totoricagüeña, "Shrinking World, Expanding Diaspora: Globalization and Basque Diasporic Identity," in W. A. Douglass et al., eds., The Basque Diaspora, 284–301.
Monique Urza, Deep Blue Memory (Reno: University of Nevada Press, 1993).

Written lesson for submission

Consider the contribution of women to the integration of the Basque immigrant community in the host country and to the maintenance of Basque cultural or ethnic identity.

Key words

GENDER MODELS: the models of women and men that, in any given society, are constructed on the basis of culturally specific stereotypes, establishing, for example, an ideal model of motherhood or fatherhood.
NATURALIZATION: the process by which gender stereotypes draw on nature for their legitimation, presenting cultural phenemona, such as the values ascribed to being "a good mother," as natural ones.

CULTURAL TRANSMISSION: the passing on of cultural traits from one generation to the next. It is an idealized aspect of "motherhood" and women's role in the family, as well as an important feature of women's contribution to community building in the diaspora.

GENDER AND NATIONALISM: political movements, such as Basque nationalism, draw on archetypes of the Basque woman to represent all Basque women—for example, incorporating symbols that project an image of the ideal woman as both mediator and transmitter of the Basque culture.

GENDER FIXING: the outcome of the use of naturalized and idealized gender models is to fix certain versions of male or femaleness, fundamental to significant social structures such as the family. By fixing the structure of the family, society is stabilized and change resisted.

17 · Rituals, traditions, and change

The area of rituals, traditions, and festivals is an important field of inquiry in Basque Gender Studies, for several reasons. First, the ethnographical context of the Basque culture is particularly appropriate for this type of analysis since it is rich in festivals, customs, and traditions and replete with ritual and symbolic acts. These elements have been considered crucial in the construction of cultural identity and are also important for understanding the way gender systems work. Second, because of its symbolic nature, ritual takes us into another dimension of meaning and enables us to perceive certain aspects of a culture or society that are not immediately obvious to us as we contemplate daily reality. Finally, since ritual occupies a symbolic and often sacred domain of significance, one related to religious acts and traditional practices, it has been less open to change than other aspects of life.

In this chapter we will be looking at Basque women's ritual role in the past and their adoption of new roles in the present, particularly in festivals from which they had previously been excluded. Examining the incursion of women in carnivals and other festivals over the past years and the expressions of resistance with which they have met, we will assess the different factors that aid or abet their incorporation. Last, we will consider the symbolic dimension of space and how it is gendered.

Nature and Functions of Ritual

A ritual may be defined as a form of standardized and repetitive behavior that responds to its own internal structure and obeys a culturally or religiously prescribed order that lays down the correct way to carry out a series of rites or solemn acts, for example in a religious or civic ceremony. Let us look at the different qualities and functions of ritual:

Symbolism. One of the overriding characteristics of ritual is its symbolic dimension. Broadly speaking, we can distinguish between the "symbolic order" that includes ritual and festival, and the "social order" of everyday life. These two spheres of significance are mutually influential and connect in relation to space, time, and ideas. A change in one order produces a change in the other. However, the change does not always occur in a straightforward manner and the change proposed at the social level may meet with opposition at the symbolic level. In gender terms, the incorporation of women in a traditionally male-dominated space may find fiercer resistance in the symbolic sphere than at the social level. We shall see some examples below.

Identity. Rituals often have the function of constructing or reinforcing a group identity either vertically (in reference to a shared past) or horizontally (in reinforcing transversal relations across the group). Where they represent certain aspects of a community's history (heroic acts, battles fought and won, ancient treaties, and the like) they establish links with their past, evoking the deeds of their ancestors and celebrating their achievements. By referring back to their common ancestry, they stress the sense of belonging to the community and celebrate the ongoing worth of the group in the present. In so doing they reinforce the notion of continuity through time, and in reenacting the past they also have a pedagogical function in transmitting to their children, newcomers, or outsiders an aspect of history that has become sacred to the people.

Religion and ritual
Traditionally women had a symbolic role in Basque religious life, custodians of the souls of the living and dead who passed through their households, and responsible for rituals and ceremonies in the family. Here a mother leaves the church after her eldest son's First Communion.
Collection Asunción Maisterrena.

The performance of a ritual or participation in a festival re-creates the community by establishing a transitional state of harmony, uniting disparate members, and overcoming differences in the fulfillment of a common end.

Social order. Rituals can also have the function of reinforcing or, alternatively, contesting the social order. Sometimes a ritual reproduces the existing hierarchies of the society in question; at other times, it overturns that order, allowing an inversion of the accepted norms and ultimately acting as a mechanism of social control in which the ritual serves the purpose of an escape valve, permitting the return to the "norm" once the festival or ritual is over. The process may be vastly more complicated than this, with different sectors competing to impose their version of reality on the ritual, giving rise to a series of ritualized discourses that may enter into negotiation or confrontation.

World order. Rituals present a symbolic interpretation of reality that can help us to better comprehend the world in which we live by establishing a logical and coherent framework through which to face the sensation of chaos and disorder roiling around us. Given the flux of change and upheaval of events in contemporary society, rituals can be comforting and reassuring, a symbolic bulwark against change and interference.

Space. Rituals reinterpret space, giving new meanings to the places where they are performed and that, in their daily reality, are occupied by a different set of people doing different things. Rituals also have the capacity to act out an ideological project through space, such as in the case of the Korrika (see Chapter 14), where we have seen the ritual dimension of this run designed to promote the use of the Basque language, Euskara, and its symbolic construction of a united Euskal Herria through the abolition of administrative, political, and geographical divisions.

Concepts of Tradition

The Basque culture is rich in traditions and festivals that are themselves ripe in ritual. This area of study provides the context of some particularly colorful analysis, which from a gendered perspective can take us beyond the purely ethnographic dimension of folklore to the symbolic sphere in which social issues are acted out on another plane from daily reality. Against the backdrop of tradition we will look at the way women have been taking up new roles in formerly male-dominated spaces of custom and tradition, and unpack the wider implications of this change. We will begin by looking at the concept of tradition and then select a couple of examples that have been analyzed by Basque anthropologists, before going on in the next section to concentrate on a contemporary case study of the opposition to women's participation in the traditionally male-dominated parades of Irun and Hondarribia.

First let us look at what we mean by "tradition," since tradition evokes a cluster of meanings that are called up in opposition to change, often contrary to women's interests. In this sense, tradition conjures up notions of stability and continuity over time, of the unchanging repetition of a series of rites or actions anchored in a stationary past and brought forward as a faithful replica into the present.

This concept of tradition is positively valued for its connections to time, identity, and history:

Time. The temporal dimension of tradition stresses length of time ("the older, the better") and continuity.

---

1. Traditions accumulate value over time, acquiring greater merit for having survived from a more or less remote past.
2. Traditions represent continuity through time by their uninterrupted repetition down the ages.

Identity. The concept of time connects with that of transmission, of handing down traditions from one generation to the next, thus establishing links with the community of ancestors whence they came and reinforcing a sense of shared identity.

History. Hailed as the cornerstone of tradition, history is perceived to be a sacred legacy to be faithfully preserved and protected; events must be reenacted exactly as laid down in history.

In opposition to this static notion of tradition, Eric Hobsbawm, in his introduction to The Invention of Tradition (1986), puts forward a dynamic vision of tradition that develops the idea that, far from being motionless and monotonous, traditions are totally flexible and constantly changing. He argues that traditions are reinvented in accordance with contemporary circumstances, evolving with the societies that practice them, and modifying the relation with the past to respond to new situations in the present. History is also deconstructed to reveal that it is no more monolithic than tradition, since it does not correspond to an "absolute truth" or a single veridical version of events, but rather is created and recreated by different subjective individuals who present events from their own perspective and often mold or shape them for specific ends.

It is this capacity for change that keeps traditions alive and saves them from becoming relics, museum pieces that stagnate on shelves. Tradition is maintained not by its mere repetition but rather by its evolution. It is the social actors who reenact a tradition and by doing so recreate their culture. They innovate, introduce new ideas, update old ways so that they vibrate with the same vitality in the twenty-first century as they did back in the seventeenth when they began. This notion of tradition is in accordance with a dynamic concept of culture that emphasizes the agency of the social actors, as explained here in the words of Carmen Díez: "Culture ... (can be defined as) as something which is constructed in interaction with historical and economic processes which integrate identity as an element which social actors assume, negotiate and redefine, selecting traits which differentiate them from other groups." (1999:159, my translation)

If we follow Hobsbawm and subject seemingly timeless traditions to a closer examination, it is probable we will find evidence of multiple changes and adaptations over the years, new elements that are woven into the fabric of the tradition, others that are eliminated as obsolete or no longer desirable. This capacity for change suggests that behind the preoccupation with losing the authenticity of certain rites or rituals by allowing women to take part, an underlying resistance is trying to shift the balance of power between men and women as symbolized in the traditional layout. A leading feminist anthropologist, Virginia Maquieira, unveils, in an inspirational article on anthropology, gender, and human rights, the way culture and tradition are used to cover up legitimate claims to equality: "The name of culture, that is to say the discourse of the supreme importance of preserving and saving cultural specificity, is presented as the globally most potent argument to de-activate the claims and demands of women in the world in which we live." (1999, my translation)

Lesson seventeen

Summary

1. The analysis of ritual reveals a symbolic dimension of meaning that works through a series of repeated acts and the transformation of space, and functions to construct or reinforce group identities, reaffirm the social order, explain the world order, and provide a stable reference in the face of change and threat of chaos.
2. Ritual connects with the notion of tradition, which is imbued with concepts of the value of time, identity, and history. A static perspective of tradition is challenged by a dynamic concept of culture that holds that traditions, as a part of culture, are constructed and reconstructed over time by specific social actors in specific contexts. Both tradition and culture are thus entirely flexible and open to change.
3. The static concept of tradition as emblematic of cultural specificity is universally used as an antidote to women's claims for equal rights.

Suggested Reading

Eric Hobsbawm, "Introduction: Inventing Traditions," in E. Hobsbawm and T. Ranger, eds., The Invention of Tradition (Cambridge: Cambridge University Press, 1986), 1–14.

Bibliography

Carmen Díez, "Sistemas de identidad, género e identidad nacional," in Pedro Albite, coord., Sociedad vasca y construcción nacional (Donostia: Tercera Prensa–Hirugarren Prentsa, 1999).

Virginia Maquieira, "Antropología, género y derechos humanos," Anales del Museo Nacional de Antropología, no. VI (Madrid, 1999).

Written lesson for submission

Apply Hobsbawm's concept of invention to a tradition you are familiar with (local festival or parade, religious ritual, family tradition at Christmas or other holiday, and so on). Look out for the qualities and functions laid out for ritual and the aspects of tradition that give value to what you are describing and that may be opposed to change.

18 · Basque women and ritual

Now we will look at the traditional role of Basque women in religious rituals before going on, in the next chapter, to consider the ways by which women have entered the symbolic spaces of festivals that were formerly exclusive to men. In a comprehensive article covering religion in women's lives, 1939–1987, Carmen Larrañaga and Carmen Pérez (1988) point to the overriding characteristics of Basques as a traditionally religious people, expressed in an equation that makes euskaldun (a Basque person) tantamount to fededun (believer). This religious dimension of Basqueness is especially associated with women and quintessentially with mothers, and just as the transmission of the language is located in the home and commended to women, so is the inculcation of religious beliefs and values. As we saw in Parts 2 and 3, in traditional Basque society the woman of the baserri was considered (in the words of Barandiaran) a "priestess." The farmhouse itself was considered to be imbued with religious meaning through the mediation of the woman of the house in the different rites carried out for the benefit of the living as well as in memory of the dead. She was especially responsible for conducting certain rites of passage in relation to birth and death. In this chapter we will be looking at ritual in relation to certain Basque festivals where women have made an incursion over the past years and will assess the different factors that aid their incorporation.

Mother Mary, Motherland. The central role of the mother in Basque culture is carried over into religion and represented by the cult to the Virgin Mary in different manifestations throughout the Basque Country.

Larrañaga and Pérez (ibid. 16) signal the institutionalization under Franco of the day of the Immaculate Conception (December 8) as a public holiday and see this as the symbolic convergence of the religious model of motherhood that is reinforced by state legislation to subject women to their husbands and the home. Basque religious culture is full of references to the Virgin, often perceived to be more important in popular belief than Jesus, and in many places masses, pilgrimages, and festivals are celebrated in her honor. In his book Basque Violence, Joseba Zulaika tells us of the cult to the Amabirjina (literally "Virgin Mother") of Itziar (Gipuzkoa), stressing her centrality to popular faith based on the medieval legend of her apparition in the village and "the intensity of the cult devoted to her that is outstanding in the daily religious experience of Itziar" (1988:273). Zulaika establishes a link between the cult to the Virgin and the salience of the mother figure in Basque culture, which in turn permeates notions of nationhood, conceived of in terms of "Motherland" rather than "Fatherland." He looks at the symbolic dimensions of the icon to postulate a relationship between the cult of the Virgin Mother and the cult of violence that takes on a sacred significance in the political activity of ETA.

The relationship among women, religion, and the nation is nowhere more powerfully projected than in the history of the women of the Basque nationalist party (PNV),[23] members of Emakume Abertzale Batza, or the "Association of Patriotic Women." Returning to the work of Mercedes Ugalde on this association, we find ample evidence of the stress on Catholicism, an intrinsic part of the PNV's political ideology, which was taken up as a special mission for the women through the family: "Their most important contribution was in the family,

Rites of passage
The rites of passage, from baptism through First Communion to marriage and ultimately death, bring into play a series of duties and rights performed by both women and men in Basque society.
Collection Asunción Maisterrena.

---

considered by the nationalists as the foundation of the homeland. It was there that, as mothers and educators of their children and as wives who could influence their husbands, they were charged with a mission of transcendental importance." (1993:103, my translation)

Together with the Catholic religion, expressed by "Jaun Goikua" ("the Lord Above"), Basque traditions ("Lagi Zara" or the "Old Laws") were the pillars of conservative Basque nationalism. The two often went hand in hand, and again emphasis was placed on women's role in going to mass and encouraging the rest of the family to do so and also carrying out the rites and rituals that accompanied the ecclesiastical calendar. The convergence of religion with custom can be seen to be played out in the organization of death rituals, which have received attention from scholars.

Death rituals. The importance of death rituals in traditional Basque society is the subject of William Douglass's Death in Murélaga, where we see the way death activates a wide range of social relationships, through family, domestic group, kin, and neighbors. Douglass finds that the participation in funerary proceedings reflects "egalitarianism between the sexes," with a strict "complementarity of male and female roles, with no indication that one is emphasized at the other's expense" (1969:203). Teresa del Valle (1997:17–18), however, emphasizes the symbolic dimension of the space occupied by women in death rituals, expressing their importance for the continuity and stability of the house and the household. In former times, death rituals were closely related to the house, and by extension to the woman of the house. It was she who, in representation of her house, took up a place by the bedside of the dying person and then played an important part in the burial, funeral, and masses.

Sandra Ott (1981:117–30) describes the mortuary obligations between the farms making up an auzoa, or neighborhood, in the Zuberoan village of Sainte-Engrâce. Neighborhood relations are found to vary throughout the Basque rural world, but on the whole the dominating concept is that of the "first neighbor." That person is differently defined in different localities, but rather than indicating physical proximity the term refers to the moral ties that bind and that make one neighbor household the first to whom one turns in times of crisis. In Sainte-Engrâce, Ott identifies three "first neighbors" for each household, and it was these three who had specific duties and obligations to fulfill, as we shall see in the case of death. It was traditional for the male "first neighbors" to take over the work that the male of the deceased's household would normally have done, dealing with livestock, the land, and so on while the women saw to the domestic work.

The female "first neighbors" performed certain specific rituals, which Ott documents for Sainte-Engrâce and Douglass for Murélaga, but which had their regional variations. For example, the first "first neighbor" in Sainte-Engrâce was to open all the windows of the house when someone died so that the soul could escape. She and the other female "first neighbors" then gave a gift of a blessed candle to the bereaved household and was responsible for making sure the candles did not go out until the corpse was taken to the church 48 hours later. It was believed that light was crucial to the dead and sustained souls in the afterlife, and in the first two days was thought to illuminate the soul's path to God. Apart from the candles, the female first "first neighbor" prepared the corpse and room, attended the neighbors who came to pay their respects, and cooked for the family of the deceased. The male "first neighbor" was responsible for helping to receive the visitors and collecting donations for masses. Both the male and female "first neighbors" kept vigil.

Formerly, the coffin was carried down to the church, accompanied by the priest and mourners, proceeding in an established order and along paths that led from the farm to the village and that (though in daily use) were known as hilbideak ("paths of the dead"). As the procession entered the church, the bells were tolled in different patterns to signify that the deceased was male or female. The positions assumed at the burial varied from place to place and according to one's relationship to the

Ritual and change
Ritual is a realm where social realities are played out on a symbolic plane. Carnival can often provide the opportunity to invert gender roles and the social order, but the rigours of ritual can also prove a restriction to change. In the Carnival plays, called Mascaradas, of Zuberoa, the combination of dance and theatre has gradually opened up to change over the years.
Photo: Imanol Ilárraz

---

deceased, as well as to whether it was a man or a woman who had died. Usually, the funeral was performed in the church and then the mourners accompanied the coffin out to the graveyard. Ott (ibid. 124) observes that in the French Basque communities it was usual for the nausi (male head of the household) or the male first "first neighbor" to lead the procession, followed by the priest, while the other male "first neighbors" or friends of the deceased carried the coffin and behind them came the other men and then the women.

One of the most obvious spatial markers of men's and women's ritual participation is the division of the church, where the women took up their places in the nave and the men stood up in the stalls. Traditionally, each farm, or baserri, had its own seat in the nave of the church, where the woman of the house would sit. It was known as jarleku, meaning "tomb," though its significance was symbolic, representing the souls of those who had belonged to the baserri. The women lit candles there for the souls of their dead, using an argizaiola (literally, "board of light"), a flat piece of wood that stylistically represented the human form and around which was wrapped a long piece of candle. In this sense, the offering of bread was also important as it was thought to provide sustenance to the souls of the dead, and, according to popular belief, during the funeral the bread offered was said to lose all its nutritive qualities, having been consumed by the soul of the dead person. In some areas, it was also traditional to make offerings of meat or live animals. In Sainte-Engrâce, Ott (ibid. 106–16) describes the ritual giving of blessed bread to the living rather than to the dead.

Although very few of these practices are still observed today (almost no people die at home nowadays, and an undertaker is typically hired to deal with the funeral arrangements), some of the old customs can still be seen. While women no longer have their specific seats in the church, and mass-produced candles have replaced the handmade tapers that curled round the wooden argizaiola, in some villages it is still common for women to sit in the nave and men in the balcony stalls. Even where people have moved away from their farms, the former first-neighbor relationships can resurface at death, where a family might return for the funeral and resume their ties with those they had been neighbors to, the woman taking a place alongside the family members, at the head of the procession from the funeral to the graveyard. Alternatively, since most people now travel by car between church and cemetery, they might just take up their place at the graveside.

Modern times. Today death is more clinical, professionally handled, and distanced from the home and family, and male and female roles are less clearly defined in relation to funeral ritual. Death nevertheless continues to activate a wide network of family and social relations in the Basque context. It is the norm for the dead to be taken to the tanatorio, or funeral parlor, where they are laid out in a coffin and members of the family stay by them, receiving visits from friends and relatives who come to pay their respects. Obituaries are placed in the local papers, often with a photograph of the deceased, and these pages are read assiduously by local people. It is usual for a wide circle of family, friends, and relatives to attend the funeral, often filling the churches to overflowing and leaving several out in the street. Rather than a notion of needing privacy, the social emphasis is on accompanying the bereaved, expressing sympathy and support through one's very presence, and this extends to both men and women.

Catholicism in the Basque Country and Spain as a whole has been waning ever since the end of the Franco dictatorship, when people grasped at the possibilities for freedom of all kinds, political, religious, and sexual. Since women had been a pivotal part of the Church, their sexual liberation—not only through access to forbidden contraceptives and abortion, but also through the change in values that gave them access to education and the workplace as never before—meant a distancing from the constraining precepts of religion. The loss of the prime agent of religious socialization continues to be a problem for the Church, but, though less apparent than before, the social weight of Catholic customs still prevails in the practice of baptism, first communion, and marriage.

Carnivals and Other Festivals

Another realm of ritual that was suppressed rather than reinforced by Franco's regime was that belonging to Basque festivals, especially carnivals, which were prohibited during the dictatorship. These celebrations have been gradually recuperated and in recent years have grown in popularity and equality.

Ituren and Zubieta. One of the first Basque festivals where the incorporation of women was documented is the carnival of Ituren and Zubieta. Celebrated on the Monday and Tuesday directly after the last Sunday of January (i.e., either the last week of January or the first of February) this carnival, like all others outlawed by Franco as potentially subversive, was revived in the last quarter of the twentieth century and has grown in popularity over the past few years, attracting busloads of visitors to these two neighboring villages in the heart of a beautiful valley of Nafarroa. One of the purposes of the carnival, before communications were improved by roads and transport, was to resume social relations between the villagers after the period of winter isolation.

The festival served to bring them back into contact in a celebratory fashion that would contribute to the maintenance of social harmony essential for the peaceful and equitable sharing of the valley's resources. As a result, the festival is conceived so that on the Monday the people of Zubieta visit Ituren and are feasted there, and on the Tuesday the roles are reversed and those of Zubieta become hosts to their neighbors from Ituren.

The rural carnivals found throughout the Basque Country share a common well of symbolic significance. Part of the winter cycle of celebration, they represent the awakening of nature after the season's hibernation. In different ways, they act out the casting out of the spirits of death and decay to renew the earth's fertility and herald in the new life of spring. The cockerel's feathers tied to the tip of the tall conical hats, decorated with white lace and colored ribbons, symbolize fertility, and the incorporation of petticoats with more lace and trimmings represents the appropriation of female signifiers in the otherwise starkly masculine world of the shepherd. In these two farming communities whose livelihood once depended on sheepherding, these animals symbolically dominate the festival as the men dress up in sheepskins and strap massive sheep bells around their waists, giving them the name joaldunak ("wearers of sheep bells").[24] The rhythmic movements of the dancers make the bells ring against their backs, and as they made their way from one village to the other the sound was said to waken the land from its winter sleep, frighten off wolves and bears from the flock, and ward off witches who, we have seen, were said to inhabit such rural areas. Teresa del Valle (1998:7) cites the case of one Maria from Ituren, burnt at the stake on accusations of strange behavior, including sexual libertinage and practicing abortions. As well as the bells, the joaldunak also carry a horsetail switch or hisopua, which was traditionally used to scare witches away.

Del Valle (1996; 1998) relates the incorporation of a small number of women into the group of joaldunak in recent years and remarks that their integration has been achieved without any difficulty. She found that the women were unwilling to draw attention to themselves and saw their participation simply as an

Gender role play
Carnival plays and performance provide a chance to play with gender, inverting roles and swapping clothes.
Photo: Imanol Ilárraz

extension of the social life they shared throughout the year with a group of friends, or cuadrilla, of both sexes. Apparently there was no resistance to their proposition, and the older members of the community were visibly moved to observe them. Rather than a break with tradition, women's participation was thus seen as a natural continuation in its evolution. Nevertheless, women are still very much a minority, with only one or two taking part in any one year, but at least the option is open to them and their presence is noted.

One other aspect of the Ituren and Zubieta celebration that is worthy of note is the riotous carnival parade that runs parallel to the bucolic and dignified image of the joaldunak. The young people don outrageous fancy dress, which sometimes looks terribly medieval as they wear old rags and sackcloth and ride on carts decorated with rusty old farm implements or machinery, throwing out handfuls of chaff and sawdust at the unsuspecting onlookers. Others follow the typical carnival guise of sexual role reversal, particularly of men dressing up as women and flaunting a loud and lurid sexuality. Or again, there may be political parodies with irreverent characterization of leading politicians. Del Valle analyses the carnival as an example of a gendered cronotope in which the past reprobation of sexual freedom, censored and punished in the form of witches, and present in the symbols carried by the joaldunak, meets the unleashing of that repression in the carnival role reversal and provocative sexuality. She locates the meeting of time and space in the fixed locality of the squares of Ituren or Zubieta, where these scenes are acted out and where gendered identities come into collision through the reenactment of past superstitions, the sending up of present stereotypes, and the progressive incorporation of women on equal terms into the parade.

The Mascaradas. Crossing the border, Kepa Fernández de Larrinoa has studied the carnival plays, or Mascaradas, of the French Basque province of Zuberoa,[25] and in his book Mujer, ritual y fiesta (Woman, ritual and festival) he documents the creation of an all-woman Mascarada by the village of Eskuila in 1992. It is not that women had been absent from the Mascaradas until then but rather that their participation, gradually increasing since the eighties, had been limited to female parts, formerly played by men, such as the cantinera, the "lady" of the village who accompanies the "lord" in presiding over the spectacle, or the "working woman" who, along with her male counterpart, also watches the performance in representation of the people. The incorporation of women had been considered a response to women's changing place in society and, given the high rate at which females were deserting the rural way of life and rejecting traditional roles in the domestic sphere, their integration in the Mascarada was perceived as a positive force to counter the pull away from the old ways by modernizing them. The changes in the carnival plays reflected change in the world beyond Zuberoa and represented the community's consciousness of forming part of a wider society with which they needed to keep up. However, the organization of an all-women carnival was seen as a departure from this progressive pattern, as it constituted a major challenge to the ascription of meanings in the symbolic universe of dance and performance.

We need to look at the structure of the Mascarada itself to understand the problems raised by the female assumption of certain roles. Basically, the Mascarada consists of two groups: the Reds and the Blacks. The Reds are the formal dance troupe who represent good and are elegantly dressed and dance beautifully.

Cultural codings of masculinity
The riotous "Blacks" whose unruly behaviour is a counterpoint to the elegant dancing of the "Reds", are considered to occupy a male domain which is unseemly for women, as shown by the negative reactions to an all-female *Mascarada* in recent years.
Photo: Imanol Ilárraz

The Blacks, on the other hand, represent the inverse: they are dirty and unkempt, shameless and unruly, thieves and liars. While the Reds gracefully perform dances such as the *Godalet dantza* in which they must dance around and on a goblet of wine without knocking it over, the Blacks provide amusement through their antics. These involve scenes played out with knife grinders, blacksmiths, castrators, gypsies, and tinkers. It is the gypsies and tinkers who are the most raucous and outrageous; they parody the Reds, tease the public, and generally provoke hilarity. As might be expected, it was found perfectly acceptable for women to take the parts of the Reds, with the exception of Zamalzain, the figure of the horse, which is one of the most outstanding because of its elaborate costume and skillful dancing, and is associated with male virility, here caught and castrated in an act of human domination and appropriation of animal forces. However, the suggestion that women could be Blacks was considered totally ludicrous, unthinkable that females could perform male-coded parts that involved such "masculine" behavior, the antithesis to all that was considered appropriate for women.

Fdez. de Larrinoa (1997:62, 69) finds two diverging currents in male opinion on the all-women Mascarada. One he calls the "radical male" position, which considers women's performance of male-coded parts as "a betrayal of the fundamental laws of local ritual expression." The other, "liberal male" version he sees as a radical change but one that goes hand in hand with many other radical changes happening all around. Beyond the resistance to women acting "unfeminine" roles such as the Blacks, Fdez. de Larrinoa detects the unwillingness to admit change in the hierarchical gendered order represented and reinforced by the carnival ritual. Male prestige is reinforced through men playing the main parts, which, moreover, connect with notions of virility and male agency in procreation (through the Zamalzain), condoning the unbridled expression of sexuality (through the farcical vulgarity of the Blacks) and maintaining male domination in the social order.

Many more carnivals can be examined across the Basque Country, and some interesting lines of inquiry can be traced to the gendering of traditional folk dance, in the context of carnival and in other types of festivals and celebrations (see del Valle, 1997:24–27).[26]

Lesson eighteen

Summary

1. The concept of religion in the Basque case has been intimately related to the cultural identity, both of which are projected in the ideal figure of the Basque mother, shrouded in the symbolism attached to the Virgin Mary. The cult to the Virgin is linked to the importance attributed to the mother and in turn to the homeland, often referred to in Basque as "motherland." In both conservative and radical expressions of nationalism, different aspects of the Catholic religion have been incorporated into the ideology of nationhood.
2. Basque cultural traditions intertwine with religious practice in the death rituals, which acquired tremendous importance in the social organization of Basque rural society.
3. Since the end of Franco's regime and the separation of church and state, the progressive acquisition of political, religious, and sexual liberty have contributed to a cooling of religious fervor. Nevertheless, the social impact of the Church still holds strong in the popularity of the standard rites of passage (baptism, first communion, marriage, funerals).
4. The incorporation of women into traditionally male-dominated rituals such as the rural carnivals of the Basque Country provide examples of the symbolic significance of ritual that can reinforce gender stereotypes or be reassigned at a moment of change.

Suggested Reading

Kepa Fernández de Larrinoa, "Carnival Performance, Gender and the Politics of Visuality in Rural Basque

society," unpublished paper delivered at the Performing Politics Conference, Loughborough, UK (1996).
Joseba Zulaika, Chap. 12, "The Amabirjina: Icon and Sacrament," in Basque Violence: Metaphor and Sacrament (Reno: University of Nevada Press, 1988), 268–87.

Bibliography

English Bibliography

William A. Douglass, Death in Murélaga: Funerary Ritual in a Spanish Basque Village (Seattle and London: University of Washington Press, 1969).
Sandra Ott, Chap. 8, "First Neighbour Mortuary Obligations," in The Circle of Mountains: A Basque Shepherding Community (Reno: University of Nevada Press, 1993), 117–30.

Spanish Bibliography

Teresa del Valle, Las mujeres en Euskal Herria: Ayer y hoy (Egin Biblioteka, 1997).
Kepa Fernández de Larrinoa, Mujer, ritual y fiesta: Género, antropología y teatro de carnaval en el valle de Soule (Pamplona-Irunea: Pamiela, 1997).
Carmen Larrañaga and Carmen Pérez, "La religión en la vida de la mujer: 1939–1987," in T. del Valle et al., La mujer y la palabra (Donostia–San Sebastián: La Primitiva Casa Baroja, 1988).

Written lesson for submission

Explain the symbolic and ritual role attributed to women in the relationship established between Basque culture, Catholicism, and nationalism.

19 · Changing the gender of festivals

One of the most polemical feminist struggles currently under way in the Basque Country is the fight for women's right to take part in a ritual march called the Alarde, which is celebrated annually in the neighboring towns of Irun and Hondarribia. The present controversy began in 1995 when a group of women sought permission to participate in the march, which has traditionally been an exclusively male event (with the exception of a privileged few female mascots called the cantineras). Their petition was officially declined, and when they decided to take matters into their own hands and force their way in, they met with violent repulsion by the vast majority of the local population. The matter has been taken to court and championed by certain governmental institutions as well as the national feminist movement, but several years down the road it is still without a satisfactory solution. Research on the reasons behind this conflict will shortly be published in a book written by Margaret Bullen and José Antonio Egido and entitled Tristes espectáculos (A sad sight). Here we will give a summary.

The conflict brings to light a number of issues regarding gender, culture, and identity and provides an appropriate case study since it both engages with many of the themes we have been addressing and poses questions for the future path of Basque Gender Studies. It is further suitable because it is concerned with broad theories of gender and at the same time fulfills our requirements of being firmly situated in the Basque context and thus reflects some of the issues of Basque cultural categories, political concerns, and especially nationalism. We will first present a brief description of the Alardes, and then go on to analyze the reasons for women being refused participation in the march. Finally, we will explain the controversy in terms of the cultural and political categories on which concepts of men and women are constructed in this particular context.

The Alardes

Originating in the fifteenth century, the Alardes were initially a "show of arms," organized annually throughout Gipuzkoa in compliance with a special set of laws called the fueros that bound Euskal Herria to the kings of Castile and committed the Basques to the defense of the borders in case of invasion. The "fueros" called on all men between the ages of 18 and 60 to form part of a local militia that was to rally in times of need and once a year for the review of arms. In the course of time, the victories won over French invaders in the border towns of both Irun and Hondarribia gave rise to the celebration of processions in thanksgiving to the patron saints and virgin of the locality. Even when the "fueros" had ceased to exist and the review of arms was no longer an obligation, these towns continued to celebrate their annual festivals, combining the military parade with the procession.

Nowadays, the parades are made up of about twenty companies that correspond to different neighborhoods or professional groups. Traditionally they have only admitted men to their ranks, except for the emblematic figure of the female cantinera, corresponding to the serving girl who accompanied the troops on their campaigns and served them from the canteen. In addition to the cantinera, each company has its own captain and other officers, who are in charge of the soldiers, divided between the musicians (playing pipes and drums) and the foot soldiers, known as escopeteros since they carry an escopeta, or air rifle.

The Alarde displays many characteristics of a ritual both in its symbolism and its hierarchical order. The troop comes under the orders of a general and his second-in-command. The companies are arranged in a set order, led by a squadron of hatxeros, or zappers, and the band is followed by the infantry, with the artillery and cavalry bringing up the rear. Immaculately dressed in their military uniforms, they form a carefully structured order, marching in time, stopping in certain symbolic places to make their gun salutes (in front of the town hall, the parish church, and so forth), following a hallowed route around the town to the cheers and applause of the public who turns out en masse to see them pass by.

The Alarde de San Marcial of Irun is celebrated on June 30 and the Alarde of Hondarribia on September 8. The festivities start early in the morning with the parade, followed by the procession to the chapel of San Marcial in Irun and to the sanctuary of the Virgin of Guadalupe in Hondarribia where a mass is conducted, and after a celebratory lunch the troop reassembles for the afternoon parade.

We do not have the space to enter into the evolution of the conflict, which in any case is documented elsewhere (Bullen 1999a; 2000b) but we will now go on to consider the reasons for the opposition to women's participation in the events we have just described.

The Reasons for Resistance

The opposition to the incorporation of more women in the parade is explained in terms of the defense of tradition, the respect for history, the expression of identity

Up in arms
The proposal for women to take part on an equal footing with men in the annual parades, called Alardes, met with unprecedented resistance from the vast majority of people in Irun and Hondarribia. As well as resting their case on the strength of their numbers, the reasons they gave ranged from maintaining tradition, being faithful to history and respect for their ancestors.
Photo: Itziar Irastorza

---

and the democratic right of the majority. Let us see how each of these arguments is articulated.

Tradition. The principal argument that has been used to deny women the right to participate in the Alardes is the defense of "tradition," conceived, as we saw above, as rooted in the past, tied to history, and emblematic of local culture and identity. It is the reason most people give for opposing women's participation in the parade and forms the basis for the movement that grew to organize this opposition: Betiko Alardearen

---

Aldekoak, meaning "Those in favor of the traditional Alarde." Betiko literally means "as always" and conveys the notion of continuity, unchanging, over time. People express their desire to see this particular tradition "as it has always been," colored by affective memories of the past that obscure the fact that the Alardes have undergone numerous changes throughout the years without posing any major problems. That the admission of women threatens the notion of tradition in an unprecedented way suggests that the reasons go deeper.

History.[27] Another factor in the arguments against female participation is the use of history to justify women's exclusion. The main thrust is that if women did not participate in the foral militia that are commemorated in the Alardes, then they have no right to participate in the parade. This has led to debate over the interpretation of history from different perspectives and for different ends. For example, people disagree over whether it is the review of arms, in which only men participated, that is most important in establishing the origins of the Alardes, or whether that distinction is held by the battles, which give rise to the processions and ensure the continuity of the parades once the foral militia have ceased to be, and in which women were found to have contributed in significant ways.

There is also a questioning of the use of history at all in the legitimization of contemporarily unacceptable inequality. The theatrical dimension also weakens the historical argument. If everyone is playing a part, representing something they are not, what difference does it make if a woman plays the part of a man, or vice versa? This issue lies at the heart of the feminists' demands to participate alongside men as soldiers, in any of the roles of the Alarde and which in Irun, which has been contested by the women who position themselves against that possibility, by creating their own female parade, prior to the central Alarde. The reactionary women reinterpret their role in history by acting out the part played by the *antorcheras*, or "torchbearers," who threw the enemy off the track by making them believe the local army was hiking along one road when in fact it was lying in ambush in another spot. While this may appear to be an inventive way to bring to light women's contribution to history, in the context of the polemic it evades the issues of equality and maintains women on the margins of the festival.

It is an issue that also stands at the center of debate in the Tamborrada of Donostia–San Sebastián, where women have been gradually incorporated into some of the drum regiments that celebrate the day of their patron saint, Sebastian, on January 20. The option taken up there was effectively that of looking up suitable historical roles and dress for women, though there is also a certain flexibility with regard to women dressing as "male" drummers. The Tamborrada of Azpeitia, held at the same time, and the Alarde of Tolosa, celebrated during the festival of St. John, have both proved to be much more open to change and inventive in their incorporation of women. However, in making these comparisons, we would need to look at the different structure of the Tamborrada, which functions through the independent parades of its component parts at different times and in different places, and the Alardes, which are far more compact, uniform, and hierarchical. The prestige of the different celebrations and the importance attributed to each by the local population are also factors to consider.

Identity. We have seen that one of the functions of tradition is to create or reinforce a sense of identity, of belonging to a particular group or people through the

Strong feelings, harsh words
Those who oppose the incorporation of women as soldiers in the parade cannot be neatly grouped as man against women, old against young, right-wing against leftists. It is a conflict which cuts right through friendship and family groups and is the cause of social tension and aggression.
Photo: Itziar Irastorza

shared celebration of the heroic acts of common ancestors, which bestow a sense of respect for one's heritage and pride in forming part of that community. The ritual performance of the past is then a way of expressing a collective identity—in the words of cultural anthropologist Marvin Harris, a "rite of solidarity."

In the case of Irun and Hondarribia, it is particularly interesting to contemplate the reinforcement of a local cultural identity in response to the proposal for women to march as soldiers in the Alarde, at a time of broad social and economic change in the area. Right at the beginning of the conflict, Teresa del Valle (1997) suggested that the Alarde performed a function of unification of the local community in the face of major structural upheaval in the area. Since the implementation of the European open frontier policy in the early nineties, Irun, which is situated on the French-Spanish border, has seen the closure of customs-related businesses with the attendant unemployment, and is currently undergoing sweeping economic reconversion and a radical reorganization of its urban layout.

Hondarribia, a picturesque fishing town and summer holiday resort, has also grown into a major tourist attraction with an expanding service sector taking over the traditional occupations of farming and fishing. Kepa Fdez. de Larrinoa's assertion that ritual provides a coherent, symbolic frame to counter the sensation of chaos and disorder in the "real" world is applicable here, for it seems that, against these changes, the Alarde represents stability in the face of change, unity and harmony in the face of disintegration, and both a remembrance of the old ways and a celebration of autochthonous culture in contrast to the customs and ways of the newcomers.

The majority. The traditionalist position defines itself as authentically "irundarra" (from Irun) or "hondarribitarra" (from Hondarribia) in opposition to those who favor change and who are defined as "outsiders." The irony of this distinction is that many of those siding with the traditionalists are not from Irun or Hondarribia at all, but rather migrants from other parts of Spain who moved to the area in the strife-torn years after the Civil War. The Alarde becomes a door that opens on to integration for those who oppose the free participation of women in the parade but leaves out in the cold anyone who supports them, including those from generations-old families of Irun and Hondarribia. In this way, a new notion of "the people" is constructed in which membership depends not on belonging in any ethnic sense, but rather in an ideological one. The traditional Alarde has come to be called "the Alarde of the people," drawing a line between those who belong on the basis of defending an Alarde with women only as cantineras, and those who do not belong because they willfully sabotage the "essence" of the event, which is understood to be defiled by the free participation of women.

At the same time, the notion of "the people" is constructed in relation to numbers, and since the majority of the residents of Irun and Hondarribia have shown themselves to be against the incorporation of women as soldiers in the parade, it is assumed that, in a democratic world, the majority must be right. According to this reasoning, no one can bend the will of a people who are sovereign, a law unto themselves, and above the rulings of courts, governments, or other external authorities. This discourse is used to crush the demands of a minority whose rights to equality are recognized by the law, the constitution, and the statutes, but whose reason is denied by an effective strategy of aligning feminist demands with radical politics on the one hand, and on the other with "deviant" gender models.

Gender Models of Women and Men[28]

The underlying reasons for resistance to women's participation in the Alardes can be found in the culturally influenced gender system of local society. Ideal models of men and women which inform attitudes and values and cement the foundations of socially accepted relations, are opposed to alternative models which challenge the assumptions of an androcentric and heterosexual order. Let us consider the different models of femininity and masculinity as ritualized in the parade.

Radicals. The defense of equal rights is discredited by association with stereotyped radical groups from the extremes of the political spectrum. The conflict is construed in terms of a sociocultural stronghold located in Irun and Hondarribia that must repel the onslaught of attackers whose only aim is to seek their own political ends. Those who defend the traditional Alarde imagine the festival to reside in the realm of the sacred and symbolic, out of time and hence immune to change, cut off from the social and political concerns of everyday life. Called on by the committees in charge to protect their patrimony, they have adopted the fight to ban women from the rank and file of the march almost as a holy crusade against the infidel. They feel the women who wish to march alongside the men as musicians and soldiers are violating the sanctity of a timeless tradition and brand them and the men who support them as radical feminists, leftists, and dangerously extreme nationalists.

Both feminism and nationalism are perceived by the defenders of tradition as being outside the agenda of the Alardes. They insist that the parade is not the appropriate forum for any kind of political claim-making and should be invulnerable to pressure groups abusing it as a means to making a statement. They argue that the parade has always put its own preservation over and above any political interests, even during the stormy years of Franco's dictatorship and the ensuing transition.

The accusation is not only that these groups want to introduce politics into the parade, but that their particular politics are subversive. This discourse detracts from the stated aim of achieving sexual equality in all areas of society, which is voiced by the different platforms supporting the coordinator of women's associations, Bidasoaldeko Emakumeak ("Bidasoa Women"), shortened to BAE.[29] Instead of focusing on the desire to improve gender relations at all levels, the dominant discourse associates the women's movement with radical minorities militating in the Basque Country with no better motive than to upturn the established social order–including the Alarde–and create havoc. The struggle is a Foucaultian one of the power to pin labels onto others. By labeling the men and women who favor free participation for all in the parade as trouble-making radicals connected to extremist groups, they disqualify their cause and discredit them completely.

Models of femininity. The basis of sexual equality is also undermined by opposing negative models of "deviant" feminists to positive, idealized images of "respectable" Basque women. The further connection of the feminist movement to radical nationalist politics adds greater weight to the process of discrediting the women's desire to parade, just as the symbol of the Basque matriarch as the supporting column of culture and society is engaged in the projection of a noble people fighting to defend a tradition embedded in their whole system of values and social organization.

The denigration of feminism, or of the women's movement in its different manifestations, is not unique to the Basque context but is found around the globe and responds to the construction of dualistic sexual stereotypes that set up a dominant model of masculinity and femininity in opposition to an array of alternatives contesting this ideal (see Bullen 1999b; 1999c). Ironically, the members of BAE have not always been in

A model woman
The cantinera is the one woman who has traditionally been allowed to participate in the Alardes. Historically representing the girl who served the troops on military campaigns, symbolically the cantinera condenses a sense of local identity and cultural pride as well as projecting an idealized gender model of woman as an object of admiration.
Photo: Itziar Irastorza

agreement with the universal reach of their cause, falling into the dominant stress on the local nature of their struggle and accepting with difficulty the application of their claim for equality in the Alarde to the defense of women's free access to any other walk of life. At one level, they invite much-needed support from other feminist groups but at the same time they want to control the terms of that support.[30]

With reference to the Alardes, the ideal female models materialize in the form of the matriarch (the mother or wife who takes a backstage role as spectator and facilitator of male participation in the parade) or the women as object (in the person of the cantinera, the pretty young girl who occupies center stage as the mascot of her company). The alternative is constructed around a series of negatives portraying the feminist as unattractive, unfeminine, and unsatisfied. The dominant male model corresponds to a hegemonic masculinity prevalent in society, whereas the alternative centers on the effeminate male.

It is interesting how Basque conservative nationalism has absorbed the dominant female stereotype and used it as both an identifier of Basqueness and an element of ethnic differentiation. The polemic over the Alarde demonstrates the assumption of matriarchal power by the traditionalist sectors of the community. Women have been some of the most ferocious opponents of the amplified participation of women in the parade and have formed their own subsections of Betiko. In their declarations and demonstrations they have affirmed their own power of decision and asserted their belief that they already participate fully in the Alarde through their part in preparing and completing the event, denying that they need any feminists to fight for their rights since they consider themselves already in complete control of these. The men point proudly at this show of strength and determination by their women, claiming their impotency to act against the will of their wives or mothers. These women thus emerge as not only the stalwart defenders of a worthy tradition but also the bedrock of their families and the social structure in which these are inserted. What we are witness to is the naturalization of sexual stereotypes that take on symbolic proportions, acquiring an aura of rightness and truth and fixing gender relations in an inflexible system in which the family, with the matriarch at its head, is presented as a stabilizing structure in the face of change.

The other dominant image of the female in the Alarde is that of the cantinera, who represents the idealization of femininity. The importance of the position occupied by the cantinera, attracting the interest of the crowd and provoking comment as to her grace and beauty—or lack of it—is used as an argument against the participation of other women. It is feared their presence would steal her limelight, diminishing the high social status and prestige attached to being elected cantinera. It is also argued that the importance of her role makes up in quality what it lacks in quantity, that is, that while there are only some twenty cantineras to seven or eight thousand soldiers, her position is such that she is able to represent all women and compensate for the numerical disadvantage.

The cantinera, then, embodies the model of femininity to which that of the feminist is opposed. The stereotype of the feminist is one of a woman of "masculine" physique, ugly, and either a lesbian or condemned to be a "spinster." It is said that the women wanting to march are embittered because they are too unattractive to have been chosen as cantineras (an assertion belied by the fact that BAE embraces several former cantineras). This is the popular explanation for female nonconformity and fits with the sociocultural construction of lesbianism as being a perversion opposed to the "normal" paradigm of heterosexuality, which relates female sexuality to reproduction. Thus a discourse of feminism-as-transgression produces a totally negative image that works in antithesis to the ideal and serves to discredit the feminist call for change in society and the claim to equality.

Models of masculinity. The same process of naturalization of gender relations and roles is evident in the

Models of masculinity
The Alarde projects the dominant model of masculinity built around the notion of the man as principal protagonist of the public arena, transmitter of certain masculine values, attached to military practice and male diversion.
Photo: Gotzone Elu

---

construction of masculinity that emerges in the debate over the Alarde and reflects the models predominant in society. The supporters of the traditional Alarde project the dominant model of masculinity built around the notion of the man as principal protagonist of the public arena, transmitter of certain masculine values, attached (in this particular case) to military practice and male diversion. Gilmore (1994:46) has noted that Mediterranean masculinity emphasizes public performance in such a way that the rest of society can properly evaluate male behavior. The theatrical metaphor is easily translated to the Alarde. Here we have the man as the privileged member of the family and of society, who has the unquestioned right to parade and whose participation is wholeheartedly approved and applauded by the womenfolk who prepare his clothes and food, wait patiently on the pavement for him to pass, and give him free rein to enjoy himself that day.

Another aspect of masculinity expressed in the Alarde is the military element, which cannot be overlooked in a parade that commemorates wars and battles and celebrates past victories won. The organization of the parade responds to that of an army, hierarchically orchestrated with its general, captains, and other ranking officers who take charge of their companies. Military uniform, music, and marching; a show of arms—guns, cannons, sabers, and other instruments of war. These characteristics of the Alarde have caused some supporters of insumisión, the protest movement against obligatory military service in the Spanish army, to argue from a pacifist or nationalist perspective that nowadays the legitimacy of such a parade should be questioned. Nevertheless, some who have themselves refused to do military service reconcile their political convictions with participation in the Alarde on the grounds that it is a festive representation in which the participants are performers whose costume and actions lack greater significance.

Rather than the outer aesthetics of the parade, some have a greater problem with the power play among some of the ranking officers who take their role all too seriously and use it as an excuse for exercising an authority that they would not normally have. A former captain of one of the Hondarribia companies and a militant member of Herri Batasuna (HB)[31] found himself drawn into the parade's military setup and resigned from his position when he found he was behaving like a military man himself. This same person was later expelled from the organizing committee of the Alarde, purportedly for his support of women's participation but also because of his alliance with HB.

It can be seen that the dominant model of masculinity is associated with male public performance, unquestioned privileges and power for men, and the desire to wield authority. The military aspect contains the potential for violence and aggression in the handling of weapons and the projection of an ideal of virility, in direct contrast to the stereotype of effeminate homosexuality. The men who support women's participation in the Alarde are overtly insulted along these lines, with taunts suggesting that their masculinity, their eligibility as men in the socially acceptable mold, is not only dubious but also deviant.

The men who fail to conform to the social standard of masculinity are thus criticized on either sexual or political grounds. They support the women because they are thought to be homosexuals and lenient toward femininity, since they themselves are effeminate. Or their support derives from political sympathies positioning them with the women in the realm of radical nationalist militancy and they find themselves branded as disrespectful toward tradition, disruptive of the festival, and dangerous to the status quo.

Lesson nineteen

Summary

1. The popular opposition to the petition of women to join the annual parades, or Alardes, of Irun and Hondarribia on the same footing as men shows that, despite the advances made toward equality in other

walks of life, the sphere of ritual with its sacred/symbolic dimensions resists change.
2. The arguments against women's right to take part in the parades are expressed in terms of the defense of tradition, the faithful reproduction of history, the respect for ancestors, and the sense of identity forged through the festival. The right of the majority, legitimated by its equation with "the people," is brought to sway over a minority right.
3. Beneath these arguments, the gender system of society becomes apparent in which hegemonic models of femininity and masculinity are extolled while their alternatives are denigrated. The defense of a fairer system is obscured by the distortion of the ideas through negative labeling of those who propound them.

Suggested Reading

Margaret Bullen, "Gender and Identity in the Alardes of Two Basque Towns," in W. Douglass et al., eds., Basque Cultural Studies, Basque Studies Program, Occasional Papers Series, no.7 (Reno: University of Nevada Press, 1999a), 149–77.

Bibliography

English Bibliography

Margaret Bullen, "Bordering on Chaos: Culture, Gender and Identity," paper presented at 1st International Symposium on Basque Cultural Studies, London Guildhall University, electronic publication, http://ibs.lgu.ac.uk/sympo (2000a).

Spanish Bibliography

Margaret Bullen, "Identidad y género en los Alardes de Hondarribia e Irun," in Ankulegi 1:38–40 (1997a).

———
Margaret Bullen, "La construcción de género en el discurso sobre los Alardes de Irun y Hondarribia," in Ankulegi 3:53–61 (1999b).

———, "Cambio y confrontación en los Alardes de Irun y Hondarribia," in Carmen Díez and Mari Luz Esteban, eds., Antropología del Género (Actas del VIII Congreso de Antropología: 2) (Santiago de Compostela, 1999c), 69–79.

———, "Hombres, mujeres, ritos y mitos: Los Alardes de Irun y Hondarribia," in Teresa del Valle, ed., Perspectivas feministas desde la antropología social (Barcelona: Ariel, 2000b), 45–78.

Margaret Bullen and José Antonio Egido, Tristes espectáculos: Los Alardes de Irun y Hondarribia, (Bilbao: Servicio de Publicaciones de la UPV-EHU, forthcoming).

Teresa del Valle, Las mujeres en Euskal Herria: Ayer y hoy (Egin, 1997).

D. D. Gilmore, Hacerse hombre: Concepciones culturales de la masculinidad (Barcelona: Paidos, 1994).

Xavier Kerexeta, "Díme de que alardeas," electronic publication, www.alarde.org.

Written lesson for submission

Assess the arguments for and against the incorporation of women in the Alardes on equal terms with men.

20 · Gender and space

As we consider the symbolic dimension of social reality and gender inequality, space emerges as significant factor in creating differential status between women and men by organizing their access to areas connected to the generation of prestige and power. It is important to reflect upon the confluence of space and time in the creation of inequality.

The analysis of the urban spaces of Basque cities reveals how women have often been excluded from urban planning and design, resulting in the construction of spaces that are "unfriendly" to women and that are symbolically reclaimed in acts and rituals.

Space and gender status.

In the introduction to her book Gendered Spaces, Daphne Spain affirms that the spatial layout of our social environment reinforces sexual inequality by segregating men and women and reducing women's access to certain resources necessary for producing and reproducing power and privilege (and thus acquiring status). She shows how taking space into account can improve our understanding of how inequality occurs: "Spatial arrangements between the sexes are socially created, and when they provide access to valued knowledge for men while reducing access to that knowledge for women, the organization of space may perpetuate status differences." (1992:3).

It is now widely recognized by geographers and sociologists that space is socially constructed and that to understand where a social phenomenon occurs enhances our comprehension of why it occurs. Some disagree as to whether spatial arrangements cause social difference, or conversely whether social structures give rise to a determined distribution of space, but Spain argues for the interdependence of the two: "My hypothesis is that initial status differences between women and men create certain types of gendered spaces and that their institutionalized spatial segregation then reinforces prevailing male advantages." (ibid. 6)

Feminist geographers were among the first to theorize on gender and space, pursuing the private–public dimension and analyzing the spatial organization of urban capitalist societies which has clearly defined masculine spaces of production and feminine spaces of reproduction. Architecture and the design of homes and other buildings are also seen to reflect gender and status assumptions about social relations.

If the family, one's education, and the labor force are found to be major components of gender stratification, then we will learn more about how that stratification works if we look at the spaces connected with them: homes, schools, and workplaces. In most Western homes today, the house is seen as a feminine space and men's domain is located outside that space in the garage, workshop, or garden shed.[32] In the Basque context, we have seen the importance attached to the traditional farmhouse, or baserri, and the association of the etxekoandere, or woman of the house, with the domestic realm, especially the kitchen. It is interesting to observe that Basque men have socialized cooking and eating through the creation of sociedades, eating societies that have traditionally been men-only clubs where groups of friends meet to prepare and eat a meal together. Although many societies now admit women or at least have a "lady's night," the kitchen usually remains out of bounds to women (with the exception, ironically, of the

Women on the move
Cronotopes link space and time in a dynamic way which can easily be perceived in the popular annual race between Behobia and Donostia-San Sebastián. Meeting points in a network of sociocultural phenomena, cronotopes provide clues to the way inequality is embedded in the social structure. Women's incorporation into different sports' arenas is a breakthrough which is questioning the qualities we ascribe as feminine or masculine and the ways we conceive of the body, issues of health and gender relations as a whole.
Collection Carmen Díez

---

cleaning lady who is paid to go in to wash the dishes the next day).

Gender, space, and time. As we saw in Part 1, on gender theory, one of the principal issues for women's studies has been the difficulty not only of making women visible and giving them a voice, but also of interpreting the symbolic encoding of what Edwin Ardener (1975) called "muted groups." Given that male bias in research has constructed androcentric models that equip scholars with tools of interpretation derived from a male world-view, women, marginalized groups, and minority groups who do not fall under the hegemonic male model cannot be satisfactorily understood.

Both Edwin and Shirley Ardener have addressed the need to seek out the models of muted groups in symbolic rather than discursive forms. In her work on space, time, and memory, Teresa del Valle has pursued the quest to comprehend the basis of inequality in Basque society and culture and has published her findings in the book *Andamios para una nueva ciudad: Lecturas desde la antropología* (1997). We can find a synthesized version of her work in English in the paper titled "At the Crossroads of Gender, Time and Space: Discovering the Basis for Inequality," presented at the 1998 conference on Basques in the Contemporary World in Reno (Nevada).[33] In her study of the two Basque capitals, Bilbo-Bilbao and Donostia-San Sebastián, she finds that women are, for the most part, absent from the symbolic representation of the cities and sets out to discover aspects that do not come to the surface because they are not picked up by the dominant models of discourse and therefore do not enter recorded, textual memory. Conversely, the search is for nondiscursive, personified, or embodied memory that connects with interiorized, emotional experience (1998:1–3).

Del Valle develops the concept of "gendered cronotopes" as a methodological strategy that synthesizes wider realities, uniting the concepts of space and time, and presenting new possibilities for the study of change. The author defines time as "an unfolding reality" and space as "an area which is physically identified through the activities, interactions and through the meanings engraved in experiences and perceptions" (ibid. 4). Cronotopes then link space and time in a dynamic way. They are meeting points in a network of sociocultural phenomena where specific actions or emotions take on a symbolic dimension. The adding of gender to this spatial–temporal relation enhances the analysis of how inequality is embedded in the social structure.

We are given three examples of where to find gendered cronotopes in our observation and analysis of social phenomena:

1. Everyday locations and situations where there is a confrontation, reenactment, or redefinition of the masculine and feminine realms (a playground, football stadium, workplace, and so on)
2. Rituals where identities are negotiated or come into conflict
3. Evocation of other people, actions, or situations which re-create the past but form part of a nondiscursive memory

The Gendered Space of Basque Cities

A growing body of work on Basque urban anthropology is evidenced in a series of conferences organized on the theme by Eusko Ikaskuntza and reflected in the publications of the proceedings. Thanks to the efforts of José Ignacio Homobono in gathering together the different contributions in this field, we have the publication *Invitación a la antropología urbana*, where we can find reference to significant works in the area of gender and urban space, among others (2000:36–37). Homobono himself has studied neighborhood relations in the fishing town of Bermeo (Bizkaia) and shows how the women take over the streets both during the local festivals and in their everyday interaction (1997). Homobono's reflections on the symbolism of the space contained by the old walled city of Hondarribia also prompted Bullen's consideration of the way space is tied into the reaffirmation of identities in relation to the Alarde tradicional.

We have seen different examples of the transforming potential of ritual and how focusing on space can help us grasp a wider picture than we would otherwise have (carnivals, Alardes). To finish, let us consider some of the other gender issues that are revealed by a closer examination of space, such as the layout of cities, shown by del Valle (1989) to be sexist, unfriendly, and unacceptable to many of the women who inhabit them. She looks at the Basque cities of Bilbao and San Sebastián and finds, from different women's organizations, that in certain spaces women's movements are curtailed by fear. She documents the Lilathon, a women's run, held on International Women's Day (March 8), as a symbolic act of reclaiming the streets for women.

Lesson twenty

Summary

1. Space is shown to be a factor in the differential status of women and men by organizing their access to areas connected to the generation of prestige and power.
2. Looking at the interrelation of space and time can enhance our perception of the creation and conditions of inequality.
3. The analysis of the urban spaces of Basque cities reveals how women have often been excluded from urban planning and design, resulting in the con-

struction of spaces that are "unfriendly" to women and that are symbolically reclaimed in acts and rituals.

Suggested Reading

Teresa del Valle, "Urban Space and the Manifestation of Gender Relations/Gender Systems in Two Basque Cities," paper given at AAA 88th annual meeting, Washington, D.C., Nov. 15–19.

Bibliography

English Bibliography

Edwin Ardener, "Belief and the Problem of Women," in S. Ardener, ed., Perceiving Women (London: Dent, 1975), 1–17.

Teresa del Valle, "At the Crossroads of Gender, Time and Space: Discovering the Basis for Inequality," unpublished paper presented at the 1998 conference on Basques in the Contemporary World, Reno, Nevada, 1998.

Daphne Spain, Gendered Spaces (Chapel Hill and London: University of Carolina Press, 1992).

Spanish Bibliography

Teresa del Valle, Andamios para una nueva ciudad: Lecturas desde la antropología (Madrid: Cátedra, 1997).

José Ignacio Homobono, "Fiestas en el ámbito arrantzale: Expresiones de sociabilidad e identidades colectivas," Zainak: Cuadernos de Antropología-Etnografía, no. 15, 61–100.

———, "Antropología urbana: Itinerarios teóricos, tradiciones nacionales y ámbitos temáticos en la exploración de lo urbano," Zainak: Cuadernos de Antropología-Etnografía, no. 19 (2000), 15–50.

Written lesson for submission

What can the contemplation of space contribute to the study of gender in the Basque Country?

Key words

RITUAL: a form of standardized and repetitive behavior that obeys a culturally or religiously prescribed order laying down the correct way to carry out a series of rites or solemn acts. Ritual has an important symbolic dimension that functions to construct or reinforce group identities, reaffirm the social order, explain the world order, and provide a stable reference in the face of change.

TRADITION: the repetition of a series of rites or action acquiring greater merit for having survived from a more or less remote past and representing continuity through time, imagined to be unchanging, but frequently admitting change. A static perspective of tradition is challenged by a dynamic concept of culture that holds that traditions, as a part of culture, are constructed and reconstructed over time by specific social actors in specific contexts.

CULTURAL SPECIFICTY VS UNIVERSAL RIGHTS: the static concept of tradition as emblematic of cultural specificity is universally used as an antidote to women's claims for equal rights.

GENDER AND SPACE: the spatial layout of our social environment reinforces sexual inequality by segregating men and women and reducing women's access to certain resources necessary for producing and reproducing power and privilege.

Part six. Basque feminism and gender studies

21 · Women in twentieth-century Spain

Before we can assess the evolution of the Basque feminist movement, we need to situate it in its historical context at the level of the rest of the Spanish State. We cannot talk about gender at the dawning of a new millennium in Spain or the Basque Country without mentioning the political regime that dominated a major part of the twentieth century and that determined women's position in society at that time. We are referring, of course, to the dictatorship of General Francisco Franco, who ruled Spain with an iron fist from his victory in the Civil War (1936–1939) up to his death in 1975. An outstanding reference for the history of women in Spain is Mary Nash, who has written numerous books and articles, including most recently Defying Male Civilization: Women in the Spanish Civil War.

However, before we come to the Civil War, which placed Franco in government, and look at what franquismo meant for Spanish women, we need to cast our eyes further back still to the Republic that saw the end of the reign of King Alfonso XIII in 1931 and that marked the beginning of a few intense years of progress in many directions, but especially in the direction of women's liberation. These periods of history are amply dealt with in the fifth volume of a series on the history of women in the West, Historia de las mujeres en Occidente, and here I will refer to those sections that discuss the situation of women in Spain in the twentieth century. Danièle Bussy Genevois covers the period from the Republic to the advent of franquismo. Much as was to recur with Franco, the Borbon monarchy headed by Alfonso XIII represented the union of Church and Crown and kept women under the thumb of Catholicism and a particularly repressive legal system. Bussy questions how women who had broken free of these chains during the Republic could allow themselves to be so tied up again under Franco.

Women's Rights in the Republic

The Republic was based on the ideas of an intellectual elite that proposed sweeping reforms to reduce inequality and render Spanish society more just. Women's rights were fundamental to this project of reform, and many aspects were seen to be in urgent need of improvement:

1. The cultural and judicial inequality between husband and wife
2. The high birthrate and the highest infant mortality rate in Europe
3. The tolerance of adultery in men
4. A high number of illegitimate children
5. Widespread prostitution and high incidence of venereal diseases
6. Poor working conditions for women

Different groups gave priority to different issues: the Socialists to the abolition of prostitution, the Anarchists to the concept of free love and availability of contraception, others to divorce (though there was not unanimity on this even among feminists). The emergent feminist groups gave precedence to the vote, the abolition of prostitution, attention to culture, and rewriting civil and penal codes.

The first reform introduced was a paid maternity leave, which, however, took some time to be accepted as many were opposed to payroll deductions toward it. The major breakthrough for Spanish women in the Republic was the right to vote, which was granted in October 1931, not without much prior debate in which misogynist doubts were expressed over women's "hysterical nature," their ability to think for themselves (having traditionally been guided by the Church), and their rationality (supposedly perturbed by their menstrual cycle). It was the radical lawyer Clara Campoamor who finally held sway by arguing for equality and carrying the vote of the Socialists (see Mujeres de España. 1988:85–86).

Over the following months, the Republican parliament also recognized civil marriage and divorce, granted equal status to all children (both legitimate and illegitimate) and gave the same weight to maternal and paternal authority. Not surprisingly, the swiftness of these reforms met with staunch opposition from the Church and conservatives. The Right urged their women to stand against the tide of change: to stop the flow of secularization of the state and education and to attract votes for the Right. Here, as we have seen in other moments of change, it is unclear whether the activity of right-wing women is a result of their subjugation to male leaders or whether it can be put down to their own initiative. Whatever the reason, women became important activists in campaigning against the Republic through groups such as Acción Católica Femenina and other associations that gathered thousands of women in rallies up and down the country. For example, when the Republicans banned religious schools and closed down the Company of Jesus, women were particularly vehement in their protest. They marched in the streets, crucifixes in hand; sent their children to school armed with crosses; signed petitions; boycotted Republican businesses; and created parallel schools. These right-wing women were later assimilated by the Falange Femenina, created in 1934.

A big family
The combination of Catholicism and conservative politics meant that under Franco, the mother figure was idealized and big families were encouraged and applauded.
Collection Maria Gabriela Fdez. de Casadevante

It was a time of intense political mobilization on all fronts. By the second half of 1934 the situation had worsened. Not only was political warring rife but economic crisis was hitting hard and bread was short in many areas. In Andalucia and the Basque Country strikes and uprisings were organized. In the midst of this unrest, the Republican president committed the fatal mistake of nominating three right-wing members to his cabinet, provoking a nationwide uproar that lasted especially long in Asturias and the Basque Country, where Dolores Ibárurri, otherwise known as "la Pasionaria," joined others in urging the wives and daughters of miners and workers to rebel. This was known as the October Revolution. The furor brought the need for elections in February 1936 and though a Popular Front alliance won by a narrow margin, uniting the different left-wing groups in support of the Republic and against repression, it was weak and unable to impose order on a country still disrupted by strikes and protests. Against this background of unrest, months of conspiracy by army officers came to a head on July 18, when Franco, Generalísimo, or Commander-in-Chief of the armed forces, backed by the Spanish troops garrisoned in Morocco, led a coup d'état that detonated the Civil War. Women who had been active in different organizations participated in the resistance, taking the place of men who had gone to the front in the factories and working alongside figures like Dolores Ibárurri to procure international aid and support.

The mythical figure of "la Pasionaria" deserves special attention.[34] This charismatic woman, loved by the people of the Basque Country and Asturias where she lived and militated, became a living legend throughout Spain and Europe. Born into a mining family in Gallarta (Bizkaia) in 1903, Ibárurri experienced the suffering and hardships of the mines and the desperation of married life in the hard times in which she lived and that cost her the lives of all but one of her six children. Ibárurri militated in the workers' movements and joined the Socialist party in Somorrostro, which later merged with the Communist Party. In 1933, she became president of "Women Against Fascism," a group formed with help from a French delegation of the World Committee against War and Fascism. The movement worked toward women's liberation during the Republic and, though declared illegal in 1934, during the Civil War the organization placed women in men's jobs so that the latter could go up to the front. Around that time, Ibárurri moved to Asturias and campaigned there for children of workers under repression. Once Franco came to power, la Pasionaria, like so many others, had to flee the country and spent thirty-eight years exiled in Russia, before she was finally able to return to her beloved Basque Country where she had always dreamed of ending her days.

Women under Franco

With regard to the history of women in Spain, Bussy (1993:216) states that the start of Franquismo has to be taken back to the creation of the Falange Femenina in December 1934 and the campaign from the Church to return to the old moral order. This involved the condemnation of women in sport, baring bodies on the beach, and general frivolity. The Falange's purpose was to involve women in propaganda and organization, calling them to the "building of a great, imperial Spain", urging their men to do the same. Franco used the women in the Falange for his own nation-building program. They were set to the task of seeing to food, making uniforms, and generally looking after the soldiers, as well as delivering propaganda on the radio and in education. The figures of Isabel la Católica and Santa Teresa de Ávila were reinstated as women to be emulated by the Falange. Historical heroines had to be subjected to God, even as women had to be subjected to motherhood.

The notion that women's place is in the home was rapidly reestablished in Franco's Spain. Men were the lords of the land that lay beyond the domestic realm, and clearly the domestic was seen as inferior to the extradomestic domain. From the declaration of war in 1936, Franco quickly took measures to "moralize" female custom and practice by doing away with mixed-sex schooling. Women were to be "freed" from work and the workshop by a ban that effectively prohibited married women from working. A whole new set of laws was passed, withdrawing the freedoms established during the Republic regarding civil marriages, divorce, abortion, adultery, and extramarital sex. The leader of the Falange Femenina, Pilar Primo de Rivera (sister of Spain's pre-Republican dictator), announced at a meeting attended by 10,000 women of the Falange in Franco's presence to celebrate his victory in May 1939 that "the sole mission that this Patria assigns to women is the Home" (my translation, 1993:217).

In the social arena, Franco's regime was oppressive and influenced largely by the moral order of the Catholic Church, responsible among other things for the severe subjugation of women in most walks of life. The Church took charge of education, which was to be managed through same-sex schools and differentiated for boys and girls, but at all times subject to Catholic dogma and morality. The Civil Code raised the legal coming of age to 25, and women were obliged to stay in their parents' home until they were married or joined a convent. A double morality measured men's and women's actions with a different yardstick and made allowances for men, whereas women were punished for the same actions. For example, if a husband killed his unfaithful wife and her lover, he was to be banished, but if the wounds inflicted were not mortal then he could be absolved.

In an article about the history of women in the Basque Country, Carmen Díez refers to the way "franquismo" (understood in its widest sense not merely as a political regime but as a whole set of social forces comprising the Catholic Church, the education system, the media, the medical profession, and many other institutions) projected and promoted a single model valid for women: that of mother and wife dedicated exclusively to her household and housework. All those who did not conform to this model were classed as "spinsters," "prostitutes," or "Reds." Even the most active women of the Falange, among whom were engineers, teachers, and politicians, accepted the exaltation of the home and cultivated a hatred for the Republican women, which Bussy thinks may explain their acceptance of the reversal of so many reforms made in women's favor (218). The right-wing press talked of left-wing women in insulting terms such as "virago" (a manly woman) and "guarra" (slut); they depicted them as bloodthirsty monsters out to destroy both the Christian home and the chastity and honor of Spanish women.

Díez (1999:108) points out that there were of course many ordinary women who did not comply with the right-wing ideal nor with the left-wing stereotype. In addition, a tremendous variety of behaviors existed among those who did fulfill the criteria of wife and mother but did so in different ways. There were housewives from the upper rungs of the social ladder who enjoyed the privileges of their position, while many others from the lower sectors struggled to keep their households going (and for many this meant combining other activities with their domestic tasks, taking paid work outside the home). The influence of the ideal woman did not, then, prevent the reality from being very different and much more varied. Nevertheless, the gender ideology that shaped the values prevailing at that time was one built on a sublimated image of mother and wife, centered in the household and according to which women endeavored to mold their lives.

Rights for women
Basque women joined Spanish women across the nation in championing women's rights in the latter part of the twentieth century. Here we see moments of a March 8th rally, organized on the occasion of International Working Women's Day.
Collection Elisa Urtizberea

The Transition
The years between the ending of Franco's dictatorship with his death in 1975 and the democratic elections held in 1978 are referred to as the "Transition." It is generally agreed that these were years in which the winds of change blew through Spain, challenging the old established order and the values upon which Franco's regime had been built. Some of the changes had already begun to occur toward the end of the regime, and Franco's death was merely the catalyst that sped up the process.

A short while before his death in 1975, a marriage reform law was passed and the permiso marital (see Chapter 13) finally abolished. This was late in the history of Europe: 56 years after similar reforms in Italy and 37 years after reforms in France. It took another three years before the adultery laws were revoked in

1978, and it was not until 1981 that the Civil Code was modified to correct the injustices done to women in terms of their control of their finances and their children. That year divorce was also to become a reality in Spain again. Hooper in The Spaniards (1987:199–201) gives us the details.

It took six full years to get a divorce law passed in post-Franco Spain. Although about three-quarters of the population was in favor of divorce at the end of Franco's regime, many people strongly opposed it, arguing that facilitating divorce would leave many middle-aged women high and dry, poor and lonely when their husbands left them for younger wives. This fear was countered by the results of a survey that showed that in fact a large number of requests for divorce came from women. Hooper, (ibid. 199), cites a study of the 1932 Republican Divorce Act, entitled El divorcio en la Segunda República, undertaken by Ricardo Lezcano, which showed that in the first two years after the passing of the law, more than half the petitions for divorce came from women, and in many places, including many rural areas, all the petitions came from women.

By 1977, it was clear that a divorce law was urgently needed in Spain, but the next issue was just what kind of law. The drafting of legislation took until 1980, when the bill was approved by the Cabinet in January and submitted to Parliament later in the year. This bill was known as the Cavero Bill after Iñigo Cavero, then Christian Democrat Justice Minister, and was in fact still highly conservative. It required petitions to be passed through the old judicial system, maintaining the insistence on apportioning blame and reaching a verdict. It did not contemplate divorce by mutual consent and allowed the judge to decide against a concession of divorce if it was believed to be detrimental to one of the partners or their children. Among other faults found in the Bill, Hooper mentions the possibility of a wife demanding alimony from her ex-husband's heirs.

The progress of this Bill through Parliament was stalled by the leader of the Transition government, Adolfo Suárez, who reshuffled his Cabinet and placed Justice in the hands of a Social Democrat, Francisco Fernández Ordoñez, who had been efficient in devising a new, modern tax system and was now to have the Cavero Bill withdrawn and a brand new one drafted. The Ordoñez Bill sped up the whole process of acquiring a divorce, making it possible in one or two years, and did away with the need to apportion blame. Finally, though it did not mention mutual consent outright, it technically made this a possibility.

This Bill met with fierce opposition from the Christian Democrats who managed to put off discussion of the Bill in Parliament till after their national conference in January 1981. Their position was understood to reflect the attitude of the new Pope, John Paul II. Meanwhile, the atmosphere generated by the rift between Christian and Social Democrats over the divorce law (among other discrepancies) led Suárez to resign, and his successor, Leopoldo Calvo Soto, only served to push the Unión de Centro Democrático (UCD) further to the right. Nevertheless, Fernández Ordoñez remained in charge of the Ministry of Justice and the bill was passed through Congress, but came under pressure in the Senate when the Christian Democrats voted for an amendment that would restore a judge's power to refuse divorce in certain circumstances. Back in Congress in June 1981, in what Hooper calls "the final, historic and tumultuous debate," the amendment was removed thanks to a group of Christian Democrats who defied their party's position and voted against the amendment.

"The private is public"
Women challenged the assumption that women's place is in the home by taking to the streets, rebelling against previous restraints and claiming new liberties. With slogans along the lines of "the private is public" they drew attention to the social dimensions of the domestic domain and to the collective concerns of seemingly individual issues such as personal relations, sexuality and self-awareness.
Collection Elisa Urtizberea

The divorce law passed was a fairly liberal one in the end. It allowed for both direct and indirect divorce. The direct method required a prior separation of two years if by mutual consent or five years if not. For an indirect divorce, you had to obtain a legal separation, on the grounds established (adultery, cruelty, desertion), or if the marriage had lasted at least a year both parties could simply approach the court together. One year after the legal separation was granted either party could initiate divorce proceedings. Even after the law was passed on July 7, 1981, the Church continued to boycott it. Many of the couples requesting divorce were those who had begun separation proceedings before divorce became legal, and, as most had been married by the Church, the papers attesting to their separation were in the ecclesiastical courts. When the civil courts requested these documents from the ecclesiastical courts, many were refused with the answer that the bishops were still considering the case. This went on for over a year, considerably slowing down the first claims for divorce.

In contemporary Spanish and Basque society divorce is increasingly common, and in the nineties the number of couples filing for divorce skyrocketed. Figures for Spain show that in 1998, 33.3 percent more couples separated or divorced than only two years previously, in 1996.[35] The reasons given are those we have been mentioning in explaining other changes in gender relations and gender systems since Franco: women's economic dependence and the change in the ideology of marriage. Marriage is no longer perceived to be forever, nor the only option for couples choosing to live together, and people feel more accepting of divorce and have more practical attitudes toward it.

Lesson twenty-one

Summary

1. The Republic characterized a period of radical change and many progressive reforms for women, among which is the right to vote (1931). The social unrest that ensued in the early thirties pitted Right against Left and brought women like Dolores Ibárurri, "la Pasionaria," to the fore in the defense of human rights and women's liberation.
2. The movement known as "Women Against Fascism" was opposed by the Falange Femenina, which fought to reverse the achievements of the Republic, cutting down women's freedom and confining them to the

home and family, which were extolled as the only proper place for women.

3. After Franco's death, the years of Transition brought with them wide, sweeping reforms and the revival of debates on such troubling topics as divorce, which had been laid to rest during the dictatorship. A new divorce law was passed in 1981.

Suggested Reading

M.A. Duran and M.T. Gallego, "The Women's Movement in Spain and the New Spanish Democracy" in D. Dahlerup (ed.) The New Women's Movement: Feminism and Political Power in the USA and Europe, London: Sage Publications, 1986.

Bibliography

English Bibliography

John Hooper, The Spaniards: A Portrait of the New Spain (London: Penguin, 1987).

Mary Nash, Defying Male Civilization: Women in the Spanish Civil War (Arden Press, 1995).

Spanish Bibliography

Danièle Bussy Genevois, "Mujeres de España: De la República al Franquismo," in Georges Duby and Michelle Perrot, eds., Historia de las Mujeres en Occidente (V): El Siglo XX (Barcelona: Círculo de Lectores, 1993), 203–21.

Antonina Rodrigo, Mujeres de España: Las Silenciadas (Barcelona: Círculo de Lectores, 1988).

Written lesson for submission

Compare the lot of women during the Republic with their circumstances under Franco. How does the issue of divorce represent the new progress made in the Transition to democracy?

22 · The Basque feminist movement

In an article on the women's movement in Spain (1965–1990), Elena Grau tells us that the changes we have signaled as significant in the Transition were not thought up overnight but were the result of an increasing consciousness of social and political oppression through the years of silence and clandestinity during Franco's regime. This consciousness had been fed by forms of resistance that took many shapes: a series of strikes at the end of the fifties, the economic crisis of the sixties (which forced women out to work or to emigrate), foreign tourism bringing in new ways of thinking and behaving. The emergence of feminism goes hand in hand with the socioeconomic changes transforming the face of Spain—industrialization and economic growth coupled with the increasing demand for democracy articulated in different social movements (the students' movements, the clandestine Communist Party, sections of the Church that questioned the hierarchy and preoccupied themselves with social concerns). These social movements sought out gaps between the severe repression of the regime and a certain permissiveness toward a social movement that could no longer be curtailed (Grau 1993:673).

We have already remarked that the growth of the labor market, together with increasing levels of schooling among women, began to shake the foundations of Franco's ideal woman, whose sole destiny was marriage and motherhood. Women began to organize in protest against the constrictions of the regime, while the political groups pressing for a return to democracy began to take into account this important social sector, which could readily be incorporated into a more general fight for freedom. In the months following Franco's death, Spanish feminism made its mark with the First Congress for Women's Liberation held in Madrid in December 1975 and the First Catalan Women's Congress in Barcelona in May 1976. The congresses took up many of the causes that had been broken off forty years previously (Bussy 220) and served to make feminism visible as a movement contesting the dictatorship while at the same time setting itself apart from the democratic opposition (i.e., it was the first time that feminism emerged as a movement in its own right in Spain [Grau 675]).

The feminist movement voiced many of the concerns of women emerging from years of oppression and championed the rights of a democratic, lay society—concerns such as divorce, abortion, family planning, and paid work. At this time, the unitary concept of "woman" served to channel collective demands, and the feminist movement came out of the anonymity to which women had been relegated to air concerns that had been hushed up in the recesses of the home, came out onto the streets of Spain to lay a claim to women's rights. What had hitherto been marked as the private, individual side of being a woman was transformed into a public, collective concern as expressed in the slogan "The personal is political" (del Valle 1997:79). Sexuality and reproduction were presented as two separate things for the first time, and the right of women to decide about their own bodies emerged as a whole new concept.

There were, of course, also differences within the movement. In the papers presented at the Madrid and Barcelona conferences, a Marxist trend came to the fore and a previously stronger progressive liberal stance receded. Radical feminism also erupted onto the scene at this point, influenced by the second wave of European and American feminism and incorporating notions of self-awareness, self-help, and aspects of materialist feminist theory. Radical feminism saw women's inequality as the result of an oppressive social relationship between the sexes that was named "patriarchy," though the emphasis was not always the same. Some stressed patriarchy's denial of females as social subjects with individual identities; others underlined the material base of patriarchy, situated it in domestic production, held it responsible for female oppression, and defined it as a form of class control (Grau 676).

The new focus on the contradiction between the sexes at the center of radical feminism was traumatic for many women who recognized themselves in the traditional order, for to accept the new ideas was to face political and personal consequences. Radical feminism was critical of both Right and Left, capitalism and socialism, since both reproduced the relation of domination between the sexes and failed to solve women's oppression. As a result, radical feminism supported "women-only" political organizations as opposed to affiliations of mixed parties or groups. It aspired to the creation of a feminist political strategy capable of nothing less than transforming society (Grau 676).

Radical feminism in the Spanish State never acquired great numerical or organizational strength, though it did influence feminist discourse. The two major currents of thought from then on became:

1. Understanding the origin and character of women's oppression in order to establish the priorities in the fight for liberation
2. Sexuality and the control over one's body

In this second area, theory and practice moved from an initially timid demand for birth control and contraception in the sixties to the outright affirmation of the right to decide about one's own body (Grau 677).

Agreeing on the need to separate sexuality and reproduction, different emphasis was placed on:

1. The rejection of motherhood as the only possible destiny
2. The exploration of sexuality as it relates to pleasure, not domination

Different groups also had different priorities. The Marxist feminists called for contraception and abortion, demanding and creating family planning centers; radical feminists stressed the discovery of female sexuality and the questioning of sexuality at the service of male pleasure, and along these lines self-help groups were set up with the aim to "win back women's bodies" through self-exploration and a rejection of medical control of women's reproductive system.

The debate continued as to whether or not feminism should join forces with other political movements. Some argued it would dilute itself by mixing with parties dominated by men, others that it would not be able to achieve anything in the wider society if it stayed on the margins of other social movements.

In the first conferences in Madrid and Barcelona, the demands were still those of the previous decade before democracy became a reality: paid work, socialization of domestic work, an end to discrimination in education, and reforms in legislation. But new concerns were added to the agenda: the right to decide over one's own body made itself manifest in the demand for sexual education, the availability of contraceptives on social security, the legalization of abortion, and the suppression of legislation banning homosexuality and prostitu-

Defending the right to abortion
The massive protests at the Basauri trial of the eleven accused of abortion marks one of the main milestones in the history of the Basque feminist movement. Here one of the demonstrations demanding amnesty for the accused is reproduced in a French magazine (1979).
Collection Elisa Urtizberea

tion An attack was also mounted on patriarchal ideology: the family, virginity, the myth of the matriarchy, women as objects, and the like (Grau 677).

The women's movement in the second half of the seventies reflected the general spirit of democratic expansion that blew through Spain after the dictator's death on November 20, 1975. Also, despite differences in emphasis, it was a time when there was space for the exchange of ideas and the possibility of working together around a series of demands. Later, the differences were to grow and cause divides in the movement.

At the end of the seventies, the Spanish women's movement entered a period of change in which fissures split the movement. Women's groups lost their space in the public arena and the theoretical debate became polarized (Grau 678). Once the new Constitution was approved in 1978, and elections were celebrated in 1977 and 1979, the movement split broadly into those who were in favor of fighting for women's rights within the political system with all its limitations, and those who believed women could only be efficiently represented by women's movements. The first group sought to apply the principle of equal rights established in the Constitution to all areas of democratic institutions. Women belonging to the Spanish Socialist and Communist parties (Partido Socialista y Obrero Español, or PSOE, and Partido Comunista Español, PCE) were most active along these lines. The second group of women distrusted parliamentary representation for the feminist cause and chose instead to work for strengthening the feminist movement. The gap between different tendencies that had already been presented widened and further fractured the movement, for now the unifying goal of fighting for democracy had been achieved and thus disappeared from the agenda. At a conference of the

State Coordinator of Feminist Organizations held at Granada in 1979, a controversy raged between adherents of "feminism of equality" and "feminism of difference," which had already been going on for some time in France and Italy (Grau 679).

The problems were related to a general disenchantment with democracy. Many women left the parties in which they had militated, while others felt that feminism had reached a ceiling in many respects. Many of its practical demands had been achieved, at least to some degree, and it was difficult to keep up a pitch of militancy. Also to be considered was the emergence of the two strains, of feminism of difference and feminism of equality. The former recognized the differences existing between women and argued against the unitarian model, common to both Right and Left, founded on the universal subordination of women. It became difficult to put into practice a model that took into account the differences between women and at the same time conceived of feminism as a global option and sought out space for debate and exchange of ideas. Then there was the brand of materialist feminism that evolved out of the radical feminism of the second half of the seventies into the Partido Feminista ("Feminist Party"), a working-women's party with the feminist revolution as its goal. The materialist element meant practical initiatives producing tangible results, whether in the form of publishers and bookshops, bars or nonprofit organizations. The aim was to create new points of reference for the movement, widening the area of activity and interrelation between women.

The eighties saw two new elements in the feminist movement: "feminismo difuso" ("broadcast feminism"), meaning the spreading of the ideas propounded by the feminist movement in the female population at

Institutionalizing the women's movement
The consolidation of the Basque women's movement made itself manifest through its institutionalization in government departments such as EMAKUNDE or the former Centre for Women's Studies, here shown at the opening ceremony in Donostia-San Sebastián.
Collection Carmen Díez

---

large; and the feminist presence in institutions and a rise in government political action directed specifically at and for women. These elements responded both to the general change in women's experience in the Spanish State from the sixties and to the recognition of diversity among women and their increased presence in all areas of social life represented by their incorporation into the public space and their greater decision-making capacity with regard to motherhood. At the same time, there was also more work to do, which meant less spare time for many and led to the realization of the limitations of the power that had actually been achieved and its capacity to transform women's lives.

The presence of feminism in different institutions was also a characteristic of this era, marked by the creation of public organisms such as the Instituto de la Mujer ("Women's institute") in Madrid in 1983, following a Socialist victory the previous year. Similar entities were created in the different autonomous communities of the Spanish State, with the objectives of ensuring the application of equal rights policies and offering information, assistance, and promotion of women's affairs. In the Basque Country, the department for women's affairs is named Emakunde, an active organism for the design and implementation of equal rights policies, for overseeing the application of women's rights in society and for continually stimulating public consciousness through a program of educational projects and publications. The eighties also saw the consolidation of academic feminism, with the establishment of numerous centers for women's studies and research institutes, such as the Seminario de Estudios de la Mujer (Seminar of Women's Studies) in Donostia–San Sebastián. This center for research in women's studies grew out of the interest and endeavors of the team that undertook the work behind *Mujer vasca* between 1981 and 1985. Over the next decade the Seminario grew, organizing numerous courses and conferences, carrying out research projects, producing its own publications, and building up its library. Owing to irremediable internal differences, the Seminario was sadly dissolved in 1994 and the library is now housed in the university.

The institutionalization of feminism has been criticized by some who see in it a weakening of the women's movement, yet it is undeniable that it has allowed the channeling of public funds into women's initiatives and permitted a different course of action that would have otherwise been unviable. Among those feminists remaining on the margins of the institutions, some have divided into splinter groups in what Grau (680) terms microfeminism. For example, a series of campaigns has been conducted in favor of free abortion and against violence; small groups have multiplied to work on specific themes, with public funding or use of public infrastructure; services run by feminists on scant funds have grown to offer occupational training, counseling, and shelters for battered women. In some instances, the influence of feminist pressure groups has forced the incorporation of these programs into public services, sacrificing control for financial and institutional support. Other groups, such as the Socialist Feminists, endeavor to make the most out of institutional support for women and believe in getting women onto voting lists and creating spaces of female hegemony.

Mary Nash, writing on the history of women in Spain (1991), discusses the developments in the field of ideas and the emergent areas of research that have been characterized by the diversity of their initiatives and issues brought up for debate, resulting in new theoretical reflections. Written production by and for women as well as discussion arenas (conferences, workshops, debates, university courses, and seminars) have proliferated, resulting in deeper reflection and a more dynamic interchange of knowledge and thought. To sum up, these are the main issues that were taken on board by Spanish feminism in the eighties:

1. Practically: incorporation into the labor force; an end to sexism in mixed schools; a freeing-up of women's time
2. Theoretically: existence of historical, social, and political female subjects; concepts of gender; sexual differ-

ence; the possibility of constructing a theoretical and political discourse based on women's experience

Milestones in the Basque Feminist Movement

In the concluding chapter of her book *Las mujeres de Euskal Herria: Ayer y hoy* (Women of the Basque Country: Yesterday and today), Teresa del Valle selects what she refers to as *hitos*, or milestones, in the recent history of feminism in the Basque Country and shows how they pave the way for what she terms a "new history" in which women's struggles, aspirations, and achievements occupy their rightful place. The events that, in her eyes, loom as milestones in the course of this new history are: three editions of the Leioa feminist congress; the Basauri hearings for abortion cases; and the collective participation of women in the Alardes of Irun and Hondarribia (see Chapter 19). Del Valle explains that the metaphor of milestones corresponds to the way women remember and relate their history, focusing on certain moments or events that stand out clearly in their memory and that follow each other, building on the ground broken by the previous one. This section is documented largely on del Valle's work along with that of Mari Luz Esteban, who also refers to this episode in the history of Basque feminism in her book *Re-producción del cuerpo femenino: Discursos y practicas acerca de la salud* (Reproducing the female body: Discourses and practices concerning health, 40–44, 52–58). In addition to the three episodes related by del Valle, we will also mention the foundation of Family Planning Centers discussed by Esteban.

Leioa. First let us look, with del Valle, at the first feminist congress celebrated in Euskadi in 1977 and successive editions in 1984 and 1994. These congresses became known by the place where they were held:

namely the Leioa campus of the Basque University. Del Valle points to the significance of holding the conference in the same place on each occasion, creating a symbolic reference between space, event, and group that functions well in a culture given to situate people, families, and groups through a relation with place names. The 1977 Basque women's congress was held during the Transition, two years after the first Spanish women's congress held in Madrid in 1975, and, as we have already seen, was fundamental in consolidating the Spanish feminist movement. Separate Asambleas de Mujeres, or Women's Assemblies, were created in the four Spanish Basque provinces of Araba, Bizkaia, Gipuzkoa, and Nafarroa, based in the provincial capitals and later multiplying and extending to other smaller towns and neighborhoods. The seventies are remembered by these groups as crucial years when women began to realize their strength as a collective and value their role within such groups.

Del Valle signals that one of the most striking things about the Basque congress was the sheer volume of women who attended, making feminism visible for the first time. Some three thousand women took to the streets, appeared in the media, and showed their agreement on some major gender issues, despite their different ideological tendencies in other areas. They discussed oppression, work, and the organization of the feminist movement, but as Esteban (2000:43) points out, many of the themes also revolved around sexuality, homosexuality and heterosexuality, contraception, and the right to abortion.

The second edition of the Basque feminist congress, held in 1984, showed a diversification of interests and a change in emphasis responding to the social changes occurring at that time. The movement was fully

New Basque men
Against the cultural backdrop of idealized motherhood, the social role of a responsible father is gaining ground in twenty first century Euskal Herria and the construction of a "new Basque man" is a theme for our times.
Photo: Margaret Bullen

---

established by that time and, as we shall see below, had come to the fore of public attention, during the abortion trials in Basauri in 1979. The themes of employment and the feminist movement held sway, while room was made for new concerns such as science, domestic abuse, health, maternity, and love. Issues that had initially played an important part such as patriarchy give way to a major debate on violence in many forms, from anti-militarism and institutional violence to sexual violence and battering.

In the third Basque feminist congress, held in November 1994, though participation was still high, the signs of a serious decrease in membership and slowdown in activity of many feminist groups became obvious. They had lost their capacity to gather women en masse as they had done before, and large numbers were only achieved at rallies for special days like International Women's Day on March 8. As noted for the Spanish feminist movement as a whole, it became difficult to find new focal points to work around, and new proposals.

The Basauri hearing.: From 1979 to 1984, one of the main issues around which Basque women rallied was the trial of nine women from Basauri who were accused of having abortions and one man and one woman who were tried on charges of carrying them out. Despite the presence of a man among the accused, the trial became known nationally as "the trial of the eleven women of Basauri."

As we have already seen, abortion was a critical and central issue in Spanish feminism, and it is true to say that it is at the center of the contemporary feminist movement throughout the world. Esteban (2001:53–54) signals the importance of the issue of abortion as an indicator by which to assess the pulse of the political and judicial position, the medical and gynecological profession, and the practice of sexual relations. The public protest against the trial marked a peak period in the history of the Basque feminist movement. Never before had there been such a mass response to a call from feminist organizations through the successful coordination of the different local Assemblies and their ability to mobilize the rest of the population. Among the different protest actions taken was the occupation of one of the main court buildings in Madrid by some three hundred women who were forcibly ousted by police; the mass meeting outside the provincial court of Bizkaia in Bilbao; and the petitions signed by over 1,000 woman declaring that they had had abortions, and another signed by men admitting to having helped arrange abortions (Hooper 1987:191; del Valle 1997:81). The protesters demanded amnesty for the accused and the right to free, legal abortion with no strings attached.

The protest marches were accompanied by slogans, painted on banners, on walls, and in the streets of towns and villages, reading "Sexuality is not maternity," "Amnesty for women," "We give birth, we decide," "Free abortion" (meaning both economically and legally), "If the bishops gave birth, abortion would be legal," "We've performed an abortion at home, illegally, to see what happens," "No more abortion trials," "The right to abortion on the national health." (my translation) Esteban (ibid. 54) sees two basic ideas represented in these slogans. First is women's right to control their own bodies, including the right to use contraceptives and to have abortions under the same health care coverage as any other medical condition and the right to separate sexual pleasure from reproduction. Second is a condemnation of the contemporary legal and judicial situation as it relates to one's own body.

Although the Basauri case was first brought in 1979, hearings were drawn out and the final verdict was not given until 1982. The tremendous public pressure almost certainly influenced the judges' decision to dismiss the case "on the unprecedented grounds that the defendants had acted out of necessity" (Hooper ibid. 191). This sentence marked the first major victory on the road to decriminalize abortion and was followed by increased pressure from the judiciary, which lobbied the government to reform the abortion law. In 1985, the Socialist government legalized abortion under the following three circumstances: rape, deformation of the fetus, or physical or psychological risk to the mother. This is the basis of the abortion law that holds in Spain

"Our bodies ourselves"
A growing awareness of the connection between body and self has multiple implications in the way women assert the right to decide for themselves in matters of sexuality and reproduction. At the same time, health consciousness together with new opportunities for women in sport, has encouraged women's participation in activities such as this canoe race between Getaria and Donostia-San Sebastián organised by the Fortuna Sports Club.
Collection Carmen Díez.

---

today, nearly two decades later, though it continues to be a bone of contention among feminist groups and political parties. The Socialist Party, now in opposition to the right-wing Popular Party, has proposed amending the law to contemplate new grounds for abortion, such as unfavorable socioeconomic conditions, or to make abortion freely available to women during the first twelve weeks of pregnancy and thereafter only on medical recommendation. However, the response from the Right is one of outright revulsion, reinforced by the position of the Catholic Church and pro-life forces, which consider abortion murder (Esteban ibid. 56).

The feminist movement has kept the issue of abortion on its agenda, continuing to assert the right to free abortions on demand as part of the national health program, on the basis that the fundamental question is the woman's right to decide for herself about her own body. At the same time as insisting on abortion, feminists in the seventies pushed for both sexual education and access to contraception (which, as Esteban reminds us, was not made legal in Spain till 1978), which resulted in the creation of family planning centers that functioned independently of the official health service and provided all kinds of information and services related to women's sexual health. Esteban includes the Family Planning Centers in the line of landmarks in the Basque feminist movement and poses new questions for their functioning and philosophy today, arguing for the need to move them in from the periphery of health care, where they have been perceived as initiatives by and for women and, as such, marginalized by the broader health system (Esteban ibid. 199–205).

Lesson twenty-two

Summary

1. The Spanish women's movement built on the concerns that had begun to germinate during the Republic and that were quashed under Franco and resuscitated after his death. The movement was varied and different lines of interest and enquiry emerged, between the proponents of feminism of difference and those of feminism of equality, between those who preferred theoretical reflection and the genera-

tion of knowledge and those who favored practical action and intervention, between those who saw a source of support in the institutions and those who thought such associations deviated from the social base of feminism.

2. Some of the main issues that were debated were the origin of women's oppression and the nature of patriarchy, necessary to understand in order to fight for liberation. Another key concept was "the personal as political," in which sexuality and reproduction were presented as two separate things, stressing women's right to decide about their own bodies and transforming the private, individual side of being a woman into a public, collective concern.
3. The history of the Basque women's movement can be plotted through different areas of mobilization, such as the first feminist assemblies held in Leioa (Bizkaia); the abortion trial of the Basauri Eleven; the evolution of family planning centers.

Suggested Reading

Mary Nash, "Two Decades of Women's History in Spain: A Reappraisal," in K. Offen, R. Roach Pierson, and J. Rendell, eds., Writing Women's History: International Perspectives (Bloomington: Indiana University Press, 1991), 381–414.

Bibliography

Spanish Bibliography

Teresa del Valle, Las mujeres de Euskal Herria: Ayer y hoy (Donostia: Egin, 1997) (Chap. 5, 75–95).

Mari Luz Esteban, Re-producción del cuerpo femenino: Discursos y prácticas acerca de la salud (Donostia–San Sebastián: Tercera Prensa–Hirugarren Prentsa, 2001).

Elena Grau Biosca, "De la emancipación a la liberación y la valoración de la diferencia: El movimiento de mujeres en el Estado español, 1965–1990," in Duby and Perrot, eds., Historia de las Mujeres (1993), 673–83.

Written lesson for submission

What are the main achievements of the women's movements in twentieth-century Spain and the Basque Country? How does the issue of abortion symbolize the struggle for women's rights?

23 · Basque gender studies

In this section, we will consider some of the most recent areas of research that move beyond the strictly Basque context and engage with relevant lines of inquiry in Gender Studies today. We will consider the work undertaken in three broad areas: the body, sexuality, health, and reproduction; masculinity and men's studies; and immigration and change.

The Body, Sex, Health, and Gender

With the development of new reproduction technologies, together with increased awareness of health issues and a greater openness to sexuality, the concept of the body constitutes a fascinating area of contemporary gender studies.

The body.[36] A relatively new field in the social sciences and humanities, the study of the body has developed considerably since the seventies and particularly in the eighties. It had previously been considered the domain of philosophical and social theory as well as anthropology. The latter had focused on the nature–culture relation, which we saw in Chapter 2, and emphasized the supposed contradictions between human sexuality and sociocultural requirements. The human body had also been studied as a surface on which marks of social status, family position, or tribal membership were displayed.

Esteban (2002:332) affirms that in Western society, the last few decades of the twentieth century have been characterized by the "cult of the body." The body is the object of many daily activities, looked after with care, and shown off in public. This is the subject of another article by the same author on "Social Promotion and

Exhibition of the Body" (2000). Esteban shows that in contemporary consumer society, the body takes main stage in many spaces, such as the media and advertising, the performing arts, the world of leisure, and sports.

One of the current theoretical tendencies is centered on the concept of embodiment, which aims to overcome the dichotomies between body and mind, subject and object, and so on. Embodiment refers to the process of social interaction in which the body is inserted. Many interesting lines of inquiry are being taken up by different scholars in relation to the body, but here we will mention three of special significance for gender studies: sexuality, health, and new reproduction technologies.

Sex and sexuality. Apart from Sandra Ott's wonderful documentation of the "cheese analogy" of conception in the French Basque shepherding community of Sainte-Engrâce (Chapter 6), we have very little information on cultural interpretations of sexuality in traditional Basque society. In *Mujer vasca: Imagen y realidad*, the writing team found that back in the eighties, when the research was carried out, silence generally surrounded the topic of sexuality among women (1985:210–14). They also found a different set of standards for women and men. They believed this to have been the norm in traditional society when the subject of sex was hushed up and only talked about in terms of "being careful," not only to avoid an unwanted pregnancy but above all to protect a girl's "virtue" (i.e., that she should remain a virgin until marriage). By the eighties, and certainly nowadays, the old emphasis on virginity is no longer relevant, and nonmarital sexual relations are widely practiced and accepted. The study also revealed a contradiction between the importance attached to communication in a couple and the evident lack of communication with regards to sex. A third of the women interviewed expressed a negative, or nonpositive, evaluation of their sex lives (ibid. 212).

In 2001, a quarter of a decade after the publication of Mujer vasca, Mari Luz Esteban published Re-producción del cuerpo femenino, to which we have already referred and in which we find the broadest and most up-to-date picture of the way women in this society experience their bodies in terms of general and reproductive health and sexuality. She finds that "sex is beginning to stop being silenced," (my translation) that while many women are open to talk about sexuality in general, they are still reticent to discuss their own personal experiences, especially when these are negative (Esteban 2001:187). Bisexuality or homosexuality are acknowledged in circles where they are accepted, but still tend to be hidden from parents or others who are not expected to approve.

Health. In an article on "Feminism and the Medical Scientific System" (2002: 132) Esteban has shown how the medical profession has constructed a particular conception of the female human body as problematic, and how the medical discourse refers to women's bodies and women as social beings according to certain stereotyped preconceptions about female sexuality and reproduction. The way menopause is approached and treated by the medical profession is a prime example of the way sociocultural conceptualizations of a biological process (the cessation of menstruation and reduction in estrogen production) problematize and medicalize a process. The issues of age and aging are also important here.

new reproductive technologies. The different stages related to reproduction (pregnancy, birth, breastfeeding, and child care) have often been taken for

Models of men
Men's studies and masculinity are growing areas of gender studies and fruitful research is being carried out in relation to sport, the military and fatherhood.

Once obligatory, military service was an experience common to most Basque men like these soldiers on exercise in the mountains of Jaca, who bear witness to the prevalence of hegemonic models of masculinity. Photo: Iñaki Ugarte.

---

granted and not considered from a culturally differentiated point of view. Nevertheless, numerous feminist authors have endeavored to convey the social and cultural construction of these seemingly "natural" processes as well as the social control exerted through them.

The development of reproductive technologies necessarily challenges the naturalization that we have seen to run across the discourse of reproduction. In English,

Marilyn Strathern (1992), and in Spanish, Verena Stolcke (1998), have produced thought-provoking and pioneering work on the subject of the new reproductive technologies. Donna Haraway is also a necessary reference in the world of science and gender, famous for her concept of "cyborgs," a half-human, half-machine hybrid that she uses as a metaphor to analyze the changes in gender relations provoked by the developments of science, as well as to resolve the dichotomies of nature–culture, biology–science, feelings–reason, man–woman. The progress of new technologies takes the distinction between natural and artificial to the limit.

Men and Masculinity

In June 2001, Emakunde organized the first congress on Men in the Face of the New Social Order in Donostia–San Sebastián, which marked a breakthrough in Gender Studies and bore witness to the growing interest in Men's Studies and the construction of masculinities. This interest has arisen from the general evolution of gender theory from its initial emphasis on women to the recognition that gender depends both on the relations between women and men and on the systems that regulate those relations in society. The focus on relations between women and men, together with the concept of gender as a cultural construct, led to the focus on the ways that femininity and masculinity are constructed. It became clear that while Western society in general operates a gender system that is structured on the basis of a dominant model of masculinity, the hegemonic model is simultaneously contested by alternative models. R. W. Connell, in his work *Masculinities* (1995), invites us to examine the different masculinities that have emerged in relation to or opposition with the hegemonic model, as do, in a similar vein, Brod and Kauffman in their work *Theorizing Masculinities* (1994). We have already seen the practical application of these theories in the Basque setting of female and male gender models in the *Alardes* of Hondarribia and Irun (see Chapter 19). The work of Stanley Brandes in *Metaphors of Masculinity* reveals the gender symbolism in a festival context in Andalucia, while an important work of reference in the Mediterranean culture is Gilmore (1994).

An interesting line of study can be traced on the reproduction of masculinity through sport, in which the work of Michael Messner is an obvious reference. In the Basque context, Carmen Díez (1996a and 1996b) has found an interesting field of study in the world of football and is currently carrying out research on why girls and young women drop out of sport at school. An obvious area where the construction of masculinity is apparent is, of course, the military, and on this subject we have the work of Joseba Zulaika, *Chivos y soldados* (1989). We have already commented on the military aspect of the *Alardes*, which contribute to reinforcing the negative attitude to women's participation as equals.

In the contemplation of "new men" in the Basque context, the reconstruction of fatherhood is emerging as an area of interest, with an emphasis on the figure of the *padre responsible* ("responsible father"). This was taken up by Carmen Díez in a paper presented at Emakunde's aforementioned conference, entitled "Nuevos modelos de hombre: Emergencia y contextualización" (New models of men: Emergence and contextualization). Given the former emphasis on the role of the mother in Basque culture and the idealized projection of motherhood in society as a whole, the construction of fatherhood has much to say about Basque gender relations today.

Migration and diversity
The increasing presence of migrants from outside the Spanish State and the European Union is changing the face of the Basque Country and is a challenge to the way we conceive of Basque society, its cultural roots, social structures and gender relations.
Photo: Iñaki Ugarte

Migration and Change

One of the most pressing factors of change in Western society and one of the most imperative issues in present-day Euskal Herria is that of migration, a factor that is increasing and that must be addressed from different perspectives, but that has implications for both Basque Cultural and Gender Studies. We have already seen that the Basques have a long tradition of emigration and that new studies have revealed the importance of women in what was presented as a predominantly male phenomenon. We have also looked at the implications of migration in a globalizing world and considered the contribution of women to the construction of new cultural identities by maintaining aspects of the "old" Basque culture at the same time as interacting with the new society into which they integrate. Now, current migration trends have reversed the situation in which there was a tendency for Basques to emigrate. The tide is turning and immigrants from other parts of the world (mainly African, Latin American, and Asian countries) are arriving and settling in the Basque Country. The phenomenon is still fairly new but, given the dimensions of its social impact, it is one that is attracting wide interest from different institutions concerned with meeting the needs of this new sector of society.

A growing body of work is delving into gender and migration issues in the Spanish State, and in the Basque context it will be important to monitor the impact of immigrants in Euskal Herria, both male and female, contemplating the particular characteristics of migration for women and men and their relative degree of access to work, social status, and cultural integration. Migration, as part of the process of globalization, challenges the way we perceive Basque culture and gender, presenting new models for analysis of changing socially structured gender relations and systems.

In conclusion, it seems obvious to say that Basque society has changed radically in the course of the past century and that gender relations today are dramatically different from what they were a hundred years ago. Yet it was not until the eighties that change began to be contemplated in its own right, as a subject for analysis and something in which social actors are implicated rather than being mere receptors. In this respect, in the context of the Spanish State, the publication of *Modelos emergentes en los sistemas y las relaciones de género* (Emerging models in gender systems and relations) by some of the same authors who worked on *Mujer vasca* is

---

innovative and enriching for the ongoing study of gender. Modelos emergentes gathers the results of research that attempts to perceive the changes currently occurring in our society and their implications for gender. Departing from a theoretical framework in which to detect change, the team looks for new models of women and men, developing the themes of work and power and bringing in novel perspectives related to the emotional universe of socialization, self-perception, and self-esteem that sheds new light on the emotional motivations of both women and men. "Emerging models" help situate ourselves in Gender Studies at the turn of the twenty-first century and point the way for future investigation.

Lesson twenty-three

SUGGESTED READING

Mari Luz Esteban, "Feminism and the Medical Scientific System," unpublished translation (1994) of "Relaciones entre feminismo y Sistema Médico-Científico," Kobie Serie Antropología Cultural (Bilbao: Diputación Provincial de Bizkaia, 1996), 17–39.

Bibliography

English Bibliography

Stanley Brandes, Metaphors of Masculinity: Sex and Status in Andalucian Folklore (1980).

H. Brod and M. Kauffman, eds., Theorizing Masculinities (Thousand Oaks: Sage, 1994).

R. Connell, Masculinities (Berkeley: University of California Press, 1995).

———, "New Directions in Gender Theory, Masculinity Research and Gender Politics," Ethos 61:3–4 (1995), 157–76.

Donna Haraway, Science, Cyborgs and Women: The Reinvention of Nature (1995).

M. Messner, Power at Play: Sports and the Problem of Masculinity (Boston, Beacon Press, 1992).

Marilyn Strathern, Reproducing the Future: Anthropology, Kinship and the New Reproductive Technologies (New York: Routledge, 1992).

Spanish Bibliography

Teresa del Valle et al., Modelos emergentes en los sistemas y las relaciones de género (Madrid: Narcea, 2002).

Carmen Díez, "Deporte y la construcción de las relaciones de género," in Gazeta de Antropología, no. 12:93–100.

———, "Deporte y socialización," in R. M. Radl Phillip, ed., Mujeres e instituciones universitarias en Occidente: Conocimiento, investigación y roles de género (Santiago de Compostela: Universidad de Santiago de Compostela, 1996b), 317–24.

Mari Luz Esteban, Re-producción del cuerpo femenino: Discursos y prácticas acerca de la salud (Donostia–San Sebastián: Tercera Prensa–Hirugarren Prentsa, 2001).

———, "Promoción social y exhibición del cuerpo," in T. del Valle, ed., Perspectivas feministas desde la antropología social (Barcelona: Ariel, 2002).

D. D. Gilmore, Hacerse hombre: Concepciones culturales de la masculinidad (Barcelona: Paidos, 1994).

Verena Stolcke, "El sexo de la biotecnología," in A. Duran and R. Riechmann, coords., Genes en el laboratorio y en la fábrica (Madrid: Trotta-Fundación 1 de mayo, 1998), 97–118.

Joseba Zulaika, Chivos y soldados (Donostia: La Primitiva Casa Baroja, 1989).

Written lesson for submission

Identify the current areas of interest in Gender Studies and assess their significance for consideration in the Basque case.

Key Words

"WOMEN AGAINST FASCISM": a movement led in Spain by Dolores Ibárurri, "la Pasionaria," that worked toward women's liberation during the Republic (1931–1936).

FRANQUISMO: a political regime deriving its name from the dictator, Francisco Franco, that extended its influence to the Catholic Church, the education system, the media, the medical profession, and many other institutions.

FALANGE FEMENINA: a reactionary women's movement in key with the Church and Franco's regime, advocating a return of women to the home and to the old moral order.

FEMINISM OF EQUALITY: a trend of feminism, that assumes the universal subordination of women, and conceives of feminism as a global option for all women.

FEMINISM OF DIFFERENCE: a current of feminism that recognizes the differences existing between women (for example, in terms of class or ethnicity) and questions the possibility of a united women's struggle.

Notes

1. The problematic is also addressed by Edwin Ardener in the article "Belief and the problem of women" (1975).
2. The book was first published in 1884; Leacock wrote an introduction for a later edition brought out in 1972.
3. This work will be referred to more than once, here and in other chapters, but rather than repeat the full bibliographical reference, Mujer vasca will be used, with the date (1985) where appropriate.
4. William Douglass is the founding father of the Basque Studies program at the University of Nevada, Reno. He has devoted his life to researching and writing about the Basques both in Euskal Herria and in the diaspora and has dedicated great energy to liaising between the Old World and the new communities of Basques across the planet. His bibliography is extensive, ranging from his works on rural culture and change in the Basque Country to diverse themes from the diaspora, including the classics (cowritten with Jon Bilbao) Amerikanuak: The Basques of the New World (1975), Beltran: Basque Sheepman of the American West (1979), Basque Sheepherders of the American West (1985), and many other collections of essays on issues of ethnicity, identity, and nationalism.
5. The Circle of Mountains was first published in 1981 but all page references here will be to the 1993 second edition.
6. See W. Douglass (1975:18–32) and S. Ott (1993:31–38) for a detailed description of the

workings of a typical baserria during the annual seasonal cycle.

7. The occupation by men of spaces associated with women can also be seen in the sociedades gastronómicas (gastronomic societies) popular in Basque society. The sociedades are eating houses containing a communal kitchen where the members meet to prepare a meal that they then share. Initially working men's clubs where people of the same trade gathered to eat together, these establishments have extended to group people at different levels of interest or activity (sports clubs, hunting and fishing societies, and the like). Although many are now open to both men and women, there are still some that continue to observe the traditional "men only" rule, allowing women to attend only on certain days of the week, and there is often a ban on women entering the kitchen. Ironically, while the men pride themselves on doing the cooking, most sociedades employ a woman to wash the dishes and clean up.
8. Pio Perez, Pasaiako arrantzaleen lan eta gizarte harremanei buruzko azterketa antropologikoa (Euskal Herriko Unibertsitatea Argitalpen Zerbitzua, 2001).
9. The information on which the remainder of this section is based is derived from Chapter V of Rubio-Ardanaz's book, "Desplazamiento de la mujer sardinera en el cambio del modo de distribución tradicional del pescado," 113–45.
10. CAPV is short for Comunidad Autónoma del País Vasco (Autonomous Community of the Basque Country), which comprises the provinces of Araba, Bizkaia, and Gipuzkoa.
11. Emakunde is the Basque governmental department of women's affairs.

12. Iparralde is the northern Basque Country, consisting of the three Basque provinces that lie in the French State.
13. The archaeologist Maruja Gimbutas has worked extensively on the goddess cults in Paleolithic and Neolithic Europe and contests the category "fertility goddess" since the deities were also symbolic of death and destruction.
14. Authorities disagree about the use of the name "Mari," chosen by Barandiaran from many others that appear in the stories, or "Maia" or "Mayi," preferred by Caro Baroja. It is an ongoing debate, in which most recently Anuntzi Arana has suggested that the title "Dama" or "Anderea" ("Lady") is more in keeping with popular tradition (Díez, 2003:1).
15. In later myths, under the influence of Christianity, the sky takes on the characteristic of heaven and the sense of being in contact with the sacred and mysterious.
16. Her ambiguous nature is later exploited by Christianity, depicting her as a fallen saint or wicked angel, witch or devil queen. In later, post-Christian Basque myths, the heroes are male, as in knights fighting a serpent or flaming bull, and often aided by Saint Michael, a Christian knightly figure.
17. The name Sugaar is reflected in the contemporary Basque word for snake: sugea.
18. The September 2002 issue of the magazine published by Emakunde (the Basque government's department for women's affairs) contains a central dossier on the subject of single-parent families, presenting them as a new model in their own right rather than a failed or incomplete version of the "normal" nuclear family.

19. As we saw (Chapter 10), some feminist sectors have seized on the matriarchal thesis for the importance it gives to women and have taken the existence of a matriarchy in the past as an incentive for the future, signifying that one day Basque women will retake the power wrested from them.
20. There is a full reference to this subject in Zulaika's work in "Basque Women and Ritual" in Chapter 18.
21. From an article on the second assembly of the feminist nationalist left celebrated in Altsasu (Nafarroa), published in *Gara*, Jan. 1, 2003, 16.
22. Pecharromán has contributed to the elaboration of exhibitions and given numerous talks and interviews on Basque emigrant women, both in the United States and back home in the Basque Country.
23. PNV stands for Partido Nacionalista Vasco (Basque Nationalist Party).
24. They are also called *ttuntturoak*, in reference to their pointed hats, or *zanpantzarrak*.
25. Zuberoa is the Basque name for the French province of Soule. See Ott.
26. One of the greatest authorities on Basque dance is Juan Antonio Urbeltz, whose book *Dantzak: Notas sobre las danzas tradicionales de los vascos* (1978) is an obligatory reference. Although the focus is not primarily on gender, Lisa Corcostegui provides some useful insights on the reinvention of Basque dance in the diaspora and its importance for continuing ethnic identity in "Moving Emblems: Basque Dance and Symbolic Ethnicity," in W. Douglass et al., *The Basque Diaspora* (1999), 249–73.
27. The history of the *Alardes* is discussed in full detail in an electronic publication, *Díme de que alardeas*, by Xabier Kerexeta.

28. The content of this section is largely reproduced from the paper "Bordering on Chaos" (2000a).
29. The river Bidasoa runs through Irun and Hondarribia and out to the sea and lends its name to the district.
30. For example, in September 1999, following the incidents in the Alarde of Hondarribia that year, a group of women from Hondarribia's mixed company, Jaizkibel, decided to go dressed as soldiers to demonstrate outside a meeting of Udalbiltza, a new formation of local councils that were meeting for the first time in Bilbao and which was to be attended by Mayor Jauregui. They asked Bizkaiko Emakume Asanblada (the Vizcayan Women's Assembly) to join them in this demonstration, but were opposed to the women of Bilbao wearing their soldiers' uniform and including on their banner the statement "Emakumeak Alardera ala Edonon" meaning "Women in the Alarde and anywhere." The group from Hondarribia wished to limit the cause to the parade, keeping it local in focus and immunizing themselves from the accusations of bringing external feminist politics into the Alarde.
31. Herri Batasuna ("United People") was the name of the radical nationalist party declared ilegal by the Spanish government in the nineties.
32. Marianne Gullestad has analyzed the construction of homes, gender, and class in Norway in an article on "Home Decoration as Popular Culture," in Gendered Anthropology, 1993:127–61, but to my knowledge, there is no comparable work on the contemporary Basque home.
33. We do have a published version in Spanish, "Cronotipos de la memoria: Cronotipos genéricos,"

in T. del Valle, ed., Perspectivas feministas desde la antropología social, Barcelona: Ariel, 2000:243–65.

34. The name "Pasionaria" was initially used by Ibárurri as a pseudonym for her writing in a miners' paper.

35. The figures come from an article by Joaquina Prades titled "Pobre san Valentín" (Poor St. Valentine) in El País, Feb. 15, 1998.

36. This section is based on Mari Luz Esteban, Revisiones, teorías y perspectivas feministas en la antropología social, unpublished teaching material presented as a partial requirement for appointment to lectureship in Social Anthropology, University of the Basque Country (UPV-EHU), 2002.

Pictures

Elena Asins, 46
Seymour Chwast, Battleground, 13, The changing face of women's work, 71
Carmen Díez, 275, 300, 308
Dover Pictorial Archives, 176
Women: A Pictorial Archive from Nineteenth-Century Sources, 176, 329
Jim Harter: Women: A Pictorial Archive. Dover Publications, New York 1978
Gotzone Elu, 266
Iñaki Edroso, 74, 79, 84, 159
Ingo Fast, 102
Maria Gabriela Fdez. de Casadevante, 282
Gari Garaialde, 107, 112, 154, 193, 200, 207, 210
Imanol Ilárraz, 242, 247, 250
Itziar Irastorza, 252, 258, 263
Jon Ander (Lurra Artesanía, Irun), 162
Asunción Maisterrena, 28, 37, 51, 61, 223, 228, 239
Alain Pagoaga, 16, 89, 92, 120, 127
Begoña Pecharromán, 218
Lola Sarratea, cover, 142
Xavier Santxotena, 137, 147
Iñaki Ugarte, 21, 40, 64, 99, 117, 130, 137, 162, 173, 185, 188, 314, 319
Elisa Urtizberea, 287, 290, 297

about the cover

In Basque culture, the eguzkilore is the "flower of the sun" and was believed to represent the sun itself. It was a symbol of daytime and of life, which people hung on their doors to ward off witches and other mischievous spirits of the night.

Index

A

abortion, 242, 285, 294, 296, 302–11
among poor people widely practiced in backstreet clinics, 177
defending the right to, 297
"add-women-and-stir method" not sufficient to vanquish deep-rooted sexist prejudice in analysis, 17
adultery, 64, 175, 280, 285, 287
a crime for women whatever circumstances but for men only if in family or living with mistress or known publicly, 174
Adur, 123
mysterious force carrying positive or negative energy acting upon other persons, 122
adivinadora (fortune teller), 59
AEK ("Coordinator for Basque Literacy"), network of language schools teaching Basque, 186, 187
agency of social actors, dynamic concept of culture as, 232
agents of change, women in modernization of Basque society as, 99
aizkolari (wood cutter), emergence of women in sports involving a show of strength, 117
akelarre, witches' sabbath, 144, 153, 164
Aker, goat who is head of lesser spirits, 144, 153, 164
Alarde. See also Alarde of the people
history of the, 326
initially a "show of arms" organized annually that bound Euskal Herria and committed Basques to defense of borders, 253
of the people, women only as cantineras, 260
those who defend festival imagine to reside in the realm of the sacred and symbolic, out of time and hence immune to change, 261
Alcedo, Miren ("Las mujeres de ETA," 1997), 202, 204, 205, 213

B

C

cyborgs, a half-machine hybrid used as a metaphor to analyze changes in gender relations, 316

D

Davis, Angela, 211
deactivate claims and demands of women: discourse of supreme importance of preserving cultural specificity, 232
death rituals, 238–42, 250
defense of tradition used to deny women the right to participate in Alardes, 255
del Valle, Teresa, 9
basis of inequality in Basque society and culture (1997), 274
Basque woman makes decisions mainly in domestic sphere (1985:7), 118
carnival as an example of a gendered cronotope, 246
cronotopes link space and time in a dynamic way (1998), 275
consortium for the study of Basque women, 223
current status of the anthropology of women (1989), 55
"Importance of Continuity and Its Different Interpretations" (1994), 195
incorporation of small number of women into joaldunak (1996, 1998), 244
in-depth study of the run ("Korrika," 1994), 186
layout of cities sexist, unfriendly and unacceptable to many women (1989), 276
masculine aesthetic and attitude, women bertsolaris who progress in art, (1997), 193
metaphor of milestone for female history (1997), 303
Mujer vasca: Imagen and Realidad (et. al, 1985), 58, 60, 66, 67, 87, 91, 100, 118, 125, 129, 134, 136, 140, 158, 301, 313, 314, 319, 323
pioneer of research on women in Euskal Herria, 46
power as the capacity to make and apply decisions (1986), 114
relationship between gender theory and feminism, 11
variable of gender, need to recognize in Basque nationalism the (1997), 197

E

G

Gilmore, D. D. (Hacerse hombre, 1994), 266, 270, 317, 321
girls most critical of village life, in village of Echalar, 83
globalization for Basque identity, implications in communities of diaspora for, 221
good mother
portrayed mostly in her participation in rites of passage, 62
stereotype, 51
Grau Biosca, Elena ("De la emancipación a la liberación," 1993), 293, 302, 311
Greenwood, Davydd J. (Unrewarding Wealth, 1976), 59, 86
"guarra," slut, 286

H

Hacker, Sally (Pleasure, Power and Technology, 1989), 97, 98, 103, 105, 109
handful of women write and publish belied by growing body of literature written by authors, 185
hard worker
male was public sphere and involved a social role that maintained into old age, 63
female focus was toward organization of household and child care, 63
Harris, Marvin, 258
Harris, Olivia, 19, 25
Harter, Jim, 329
hegemonic model
Connell invites us to examine different masculinities emerged in relation to, 316
of masculinity, prevalence of, 315
Heiberg, Marianne (The Making of the Basque Nation, 1989:225), 98, 109
Henningsen, Gustav (The Witch's Advocate, 1980), 152, 167
Herri Batasuna ("United People"), 267
name of radical nationalist party dissolved by Spanish government in nineties, 327
Hidalgo, Fabian, 9
hilandera (seamstress), 59

I

J

K

Kasmir, Sharryn ...
"From the Margins" (1999), 207–9, 211, 213
"Ke Taldea," pioneering group of Basque women scientists and technologists from different fields, 106
Korrika, 195
run organized as a relay, groups sponsor kilometers of run through the seven Basque provinces nonstop for several days, 187
sponsored run to raise consciousness and awareness for Euskara, 186, 188, 194, 222, 229
women run in connection with family role, 187
Korrika women
demonstrate their own strength and staying power, 189
participation within symbolic universe of domestic environment and family, 190

L

Lady of Anboto, 130, 138
lamia, supreme and above all other beings and spirits, 139, 145, 147
Lancre, Pierre: French judge who sent 80 people to the stake in 1610, 157
Landa, Mariasun, author, 185
language learning presented as something natural when related to women, 183
La Pasionaria, 283, 284. See also Ibárurri
Lapurdi: part of France and neighbour to Spain, 158
large-scale commercialization and mechanization of fishing industry pushed women out of traditional roles while overfishing reduced stock, 87
Larrañaga, Carmen ("Del bertsolarismo silenciado," 1997), 192, 196
Larrañaga, Carmen, and Carmen Pérez ("La religión en la vida de la mujer," 1988): institutionalization of Immaculate Conception as a public holiday, 235, 236, 251
layout of cities: sexist and unacceptable to many of women who inhabit them, 276

M

Miller, Patty: director of Basque Museum embraces children
in typical Basque dress, 216
Mintegi, Laura, author, 185
model for women: forces comprising Catholic Church, education system, media, medical profession and many other institutions promoted a single, 285, 286
model mothers, 171
models of masculinity: protagonist of the public arena, attached to military practice and male diversion, 266
Mondragón. See also Arrasate
cooperative system where condition of women workers is only somewhat better relative to men, 100
group of cooperatives characterized by decentralization of industry and often considered heart of "Basqueness" in terms of language and culture, 98
system is rooted in antihierarchical values and behavior, 98
money as a resource may access virtually and that makes a good marker of gender stratification in modern complex societies, 49
moon: fertility, menstruation and conception, 145
Moore, Henrietta (Feminism and Anthropology, 1988), 14, 25, 39, 170
overlooked in way represented, 14, 15
rejects "women's status ... related to ... giving birth" and "'domestic'/'public' distinction ... valid," 39
"The Differences Within and ... Differences Between," (1993), 55
mother, stereotype of a good, 51
mother-daughter relationship: Mari jealous of, 127
motherhood is historical and culturally specific rather than universal, 171
mothering as a culturally defined activity, with regard to centrality to family and role in childcare, 40
mother status depends upon access to resources, conditions of their work, distribution of the products of their labor, 39, 41
Muguruza, Fermin: singer who brings together the ideas of feminism and nationalism, 210

———

Mujer vasca: Imagen y realidad (1985). See del Valle et al. (1985)
Murray, Margaret, 153
"muted groups," 274
muting, theory of, 18
myth: fragment of collective experience that exists outside of time and space, 131
myths: cultural constructions that are produced at specific moments in history and in particular socioeconomic contexts, 150

N

Narotzky, Susana (Mujer, Mujeres, Género, 1995:36–39), 50, 56
Nash, Mary
  "Two Decades of Women's History in Spain" (1991), 302, 310
  Defying Male Civilization: Women in the Spanish Civil War (1995), 279, 292
nation, double symbolism as both homeland and mother, 199
naturalization: process by which gender stereotypes draw on nature for their legitimation, 224
nature
  common to all cultures that values women to a lesser degree than men, 29
  healers whose treatments had failed and were accused of witchcraft by unlucky dissatisfied customers, 155
nature-culture dichotomy problems, 31, 32
negative evaluation of their work on baserri: a positive view of working at home and with children in town, 86
neskato or "female servant" assistant responsible for menial domestic chores, 76
new reproductive technologies, thought-provoking pioneering work on, 316
notion of "woman" is associated with that of "mother" in most societies, 170
notions of nationhood in terms of "Motherland, link between cult to Virgin and mother figure in Basque culture which in turn permeates," 236

O

P

Pagoaga, Alain, 16, 89, 92, 120, 127, 329
paid maternity leave
first reform introduced in Republic, 280
many were opposed to payroll deductions toward it, 280
partera (midwife), 59
participation of women and children in Korrika, run to promote awareness of the Basque language, 188
Partido Feminista was working-women's party with feminist revolution as its goal, 299
Partido Nacionalista Vasco, 326
model of strong female figure epitomized by "matriarch" and used as identifier of Basqueness, 169
"Pasionaria": used by Ibárurri as pseudonym for her writing in miners' paper, 328
patriarchal structure, 103, 129
the distribution of resources to the family as a unit reinforces, 104
patriarchy
radical feminism saw female inequality as result of oppressive social relationship between sexes, 295
system of society ruled by men and characterized by patrilineal descent, 168
Pecharromán, Begoña, 215, 329
contributed to elaboration of exhibitions and given numerous talks/interviews on Basque emigrant women, 326
performance of a ritual recreates community by establishing transitional state of harmony, 229
permiso marital, 172
Pio Perez (Pasaiako arrantzaleen lan eta gizarte harremanei buruzko azterketa antropologikoa, 2001), 78, 324
PNV. See Partido Nacionalista Vasco
"Pobre san Valentín" (Poor St. Valentine) in Prades, Joaquina (1998), 328
"political matriarchy": women exercise political power even in the face of opposition, 113
in the public arena, 126

R

riotous carnival parade: past reprobation of sexual freedom meets unleashing of that repression in carnival role reversal and provocative sexuality, 246
"rite of solidarity," alardes as, 258
rites of passage: series of duties and rights performed by both women and men, 237
ritual
defined as form of standardized and repetitive behavior and obeys order laying down correct way to carry out rites or solemn acts, 278
important symbolic dimension that construct/reinforce group identities, reaffirm social order, explain world order and provide stable reference, 278
occupies a symbolic and often sacred domain of significance less open to change than other aspects of life, 226
perceive certain aspects of culture or society that not immediately obvious, 226
provides coherent symbolic frame to counter sensation of chaos and disorder in "real" world, 259
realm where social realities are played out on a symbolic plane, 240
reinforcing or contesting the social order, 229
roles, the social construction of gender, 38
rowing, coastal women participation in, 79
Rubio-Ardanaz, Juan Antonio, 78
"Las sardineras de Santurce" (1993:34), 88
"Desplazamiento de la mujer sardinera en el cambio del modo de distribución tradicional del pescado" (1994), 79, 88, 324
rural counterparts, fishermen and women had greater mobility and wider social network than, 80

S

Sacks, Karen ("Engels revisited," 1974), 39, 44
Sainte Engrâce, study of village of, 60
Sanday, Peggy (Female Power and Male Dominance, 1981:113–14), 114, 124
Santxotena, Xavier, 147, 329

social inequality, a shift in focus and a wider angle on systems that support, 16
Socialist Party: amending law for new grounds for abortion or making abortion freely available during first twelve weeks of pregnancy, 308
socialization process, importance of, 53
social order of everyday life, 227
  rituals can function as reinforcing or contesting, 229
social power, capacity to maximize sociocultural values attached to certain areas of responsibility by making decisions in those fields, 115
social sciences, way women represented in, 14
social transformation requires unpaid work of women should be contemplated at community level, 104
socioeconomic contexts of rural and urban environment, difference between, 93
sorgiña, kind of midwife who attended women in childbirth, 146
Sorkun, singer who brings together the ideas of feminism and nationalism, 210
space
  area physically identified through meanings engraved in experiences and perceptions, 274, 275
  reinterpret giving new meanings to places where performed and act out an ideological project through, 229
  socially constructed and that to understand where a social phenomenon occurs enhance our comprehension of why it occurs, 271
Spain, Daphne (Gendered Spaces, 1992), 271, 272, 277
Spanish feminism in the eighties, main issues of, 302
spatial layout of our social environment reinforces sexual inequality, by segregating men and women and reducing female access to certain resources, 271
Spring, turning soil for planting and raking and fertilizing of pasture lands, 73
stereotypes: "characteristics applied in fixed mode as representative of person, group, collectivity," 50
stereotypes and attributes, need to distinguish between, 52

T

U

V

X

Y

Young, Kate, 19, 25

Z

Zamalzain, elaborate costume and skillful dancing which is associated with male virility caught and castrated in an act of human domination, 249
Zuberoa, Basque name for the French province of Soule, 326
Zulaika, Joseba, 9
  Basque Violence (1988), 134, 201, 236, 251
  Chivos y soldados (1989), 317, 321

Colophon

This book was edited by Mark Woodworth and indexed by Lawrence Feldman. It was laid out and produced by Gunnlaugur SE Briem, who also designed the typeface, BriemAnvil.

It was printed and bound by Fidlar Doubleday of Kalamazoo, Michigan.

The Basque Studies textbook series

1. Guggenheim Bilbao Museoa: Museums, Architecture, and City Renewal
2. Modern Basque History: Eighteenth Century to the Present
3. Basque Economy: From Industrialization to Globalization
4. Basque Cyberculture: From Digital Euskadi to CyberEuskalherria
5. Basque Culture: Anthropological Perspectives
6. Basque Sociolinguistics: Language, Society, and Culture
7. Basque Cinema: An Introduction
8. Basque Diaspora; Migration and Transnational Identity
9. Basque Gender Studies